ATTLEE

. . . .

ATTLEE

Robert Pearce

LONGMAN
London and New York

Addison Wesley Longman Limited
Edinburgh Gate
Harlow
Essex CM20 2JE
United Kingdom
and Associated Companies throughout the world

*Published in the United States of America
by Addison Wesley Longman Inc., New York*

First published 1997

ISBN 0 582 25691 7 CSD
ISBN 0 582 25690 9 PPR

British Library Cataloguing-in-Publication Data

A catalogue record for this book is
available from the British Library

Library of Congress Cataloging-in-Publication Data

Pearce, R. D. (Robert D.)
Attlee / Robert Pearce.
p.   cm. – (Profiles in power)
Includes bibliographical references and index.
ISBN 0-582-25691-7 (hardcover). – ISBN 0-582-25690-9 (paper)
1. Attlee, C. R. (Clement Richard), 1883–1967.   2. Great Britain –
Politics and government – 20th century.   3. Prime ministers – Great
Britain – Biography.   4. Labour Party (Great Britain) – Biography.
I. Title. II. Series: Profiles in power (London, England)
DA585.A8P43   1997
941.085′4′092–dc21
[B]   96-44365
                                                                      CIP

Set by 8 in 10½/12pt New Baskerville
Produced by Longman Singapore Publishers (Pte) Ltd.
Printed in Singapore

CONTENTS

CONTENTS

. . . . . .

ACKNOWLEDGEMENTS

Every work of history is a collaborative venture, and I therefore wish to thank the historians, mostly unknown to me
personally, from whose work I have profited. Some of them,
but alas not all, are mentioned by name in the references and
bibliography. My interest in Attlee goes back over twenty years
and has occasioned numerous archival forays on his papers
and those of his contemporaries. Thanks go to the many
librarians and archivists who have aided my work, and especially to those at the Bodleian, the British Library and
Churchill College. I am grateful to Bill Golant, for first stimulating my interest in Attlee, as in so much else, to Kenneth
Harris, for advice on sources, and to John Swift, for acting as a
diligent research assistant during the early part of the work. I
am also appreciative of the stimulating comments provided by
the general editor of this series, Professor Keith Robbins, and
the staff at Addison Wesley Longman. As so often in the past,
Martin Anthony and Roger Butler generously provided accom-
modation and hospitality during my trips to London and
Oxford respectively. My greatest debt of all is to Janet
Copeland, to whom this book is dedicated.

Lancaster,
July 1996

FOR JANET

INTRODUCTION: IMAGES OF ATTLEE

> *Questioner: Lord Attlee, looking back over your massive career in the Labour Party in terms of statesmanship, what do you think history will judge you best for?*
>
> *Attlee: I don't know.*[1]

Clement Richard Attlee (1883–1967) was the longest-serving leader of any major political party in twentieth-century Britain: he led Labour for twenty years. In addition, he was Prime Minister, from 1945 to 1951, during a period of unparalleled and highly controversial reform in domestic, foreign and imperial affairs: the welfare state was completed, a substantial portion of industry was nationalised, the Cold War started and the Empire began to be transformed into the multiracial Commonwealth. Without doubt he was one of the most successful figures in Labour history and one of the most significant in modern British politics. Yet he is also one of the most inscrutable.

Most students feel ambivalent about Attlee. This is partly because he was deliberately elusive. He was unwilling, or perhaps unable, to open himself up to questioners, his three stock answers being 'Yes', 'No', and 'I don't know', while his memoirs, *As It Happened,* constitute one of the least revealing autobiographies ever written. He was virtually a stranger to many of his colleagues, some of whom misjudged him entirely. For instance, while Attlee was an agnostic, who could not believe in the 'mumbo-jumbo' of religion, several figures believed him to be a convinced Christian. Arthur Moyle, his PPS, once remarked that he had 'worked for that man for

1

twenty years, yet still know nothing about him'.[2] Into his impenetrable silences could be read delphic understanding, personal inadequacy or anything in between – leaving plenty of room for misunderstanding. Hence it is not surprising that several Clem Attlees stalk the pages of modern history.

There is Attlee meek and mild, the modest man who, as Churchill quipped, had plenty to be modest about. He was the shy and retiring sort who did not angle and plot for political advancement, and nor did he particularly deserve it. He had greatness (of a sort) thrust upon him by a series of lucky breaks and by the unsuitability of his rivals. Bathos might almost have been his middle name: 'determined to make a trumpet sound like a tin whistle', as Nye Bevan believed, he brought 'to the fierce struggle of politics the tepid enthusiasms of a lazy summer afternoon at a cricket match'.[3]

There are several variations on this theme, in all of which Attlee is so colourless, characterless or self-effacing that he disappears as a human being. In the first, he is simply a void. The classic exposition of this came in Angus Wilson's short story 'The Wrong Set': 'An empty taxi drove up to No. 10 . . . and Mr Attlee got out.'[4] He may have attended, or even chaired, numberless meetings, but it is almost as if their official records have been doctored to omit all mention of him. Similarly, he may have been a member of the Simon Commission on Indian constitutional reform, appointed in 1928, but one may search the memoir of his fellow commissioner Edward Cadogan in vain for any acknowledgement of this fact. He was often next to invisible. At best, he was a small man in every respect: drab, dreary and little, according to the head of the Foreign Office during the Second World War.[5]

In the next variation, Attlee is not a man but an animal, though not, of course, any marauding king of the jungle. To Hugh Dalton he was 'a little mouse', or 'poor little Rabbit', and to Malcolm Muggeridge a 'small mouse'; to Neville Chamberlain he was a 'cowardly cur' and to Beaverbrook a 'sparrow'. Lansbury's daughter thought of him as the white rabbit, while Chips Channon depicted him as 'a black snail'. Sometimes he was an insect, occasionally merely 'a buzz'. Orwell said that Attlee reminded him 'of nothing so much as a recently dead fish, before it has had time to stiffen'.[6] There was no phallic penetration here. But it was, of course, Churchill who put it best: Attlee was a sheep in sheep's clothing.

Alternatively, there is the Attlee who lacks all animate qualities. He is a machine, 'a desiccated calculating machine' Nye Bevan once called him.[7] Many found that there was something mechanical about Attlee, as he sat in committee monotonously puffing away at his pipe. In cabinet he would canvass views, while rarely venturing an opinion himself, and then sum up the consensus of the meeting. An intelligent robot might have done the same, and with as little animation. Certainly there is little show of emotion in his autobiography, where a brief mention of his father's death is immediately followed by details of income and lodgings.

Nevertheless, more favourable variations of these themes do exist. Leonard Woolf drew the paradox that, although Attlee was indeed a mouse, he could, when one least expected it, be 'a masterful or even savage mouse'.[8] Similarly, David Low, in a celebrated cartoon of 1947, depicted Attlee as a 'Tough Lamb'. Others decided that if Attlee was small, and somehow inhuman, then he was a wasp, and moreover one capable of delivering a sharp sting. Indeed, some commentators have decided that Attlee was a consummate political performer. The traditional, sneering views, it has been said, are not merely wrong-headed, they are the exact opposite of the truth. Churchill's view of Attlee as a modest man with much to be modest about could not be more misguided: he was in fact, in Kenneth Morgan's neat reformulation, 'an immodest little man with plenty to be immodest about'.[9] Indeed Peter Hennessy, while comparing Attlee's physical presence to that of a gerbil, vaunts him as his ideal 'of what a premier should be'.[10]

The cleverly expressed opposite of any generally accepted interpretation makes for lively controversy, but it does not always produce sound history. It may, indeed, merely replace one caricature by another. Attlee has been the victim of such stereotyping for too long. Judgements about him have tended to be excessive. What are we to make, for instance, of Hennessy's depiction of Attlee as 'a real-life Captain Mainwaring' (from *Dad's Army*)?[11] Was he really, as the comparison implies, humourless, pompous and comically but endearingly ineffective? This comparison, from an admirer, backfires badly. More importantly, there is the controversial issue of the place of Attlee's 1945–51 governments in British history. On the one hand, Paul Addison has insisted that the war years saw the real revolution, so that Attlee and his colleagues merely implemented the wartime consensus. (Indeed Addison sees Attlee as essentially a little man, punctilious as a chairman of committees but 'no heavyweight', unable to dominate powerful departments and having little influence on Churchill's wartime government.) Yet, on the other hand, Kenneth Morgan has praised Attlee's premierships, judging that the 1945–51 governments laid down the consensus that dominated British politics until the advent of Margaret Thatcher, so that the 'Age of Attlee' lasted until 1979.[12] In fact, neither of these judgements does full justice either to the complex reality of British history or to Attlee's role in it. Both are over-simplifications.

What of Attlee as presented by his biographers? Have they provided us with less one-sided interpretations? The first effort, by Cyril Clemens for an American audience, is a scissors-and-paste affair containing an unusual combination of contradictory viewpoints: Attlee was living proof 'that men of genius can be men of character', and yet little that smacked of either genius or character emerges from the book: indeed Labour's leader is described as 'the poor man's Baldwin'.[13] The 1948 study by Roy Jenkins is much more lucid: but it is admittedly no more than an interim biography, and one moreover based on Attlee's own autobiographical jottings. Attlee had to wait until the 1980s before full-scale treatment from Kenneth Harris and from Trevor Burridge. Harris's work contains many personal details, while Burridge has written essentially a political biography. The two volumes therefore complement each other; and both have a similarly sympathetic view of their subject.

Both biographers depict Attlee as a great Prime Minister. There is no nonsense here about Attlee the nonentity, though Burridge – in his depiction of Attlee the realistic, practical and moral socialist servant, with no ego and no weakness – does in fact come close to depicting a somewhat inhuman automaton. Every student of Attlee is indebted to their scholarly labours, and their achievement should not be belittled. Yet both surely suffer the occupational hazard of the biographer, lack of perspective: they see their subject through his own eyes and give the impression of him which, at his best, he hoped to convey. Many may judge that their versions of Attlee – a man from whose dictionary the word ambition had been expunged – are too good to be true. In reality, Attlee was surely neither a saint nor the perfect premier, and we have to return to him his essential humanity, which means his foibles and failures as well as his positive qualities. Contrasting, but decidedly one-dimensional, depictions of Attlee emerge from the biographies of his colleagues. It is almost as if biographers cannot avoid becoming like their subjects, vicariously sharing their triumphs and disasters, resuscitating old quarrels and settling old political scores in print.

Must a biographer be a partisan? Where is the biography that can realistically portray Attlee without diminishing Morrison, or do equal justice to both Attlee and Bevan? It is the rationale of the 'Profiles in Power' series that a more dispassionate biographical essay provides an alternative, and valuable, angle of vision from the over-sympathy of the biographer and the often over-critical narrative of the political historian.

. . .

REFERENCES

1. *Clem Attlee: Granada Historical Records Interview* (London, 1967), p. 54.
2. Roy Hattersley, *Between Ourselves* (London, 1994), p. 336.
3. *Tribune*, 30 March 1945.
4. Angus Wilson, *The Wrong Set* (Harmondsworth, 1949), p. 89.
5. David Dilks (ed.), *The Diaries of Sir Alexander Cadogan, 1938–45* (London, 1971), p. 761.
6. Ben Pimlott (ed.), *The Political Diary of Hugh Dalton, 1918–40, 1945–60* (London, 1986), pp. 196, 282; Malcolm Muggeridge, *The Thirties* (London, 1967 edn), p. 10; A.J.P. Taylor, *Beaverbrook* (Harmondsworth, 1972), p. 605; Kenneth Harris, *Attlee* (London, 1984), p. 103; R.R. James, (ed.), *Chips; The Diaries of Sir Henry Channon* (London, 1993), pp. 49, 200; *The Collected Essays, Journalism and Letters of George Orwell*, II (Harmondsworth, 1970), p. 481.
7. Harris, *Attlee*, p. 522.
8. Frederick Spotts (ed.), *Letters of Leonard Woolf* (London, 1992), p. 425n. I am grateful to John Swift for drawing my attention to this quotation.
9. Kenneth O. Morgan, *Labour People* (Oxford, 1987), p. 147.
10. Peter Hennessy, 'Clement Attlee', *The Independent Magazine*, 23 January 1993, p. 46.
11. Peter Hennessy, 'The Attlee Governments, 1945–51', in P. Hennessy and A. Seldon (eds), *Ruling Performance: British Governments from Attlee to Thatcher* (Oxford, 1987), p. 52.

12. Paul Addison, *The Road to 1945* (London, 1975), pp. 270–3, 280; Kenneth O. Morgan, *Labour in Power* 1945–51 (Oxford, 1984), p. 494.
13. Cyril Clemens, *The Man from Limehouse* (Missouri, USA, 1946), pp. 27, 140.

Chapter 1

THE CHILD AND THE MAN

We were, I think, a typical family of the professional class brought up in the atmosphere of Victorian England.[1]

Wordsworth, a romantic poet favoured by both Attlee and Baldwin, judged in 1802 that the Child is Father of the Man. The words have become a truism – which does not mean that they are untrue. What did Clement Attlee owe to his childhood, and how significant were the child's early years for the adult Labour leader and Prime Minister?

Clement Attlee was born on 3 January 1883 in Putney, only half a dozen miles from Charing Cross, but still essentially in the countryside. The only traffic noise then was the sound of horses' hoofs. He was the seventh of eight children. His father, Henry Attlee, from a family of millers and corn merchants, was a successful, hardworking London solicitor, who became president of the Law Society in 1906. Henry was a committed Liberal, idolising Gladstone, and at one time thought of standing for parliament himself. Yet politics were not discussed very much in the household, perhaps because his wife, Ellen, who came from a more academic and artistic background, was a Conservative. Yet there was substantial harmony between the parents, founded on a commitment to Christianity and philanthropy. There was none of the harsh, repressive discipline traditionally, but often erroneously, associated with the Victorian family unit.

Henry Attlee amassed a substantial fortune – at his death he left £70,000 – and the family enjoyed the affluence and security of the Victorian middle classes. The Great Depression was unknown to them, as were notions of Britain's relative economic decline. Their large, comfortable home boasted a tennis court and a full-sized billiards table, and there were three full-time live-in servants, as well as a gardener and a governess who came in daily. Clement Attlee later judged that the virtual disappearance of domestic servants epitomised a social revolution, but such thoughts were far from the mind of the boy. It is true – as it is always true – that the times they were a-changing, so that his early years witnessed the famous dockers', gas workers' and match-girls' strikes, as well as the election to parliament of Keir Hardie and the formation of the Indian National Congress, but the future Labour Prime Minister who conceded independence to India was, before the First World War, imbued with patriotism and imperialism not socialism. The first public event he could recall was Queen Victoria's Golden Jubilee of 1887. He also took part in the Diamond celebrations, and found the death of the old Queen a shock in 1901. He later recalled being intoxicated, as a schoolboy, 'by the vision of large portions of the school map coloured in red with people ruled for their own good by strong, silent men'.[2] He imbibed heady draughts of Kipling, became a romantic imperialist and even accepted a caning at school in order to celebrate the relief of Ladysmith.

Attlee's conventional upbringing extended to his education. He attended a prep school in Hertfordshire, where, despite doing no more than hover hopefully on the edge of the team, he began a lifelong devotion to cricket; and then, from 1896 to 1901, he went to Haileybury public school, originally founded to prepare boys for service in India. The atmosphere here was far too spartan for his liking, and he was also the victim of some bullying. But he reacted manfully, and though winning no prizes or house colours was an enthusiastic member of the school cadet corps. He also, like all sixth-formers, became a prefect, keeping order in a dormitory of over forty boys. In his final school report he received that terse but none the less definitive public school accolade: 'I believe him a sound character'.[3]

The next preordained venue was 'the university'. Attlee became a student at University College, Oxford. This was as much a social as an educational experience. Certainly the teaching left much to be desired, the tutor for the Italian Renaissance often turning up rigged in hunting gear and frequently postponing sessions when the local Bicester Hunt was meeting. Attlee studied history. Apparently he might have got a First had it not been for his growing penchant for literature. As it was, he received Oxford's unclassified Second, as well as a half-blue in billiards and a tutor's reference: 'He is a level-headed, industrious, dependable man with no brilliance . . . but with excellent sound judgement.'[4]

Attlee was being groomed to take his place as a member of the governing elite. Even at his prep school he rubbed shoulders with those destined to be his colleagues in later life, including future politicians William Jowitt and Edward Hilton Young, and the same was true to a greater extent at Haileybury and Oxford. The world of the establishment at the turn of the century was a small and homogeneous one. He also accepted public school values, including loyalty and conformity. He was at this time a Tory, professing incredulity that any educated person could admire Keir Hardie. Attlee was never an outsider in political life. Perhaps he later understood his opponents in the Conservative party because he had so much in common with them. It is true that he seemed to most observers to have extremely limited leadership potential, and little of the self-confidence from which such a quality could grow; but appearances were deceptive, as his future was to make clear.

In later life the Man was indeed marked by the experiences of the Child. He was a lifelong monarchist, and two of his very best speeches were delivered on the deaths of George V and George VI. Some even believe that he bowed to the feelings of the latter in sending Bevin rather than Dalton to the Foreign Office in 1945 and in the timing of the 1951 general election. In addition, Attlee maintained a lifelong belief in Britain's image as a great and beneficent world power. His favourite contemporary historian, revealingly, was that chronicler and sentimentalist of English glories Arthur Bryant (who 'writes awfully well and made me quite excited with old tales of battles'), and he used to read Kipling and Buchan – though with a leavening of J.B. Priestley – to his own children.[5] His patriotism was never in doubt, and it was entirely predictable that he would volunteer to fight in 1914 and to take his place in government in 1940. He also retained very middle-class tastes and standards throughout his life. He always dressed soberly in a dark suit and he employed a male servant even when living in the East End. Indeed he was said to shudder when the port was passed the wrong way round the dining table. He also, letting his egalitarian guard drop for a moment, once insisted that a feature film on war might constitute valuable propaganda 'if done sufficiently crudely for the popular taste'.[6] Attlee's vision of socialism was, essentially, a raising of the poor much more than a scaling down of the rich. He was to sow quasi-revolutionary wild oats on several occasions, but here was no iconoclast and certainly no temperamental rebel.

On leaving Oxford, he looked round for a suitable career. He would have liked to remain as a Fellow of 'Univ' but had not made the grade. Instead he looked to the bar, perhaps as a well-established stepping stone to a political career. Certainly he later recalled a 'sneaking affection' for politics; but though he admired the 'strong ruthless leaders' of the Renaissance and sometimes dreamed of doing 'impossibly brilliant things', he felt too diffident to envisage, in the cold light of day, that he would ever become prominent.[7] His ambitions undoubtedly existed – a fact that needs to be emphasised because so few have ever drawn attention to it – but for the present they seemed too remote to be other than impractical dreams. The law it would have to be. He passed the necessary exams in 1905 and the following year, after gaining experience in solicitors' offices, was called to the bar. Yet he appeared in court only four times and earned no more than £50 as a barrister. The fact is that this 'typical' product of the Victorian establishment did not fully fit in with the world for which he seemed destined. For several years he appeared to be no more than a dilettante, taking many trips abroad, including a month in the United States in 1907, learning to ride, learning to shoot and, withal, avoiding commitment. With a private income of £200 before his father's death in 1908, and £400 afterwards, no commitment was necessary. Might he remain a gentleman and nothing more? Yet when he did finally choose a career, it was that of a social worker and political activist among the poor of London's East End.

. . .

ATTLEE'S CHARACTER: THE INSIDER-OUTSIDER

What set Attlee apart and impelled him in a direction so different from that of the vast majority of his public school contemporaries? The answer lies partly in his family. His parents took philanthropy very seriously. His father helped to build St Paul's church in Dorking and served on the councils of Dulwich and Haileybury schools and of Bart's Hospital, while his mother helped with poor relief in Wandsworth. Their actions stemmed to some degree from their religious convictions. Family prayers began at 7.30 a.m. every day, each child possessed a bible, and the Sabbath was strictly observed. Attlee never, then or later, disputed Christian ethics or the high-minded Victorian conviction that privilege – of which he and his kind enjoyed a disproportionate share – meant responsibility towards those less fortunate. Many of his siblings took up some form of philanthropic work. Even his eldest brother, Robert, who took over the family law firm, retired early in order to devote himself to charity. Most important of all was the commitment of Tom Attlee, two years Clement's senior and very much his mentor at both Haileybury and Oxford: judging that we find ourselves only by losing ourselves in the service of others, he embraced Christian Socialism and took a job at a working men's hostel in London.

Yet even in his family Attlee was often the odd one out. He reacted against Christianity from an early age, apparently because of his dislike of church services, and became an agnostic at the age of sixteen. He was also a shy boy. Perhaps this was because he was much smaller than his brothers, even, embarrassingly, than his younger brother; perhaps it was due in some measure to an early illness which meant he had to be educated at home until the age of nine. But at all events there can be no doubt about his shyness. All commentators on Attlee have drawn attention to it, and almost all his contemporaries pointed it out; yet few have considered its full importance. In fact, his shyness set him apart and marked him out for life.

Usually so reticent about personal feelings, Attlee in his memoirs referred on several occasions to his 'painful' shyness, recalling that for a time it was a positive 'torture' for him to do anything in public.[8] It was this which accounted for his lifelong love of books and reading. As a lonely schoolboy he devoured an average of four books a week, and later, during his frenetically busy period as Prime Minister, he read through the whole of Gibbon at Chequers. Nor did his characteristic shyness wear off, though it no doubt wore down as the years passed. A contemporary at Oxford described him as 'terribly shy', recalling that when a 'blood' (i.e. a popular personality) came into the room Attlee would 'twitch with nervousness'.[9] Later, in the House of Commons, several MPs noticed that he would shake, and that his fingers would twitch, before making a speech. As Prime Minister in 1945, he told junior ministers that he was a very diffident man who found it hard to carry on a conversation, and that they were not therefore to mistake his silences for indifference. When an assistant whip admitted to feeling nervous before a speech, Attlee reassured him with the words: 'Don't worry, I'm always nervous.'[10] But his shyness was seen most visibly towards the end of his political career with the dawn of the television age. He would chuckle nervously, answer questions monosyllabically and do his best to beat a hasty retreat before the cameras. In fact, he was an interviewer's nightmare. On one occasion, a live party political broadcast for Labour, Percy Cudlipp was armed with twenty-eight questions for the fifteen-minute programme: but, with Attlee as the interviewee, he used them all up in a mere five minutes. Even in his seventies, Attlee was described as making 'little quick, nervous movements as if he were not sure of himself'.[11]

The disadvantages of his shyness are obvious enough. As a self-effacing man of remarkably few words – dubbed by George VI 'Clem the Clam'[12] – he was a naturally poor speaker. Most of his speeches in the House of Commons, generally brief and delivered in staccato style, summarised conclusions instead of exploring ideas. What could not be said in few words was, in the manner approved by Wittgenstein, passed over in silence. Speech-making was an ordeal to be survived, not a delight to be savoured. Similarly in private conversation he lacked all small talk, at least outside the family circle. He did sometimes make an effort, as when he asked his dedicated Colonial Secretary Arthur Creech Jones, somewhat incredulously, whether he were still interested in colonies. But this was certainly not the way to win friends and influence people.

He seemed to many contemporaries to lack human warmth, another handicap to political intercourse, and at times his habitual terseness gave the appearance of bad manners. Certainly his notoriously curt dismissals of colleagues – he reportedly told one that he did not 'measure up' as a minister – made him seem unemotional and unfeeling, if not downright cruel. Even his dismissal of his comrade Ernie Bevin from the Foreign Office in 1951 did not seem to have been done feelingly. Yet in fact Attlee was genuinely fond of Bevin and found the necessity of removing him quite 'heartbreaking':[13] he had simply been unable, as so often before, to express emotion, because emotion, especially his own, was embarrassing. Attlee seemed an unfeeling butcher only because, in Richard Crossman's perceptive phrase, he was 'shy to the point of incivility'.[14]

No one in politics quite broke through the reserve of perhaps the most silent figure in modern political history, though some tried. The easiest way to put him at ease was to get him talking about cricket or his public school. Others found alcohol an asset. Certainly Hugh Gaitskell judged that he was always in much better form after a few drinks, though it was not often that he could be tempted to have more than one medium sherry.

Attlee's mild and diffident carapace represented a considerable effort on his part to overcome his innate shyness: beneath the surface there was an even milder and more diffident man struggling to hide himself. Yet this is not the whole story. At a deeper level of his personality, there was a dominant and formidable Clement Attlee struggling to get out. Certainly it is quite wrong to associate shyness with a lack of intellectual self-confidence. Indeed his final Haileybury report accused Attlee of being 'very self-opinionated'.[15] He undoubtedly had a good deal of faith in his own ability, and especially in his ability to learn. Recognising his limitations, he made himself by dint of practice and hard work into a competent speaker. He was even in demand after 1945 as a witty after-dinner speaker. He could be particularly good in debate, where his terse one-liners were sometimes formidable weapons against more loquacious and pompous opponents. Nor was it a bad thing for a Prime Minister to seem cold, and a little inhuman, to colleagues. Many found his silence truly intimidating and held the premier in awe. Shyness also made Attlee a loner in politics, as close to being an outsider as an insider can be, and remarkably self-sustained. He once said that he would have survived the rigours of solitary confinement in prison very well.

Attlee's shyness was obviously a disadvantage, but it was also, in many ways, a remarkably effective political weapon. His solitary position in the Labour Party meant that in his governments there were no 'kitchen cabinets', no late-night gossiping sessions with a favoured few cronies. There were therefore no interest groups to appease: he was always his own man. His avoidance of political gossip also meant that he made few enemies. Furthermore, it made him appear more efficient and decisive than he really was. Because he would never think aloud, he announced conclusions – which may often have been a long time gestating – with a bullet-like force which made them seem spontaneous. As a result, observers of his premierships have tended to depict a far more brisk, decisive and resolute figure than the real-life Clement Attlee. So have historians, led astray partly by transcripts of the interviews he gave late in life, in which his always terse opinions occasionally blossomed into mature, pungent epigrams. 'Dithering' has never been considered an Attleean quality: he is generally depicted as operating with a super-efficient economy of effort. Yet he did dither at times. But above all, perhaps, Attlee's tendency to self-effacement meant that he was generally overlooked so that, in the key period of his political apprenticeship, when he was climbing the Labour party hierarchy, he seemed to pose no threat to those – his seemingly more able and certainly more obviously, and flamboyantly, ambitious colleagues – who were apparently destined for the leadership. Attlee was a man fatally easy to underestimate.

· · · ·

REFERENCES

1. C.R. Attlee, *As It Happened* (London, 1954), p. 3.
2. Lord Attlee, *Empire into Commonwealth* (London, 1961), p. 6.
3. Kenneth Harris, *Attlee* (London, 1984), p. 9.
4. Ibid., p. 15.
5. Ibid., p. 142. Attlee to Patricia Beck, 2 July 1965, Attlee Papers, Bodleian Library, Oxford.
6. Attlee to Tom Attlee, 18 October 1934, Attlee Papers, Bodleian Library.
7. William Golant, 'The Political Development of C.R. Attlee to 1935' (unpub. Oxford B.Litt. Thesis, 1967), p. 14.
8. Attlee, *As It Happened,* pp. 12, 19.
9. Harris, *Attlee,* p. 12.
10. Robert Pearce, *Attlee's Labour Governments 1945–51* (London, 1994), p. 19.
11. Lord Moran, *Churchill: The Struggle for Survival* (London, 1968), p. 677.
12. Trevor Burridge, *Clement Attlee: A Political Biography* (London, 1985), p. 2.

13. Francis Williams (ed.), *A Prime Minister Remembers* (London, 1961), p. 243.
14. Janet Morgan (ed.), *The Backbench Diaries of Richard Crossman*, 21 January 1952, p. 68.
15. Harris, *Attlee*, p. 9.

Chapter 2

ATTLEE'S APPRENTICESHIP, 1905–31

What can be done in the service of death can be done in the service of life.[1]

· · ·

SOCIAL WORK AND SOCIALISM

After leaving university, and while training for the bar, Attlee undertook a spot of social work. He seems to have been motivated as much by curiosity as conscience. With his brother Laurence, in October 1905, he visited the Haileybury Club in Stepney. This was a working-class version of the Officers' Training Corps, open to boys aged from fourteen to eighteen who were junior members of the Territorial Army. It was Haileybury's venture into Christian charity and, at the same time, its effort to put some grit into the working classes. After this first visit, Attlee went once a week and then more often. A few months later he was helping to run the club, and within eighteen months he was its manager, living on the premises, at a salary of £50 a year. Laurence pursued a similar course at a boys' club in Islington. For Clement it was the beginning of fourteen years in the East End and of an important, though not a complete, change in his mental outlook.

At first the boys probably regarded Attlee as a curious do-gooder. But soon it was they who must have been curious. Here was a strict disciplinarian, expelling several members in order to encourage the others, but also remarkably solicitous of their welfare, even tender-hearted, being generous with both his time and his money. While most of the boys were determined to 'raise' themselves socially, so that many ended up as Conservatives, Attlee was making another transition. He did not define the term with any precision, and throughout his life he resisted rigid definitions, but by 1908 the former Tory was calling himself a 'socialist'.

There are several explanations for his new commitment. First, there was the shock of seeing London poverty for the first time. Stepney, in London's dockland, was at the centre of the capital's slums. Charles Booth had recently estimated that 38 per cent of its population were living in poverty. Second, he was profoundly impressed with the people he found there. Forming class prejudices, Attlee judged, is as natural as breathing; but gradually he began to shed his, or at least some of them.

Attlee entered the East End with several preconceived notions. He believed that poverty was caused by fecklessness and that therefore, while the charity of the wealthier classes was virtuous and to be encouraged, the only real cure was individual self-help. He was highly critical, for instance, of expensive working-class funerals, which to his mind were a gross self-indulgence. Instead, he expected that people should exercise frugality and pull themselves up by their bootstraps. Certainly action by the state, identified in his mind with the prison and the workhouse, was not to be encouraged. *Laissez-faire* was his favoured policy. What need was there for collective action when the fundamental problem was with the individual?

Perhaps the first breach in the dike of middle-class complacency was on a personal level. As a public school man, Attlee would have automatically felt superior to his charges; but his shyness also meant that he felt awkward, almost at times, as his autobiographical writings attest, a fool. He was thus less clouded with conceit than many others would have been, with the result that the more he got to know the boys in the club, the more he appreciated their humanity, their decency and even their wisdom. On several occasions in later life he quoted the views of the East End lads: 'a pal is a bloke wot knows all about yer and yet loves yer'; 'a gentleman is a bloke who's the same to everybody'. He was told that women should have the vote because 'only a working woman knows what a working woman has to go through'. He also recalled the response of a small boy who, to his statement that he was going home to tea, replied, 'Oh, I'm going home to see if there is any tea.'[2]

Soon he concluded that all people are animated by the same human passions. No doubt he could have learned this, theoretically, from reading Wordsworth, who recognised that we have all of us one human heart; but some things, to be learned deeply, have to be learned from personal experience. His knowledge led not only to understanding but to trust and affection, and to the certainty that working-class people were the equals of anybody. In short, he achieved some sense of fellowship with the East Enders. By realising that all human beings are individuals, all different from each other, Attlee realised that the classes are the same. Hence expensive funerals no longer merited his ire. They were not a profligate excess but a welcome sign of pride in family traditions, comparable to the middle-class trait of dressing for dinner.

It followed from this that he could no longer accept the notion – all too comforting to the middle-class conscience – that poverty was a result of the moral failings of individuals. Hence thrift was not the key to social betterment: indeed, in the conditions of Stepney, thrift was meaningless and often meant meanness. It is the sty that makes the pig, he insisted, in a pointed though ungenerous metaphor, not the pig the sty, except in very exceptional cases.

But what should be done about poverty and poor conditions? Certainly there was no case for doing nothing. The *laissez-faire* approach, stressing that all would be for the best if individuals followed their own economic self-interest, was obviously faulty: not only had it done much to destroy a sense of fellowship, but it had manifestly failed to produce equitable standards of living. It simply allowed the middle classes to remain comfortable in their consciences, and to label the victims of poverty as the culprits. Individualism was the rich man's alibi for a multitude of sins. There was still a place, the public schoolboy believed, for the *noblesse oblige* tradition, which was based on the desire to share advantages with those less fortunate than oneself, and it was all too easy to sneer at those who undertook unpaid voluntary work. But such work had to be done in the right spirit, whereas all too often the real object of charity was the well-being of the giver, whose ego was massaged by the gratitude of the poor. No one, Attlee believed, should expect gratitude – not for what, in essence, were merely the crumbs from the rich man's table. Only between equals could charity be given and received without loss of dignity, and therefore social work had, ideally, to be done with, not to, the poor.

Yet charity could not touch the fundamental causes of poverty, and social work could only ameliorate the situation not rectify it. The real cure was not charity, social work, do-gooding or generosity – it was social justice. Instead of beating their breasts and evincing sympathy with the downtrodden, the wealthy should, in Tolstoy's formula, simply get off their backs. This demanded a fundamental political change in society. Attlee insisted that, while social workers should press for practical, piecemeal and immediate improvements, they should also be agitators, pressing for social change by means of collective action. Those who insisted that non-contributory benefits sapped the self-respect and enfeebled the wills of the recipients, he noted shrewdly, never seemed to say the same about the rents, profits and unearned income of the rich. He thus favoured a dual approach – individual and also political action. He had thus shed his former antipathy to collective action by the state. In short, he came to see that poverty was essentially a political issue. In Britain there were all the necessities for producing a good life for all the people: the problem was how to organise society to achieve this.

Attlee's thinking was not brilliant or revolutionary. It was too general for that, too lacking in critical rigour. But it also made sound practical sense, showing both an awareness of society's ills and a commitment to doing something practical about them. His emotions impelled him in the direction of socialism: as he put it, heart first ('Man cannot rest until mankind is freed', he wrote in a poem of 1908), head after-wards.[3] His was essentially an ethical motivation, which his reading of William Morris and John Ruskin confirmed. Like them, he saw the need to treat people as individuals, not as cases, categories or statistical tables.

Observers probably felt that the reticent social worker's sense of fellowship with the East Enders was incomplete and distanced. Yet in his poetry he spoke most truly from the heart. His first published poem, in the Haileybury magazine in 1899, had been a vigorous attack on the striking London cab-bies, ending with the stern certainty that the hunger of their wives and children would drive them back to work, so that they would eventually 'beg for a fare at our feet'. Perhaps such deeply-held childhood feelings could never be entirely eradicated; but it is certain that his East End experiences altered his conscious outlook. In 1910 he had another poem published, this time in the *Socialist Review*.

> In Limehouse, in Limehouse, before the break of day,
> I hear the feet of many men who go upon their way,
> Who wander through the city,
> The grey and cruel city,
> Through streets that have no pity,
> The streets where men decay.
> In Limehouse, in Limehouse, by night as well as day
> I hear the feet of children that go to work or play,
> Of children born to sorrow,
> The workers of tomorrow,
> How shall they work tomorrow
> Who get no bread today?[4]

This growing political awareness took Attlee and his brother Tom into Labour politics. They could not join the Labour Party as such, though the Labour Representation Committee of 1900 had adopted this name in 1906, since there was no provision for individual membership: only trade unions and socialist organisations could affiliate before 1918. Hence they turned, with the approval of their parents, to the highly respectable Fabian Society, originally founded in 1884. Yet they found the intellectual theorising of Webb, Shaw and Wells uncongenial as well as patronising to working people. The revolutionary Social Democratic Federation had even less appeal. Attlee was of too practical and pragmatic a cast of mind to adhere to Marxist orthodoxy, and later in life he almost boasted of never having read any Marxist stuff. His aim was not to foment violent revolution as conditions deteriorated further and further, but to bring about practical, tangible improvements. Yet the Attlee brothers did find their niche, despite parental disapproval, in the working-class Independent Labour Party, founded by Keir Hardie in 1893. Tom became active in Wandsworth, while Clement joined the local branch in Stepney in 1908. The existing members, not many more than a dozen of them, were all trade unionists in full-time employment. Hence despite his lack of experience, Attlee, whose work at the Haileybury Club left him plenty of spare time, was quickly made branch secretary. There were advantages in being a bourgeois in a working-class party.

The next period in Attlee's life was of momentous importance for his later successful career. He learned about labour politics at the grass roots. With his comfortable private income, there was no urgency for him to settle down to permanent employment, and he therefore undertook a variety of jobs, none of which seemed likely to be permanent but all of which provided valuable experience. He took part in a campaign to publicise the sweated industries; he organised propaganda for the Minority Report of the Webbs, which argued that poor relief should be a responsibility of central, rather than local, government; he campaigned for the suffragettes; he supervised free school meals for needy children; he acted as an 'official explainer' for Lloyd George's National Insurance Act of 1911 which, while doing nothing to rid the country of unemployment, nevertheless substantially eased the plight of the unemployed; and he helped distribute food during the dockers' strike of the same year. In fact, no task seemed too menial, even buttering bread or licking envelopes, and, as Harris has noted, he was 'always the servant'.[5] In 1912 he did get paid employment, as tutor in social services at the London School of Economics, defeating a younger but academically better qualified candidate, Hugh Dalton. Attlee got the post, much to Dalton's lasting chagrin, because of his greater experiences with the East End poor. But he did not intend to devote himself to academic life. Politics was taking up too much of his time.

As secretary of the ILP in Stepney, his political horizons were widened. He attended several meetings of international socialists in London; and he also made the acquaintance of George Lansbury of Poplar and of a rising figure in London labour politics, Herbert Morrison. Five years his junior, Morrison was chairman of the Brixton branch of the ILP when he met Attlee in 1910. The following year they both spoke at a joint Fabian–ILP series of lectures on political history. But more characteristic of Attlee's life at this time was a large number of tedious chores – collecting subscriptions, trying to sell pamphlets and organising speakers. At most meetings he himself, as the only one who could be certain to turn up on time, was usually the first speaker. He was not a good or a natural public speaker, but the fact that his first efforts were after dark, in the open air, must have helped his nervousness. At any rate, early shortcomings were reduced as a result of constant practice, as he addressed one or two meetings a week for several years. There is evidence of a growing expertise with hecklers.

Once again Attlee was part of a fellowship, and he gave little thought to personal advancement. But perhaps some. It is not true to say, as his later supporters did, that he was always perfectly content to tackle whatever task was before him. He gave at least some thought to the morrow. Certainly the idea of securing a place on a local council appealed to him. In 1908 he secured the ILP candidacy for Stepney borough council. Attlee had impressed no one with his brilliance, but no one else seemed to have any prior claim – and indeed no one else, if elected, could afford to take up such a time-consuming, unpaid post. Yet he polled a mere 69 votes. It was an inauspicious start, and to a colleague's hearty 'Are we down-hearted?', he barked 'Of course we are.' Yet little more could be expected. The Reform Act of 1884 had denied the vote to all women and to over one-third of men, and only about 4,000 out of Stepney's total population of 300,000 voted for a national party. The local council was dominated by the Union of Stepney Ratepayers, whose primary aim was to keep the rates as low as possible. He was defeated again in subsequent years, both for the borough council and the Limehouse board of guardians. Nor could anyone be certain that the future lay with Labour. The Labour party had won 30 seats in the 1906 election, but this was with the electoral support of the Liberals, and reforming Liberal legislation seemed likely to undermine Labour support. Certainly the pattern of by-election defeats after 1910 was ominous.

In 1914 Attlee's future was very uncertain. None could have predicted what the next years held. In fact he and his brother both ended up in Wandsworth – Tom in the gaol, Clem in the hospital.

· · ·

THE FIRST WORLD WAR

Like many socialists, Tom Attlee was a pacifist and conscientious objector. Clement Attlee, like an even greater number of socialists, felt that his country needed him. At thirty-one, he was a year too old to enlist, but string-pulling, and his experience in the cadets and OTC, led to his appointment as a lieutenant in the 6th battalion of the South Lancashire Regiment with command of a company of seven officers and 850 men. Once more, Attlee owed a good deal to his class.

Attlee had a good war: he managed to survive. Luck was therefore with him. A Winston Churchill might well have interpreted this good fortune as a sign that the gods were reserving him for an heroic and glorious future. But Attlee had not the egotism for such flights of fancy. His feet were planted firmly on the ground. He knew that he had just been lucky, and that others had not.

In June 1915, as a captain, he sailed as part of the ill-fated Gallipoli expedition. What was, theoretically, an attempt to break out of the stalemate on the western front turned out, for the men involved, to bear a strong resemblance to the familiar pattern of trench warfare – heat, flies, stench and dysentery, a bad case of which led to Attlee's collapse and his despatch, unconscious, for home. In fact he disembarked at Malta, complaining at this evacuation without consent, and returned to his men; but he had missed an assault in which half the British forces were killed. Quite possibly dysentery had saved his life. In January 1916 he was the last man, apart from General Maude, to leave Gallipoli when the expedition was recalled. Apart from the evacuation, the campaign had been a fiasco, but Attlee never joined the chorus of criticism which damaged the reputation of the First Lord of the Admiralty, Winston Churchill. Indeed he always approved the broad conception of Churchill's scheme.

The regiment was then posted to Mesopotamia, where Attlee led his men over the top against Turkish forces at El Hannah. In the process he received a bullet in the thigh and sundry burns, so that for a time it seemed he might lose the use of his legs. He was put on a hospital ship bound for Bombay and from there was invalided back to Britain. During his four months at home he worked hard to get back to the action. He was promoted major, but even so had to change battalions in order to get a posting to France in June 1917. In August 1918 he was wounded again, falling timber striking his head as he captured a German trench, and he spent the armistice in hospital in Wandsworth.

The war undoubtedly boosted Attlee's political career. There was kudos to be gained as a returning officer, and he kept the title 'Major Attlee' for most of the interwar period.

The war also affected his ideas, strengthening his conviction that society had to be improved: those who had been good enough to fight for their country and risk their lives ought to have a decent chance of a reasonable standard of living afterwards. In particular, they should have a job. He was convinced that government action, which had provided jobs during the war, could do the same in peacetime. Wartime experiences also strengthened his belief in the importance of fellowship and in the possibility of class collaboration rather than confrontation. Thus the war, though a disaster, need not be an unmitigated one – especially if it could be followed by a more rational system of international relations. The war opened out the prospect of changing society fundamentally and for the better, if only the opportunities could be grasped.

In addition, the war had strengthened Attlee's self-confidence. Already a leader of boys, he had now shown that he could be a leader of men. He wrote to Tom in 1918 that 'this soldiering business is only tolerable when one has a definite unit under one's command'.[6] On one occasion he had even threatened to shoot an officer who refused to advance. This did not betray callousness: the man did indeed advance, and though he fainted in the process Attlee argued against his commanding officer's judgement that he should be shot anyway. Instead, it showed leadership. On another occasion, he gave a man sixty seconds to obey orders, and took out a stopwatch to time him; after forty-five seconds he returned to duty. A ploy Attlee had used with boys in Stepney had once again proved its worth. Though still devoted to his family, Attlee was emerging from the shadows of his elder brothers.

· · ·

LOCAL GOVERNMENT

After demobilisation in 1919, Attlee returned to his post at the London School of Economics, where he wrote his first book, *The Social Worker* (1920). Attlee was considered by many within Labour ranks to be an intellectual, but here was no brilliant academic treatise: it was based too squarely on his own experiences for that. While reflecting his romantic faith in human nature, which he was loath to speak about openly, it was also an extremely practical book, stressing the need for both individual initiatives and collective action to change society. He called for trade unions to have a share in controlling industry, and he did not shy away from insisting that the legal profession was a powerful, blackleg-proof trade union. He also gave detailed, practical advice. In running a boys' club, for instance, one should never show favouritism towards a clique or an individual. As for chairing a committee, it was essential to remember that such bodies existed to make decisions, not to provide a forum for speech-making: therefore, the chairman – who should be polite, impartial and well-informed – had to keep members to the point, to canvass views efficiently and to get through an agenda. This was simple but practical advice, and it was to stand Attlee in good stead throughout his career.

The book did not herald his immersion in an academic career. As before the war, he combined teaching with East End activities, but it was not long before politics predominated. After all, there was now a real chance of power for the left. The number of trade unionists had increased by 50 per cent during the war; Labour had gained some ministerial experience as part of the Asquith and Lloyd George coalitions; and in 1918 the party had a new constitution, *Labour and the New Social Order*. Provision was made for individual membership and, moreover, the party had a new, distinctively 'socialist' position: it would replace a society based on conflict and inequality with one based on 'deliberately planned co-operation'. Furthermore it was pledged to bring about 'the Common Ownership of the Means of Production, and the best obtainable system of popular administration and control of each industry and service'.

Whenever Attlee used the word socialism he did so loosely, as a term of approval – as loosely as did his opponents, to whom it was a general term of abuse; but there is no evidence that he ever quarrelled with Clause IV. He was concerned not with terminological exactitude but with entering the political world.

The other great change of 1918 – the Representation of the People Act – was perhaps the most important factor in giving Labour a chance of power. The vote was now extended to men at the age of twenty-one and women at thirty. At a stroke the electorate was virtually tripled and so, at long last, the people's voice could be heard. In the general election of December 1918 the Lloyd George coalition won a huge majority of seats, 478 to Labour's 63. But, even so, this represented a breakthrough for Labour, whose percentage of the vote had increased dramatically from 7 per cent, at the previous elections in 1910, to 22 per cent.

Increased representation at Westminster was one thing, but real political power was to be won first in the field of local government. There had never yet been a single Labour councillor in Stepney; but now all could be changed. There was a prospect of a Labour-controlled East End. Attlee joined the fray, and in March 1919 his hat was in the ring, contesting the elections for the London County Council, the upper tier of local administration in the capital. The dominant groups in Stepney were Jews and Irish, each of which had their own prospective councillors: Attlee was chosen as a compromise who, though neither Jewish nor Irish, was respected by both groups. No one disliked the hardworking, self-effacing Attlee, and in addition he had a good war record, a fine history of social work in the East End and the blessing of a private income. As in 1935, when he became leader of the Labour party, he was not an outstanding or exciting choice, but he was, in Golant's phrase, the 'appropriate one'.[7] His career seemed to be making progress – and it did so, despite defeat in the LCC contest. The fact that Attlee had done well, losing by fewer than a hundred votes, meant that he was able to secure adoption as prospective parliamentary candidate for the Limehouse division of Stepney.

This defeat may well have been crucial in Attlee's rise to power. Without it, he might have pursued a career in local government. Yet he involved himself in local politics nevertheless. He leased a house in Limehouse, where he was looked after by an ex-member of the Haileybury Club, and this became the Labour headquarters from which he helped organise the party's campaign in the borough council elections of November 1919. As a prospective Member of Parliament he did not stand himself, but he threw himself without reserve into the contest. He wrote the election address for all the candidates, calling for practical reform – for more open spaces, for cheap and clean milk for infants and expectant mothers, for better street cleaning, and more public baths and washhouses. Voters were urged to give Labour a chance to make the borough a place worth living in. The chance was duly given. Labour won control by a large margin in Stepney: having never won a single seat before, the party won 43 seats out of a possible 60, including all 15 seats in Limehouse. Attlee's prospects for the general election thus looked very good.

The first duty of the new council was to select a mayor, and Attlee was chosen. This co-option of an unelected figure was unusual. Several factors were involved. Attlee had certainly been highly successful as campaign manager and so had earned the gratitude of the councillors; in addition, it was expected – quite correctly – that his common-sense moderation would win the support of some of the Tory councillors. But there is a third factor. Once more he was a good compromise candidate: only he would be acceptable to the powerful interest groups in Stepney, the Jewish garment workers, the Irish Roman Catholics and the Protestants in the Transport and General Workers' Union.

The next few years were remarkably full ones. Attlee proved himself an adept chairman of the council. The local press reported that he ruled statements out of order with 'firm – almost curt – precise and unmistakable sentences, like the slamming of a railway carriage door'.[8] He was also instrumental in securing rate rises, for landlords and businessmen, which helped to bring about health improvements in the borough. Better antenatal facilities led to lower rates of infant mortality; and the appointment of new sanitary inspectors resulted in over 40,000 demands for owners to repair their property. Attlee also gained experience outside Stepney. He became chairman of the association of London Labour mayors and a member of the executive committee of the London Labour Party, whose efficient and dynamic secretary, Herbert Morrison, had recently, like Attlee, been co-opted as mayor, in his case of Hackney. Attlee also led a deputation of London mayors to the Prime Minister to press the needs of the unemployed. Lloyd George was less than forthcoming, but Attlee gained national publicity when police clashed with a group of demonstrators and the situation threatened to become ugly. He ordered the Stepney contingent to halt and turn about, and he led them in perfect order away from the trouble.

After his mayoral year, a timely death left a vacancy for an alderman in Stepney, which Attlee filled. He now had a stable, and highly respected, five-year niche, and so was able to continue his council work. Yet there were signs that he was not the moderate many assumed. Already he had criticised the lord mayor of London for failing to support bold measures to tackle unemployment, and he had also spoken in favour of workers' control in industry. Each industry, he argued in a 1922 ILP pamphlet, taking his lead from the guild socialists, should be in the hands of its workers in a socialist state. Now, in addition, he took his stand behind George Lansbury on 'Poplarism'. The government's system of unemployment relief, administered by the LCC, threw a disproportionate burden on the poorer boroughs of the East End, while the richer boroughs of the West End were let off relatively lightly. In protest, Lansbury and councillors from Poplar refused to contribute to LCC funds, and were promptly imprisoned for their effrontery. Some Labour figures, including Morrison, repudiated Lansbury's unconstitutional tactics, but Attlee voted in Stepney to follow his lead: he too was willing to go to prison rather than support an unjust law. In fact the LCC soon redistributed the burden of rates more equitably, but Attlee's stand had been a defiant one. Even so, he was clearly aware that local government resources were insufficient to cure the twin evils of poverty and unemployment. Unlike the guild socialists, he recognised that action at the national level was also needed.

Yet if Attlee was fully aware of the needs of the East Enders, he by no means identified with them. In January 1922 he moved away from Stepney and bought a semi-detached house in the middle-class suburb of Woodford Green. In fact this was a turning point in his life: increasingly lonely since the death of his mother in May 1920, so that there was no family home in Putney to which he could return at weekends, he found a wife. At the age of thirty-eight, he married the twenty-five year-old Violet Millar, the sister of a friend of Tom Attlee's. The man who was so reticent about his feelings that many half-suspected that he did not have any, admitted privately to being 'as mad as a march hare with joy'.[9] They married, and moved to their new house, after Attlee had taken the precaution of inviting Violet to hear him speak: she was not put off. To the press she became notorious for her driving, though in fact her husband's was even worse; but perhaps her most significant quality was that, despite being Conservative-minded (with a taste in the 1940s for the novels of Angela Thirkell), she was essentially not a political animal. Hence she was able to provide what Attlee most needed, a refuge where he could relax from the incessant demands and strains of politics. The lonely bachelor was transformed into the family man, soon with four children. The family also provided a spur to Attlee's ambition, as the income from his father's estate dwindled. His first child was due three months after the general election of October 1922. If he won in Limehouse, he would have a salary of £400 a year.

. . .

MEMBER OF PARLIAMENT, 1922–29

The incumbent Member in Stepney, Sir William Pearce, had held the seat since 1906, and there was no guarantee that Labour would win this time. They lost in Mile End, the other division of Stepney. But in Limehouse Attlee was home by 1,900 votes. His election address stressed the degree to which the Tories and the Liberals, both represented in the former coalition government, had failed to bring about the social improvements they had promised: unemployment, poverty and slums still existed.

> I stand for life against wealth. I claim the right of every man, woman and child in the land to have the best life that can be provided. Instead of the exploitation of the mass of the people in the interests of a small rich class, I demand the organisation of the country in the interests of all as a co-operative commonwealth in which land and capital will be owned by the nation and used for the benefit of the community.[10]

This was a simple message, but a clear and effective one – and one which Attlee consistently espoused. As late as 1964 he was still insisting that, at bottom, the Conservatives stood for profit, while Labour existed for serving the community.

It was a good election for the party, which won almost 30 per cent of the popular vote and 142 seats. They were now the official opposition. The Conservatives, under Bonar Law, had won 345 seats, and so there seemed little likelihood of Labour forming a government in the short term, but in fact the Conservative majority stemmed from only 38 per cent of the popular vote. If Labour maintained momentum, they could well be in office in the foreseeable future. Labour MPs were therefore in buoyant mood when they assembled at Westminster, and as leader they chose James Ramsay MacDonald. Attlee certainly cast his vote for MacDonald, who was to be perhaps the foremost political influence on his life.

A founder of the Labour Representation Committee in 1900 and the Chairman of the Parliamentary Labour Party in

1911–14, MacDonald had resigned rather than support the war. For a time he had been vilified; but now, in the postwar revulsion against war, his stand seemed to have been justified. He was also a leading theorist of socialism, opposing notions of class war and believing instead in peaceful, evolutionary change. He also expressed his vision with great fervour on the platform, having a rhetorical and parliamentary skill which the more tongue-tied and inexperienced Attlee could not but admire. In retrospect, MacDonald and Attlee were to seem total opposites, but, despite the contrast in their personalities, differences in policy and principle did not yet exist. Attlee's admiration for MacDonald knew no bounds, especially when he was made one of his Parliamentary Private Secretaries.

MacDonald's decision to utilise Attlee's services is easily explained. The party leader approved the fact that now the Parliamentary Labour Party had more middle-class and upper-class MPs: but he still feared that, if the left continued to talk of revolution, Labour would not manage to shrug off its reputation as the party of rabble-rousing malcontents, representative not of the nation but only of the industrial workers. Philip Snowden, another key figure in the party, had similar ideas: the wonder, he wrote, was that Labour was doing so well when there were 'so many fools doing their best to make the party ridiculous'.[11] Attlee was therefore exactly the sort of man these two Labour leaders wished to see in prominent positions in the party – well educated, moderate and, above all, respectable. It was MacDonald who advised that he refer to himself as Major in parliament. In short, he was a welcome contrast to the left-wing Clydeside MPs who, in true Marxist fashion, were now accusing the government and the governing classes of the indirect murder of the exploited workforce and their children. Paradoxically, Attlee himself, at the end of the war, had called the middle classes 'accessories, before and after the fact', in the premature deaths of the workers,[12] but now such views were tactfully put aside. Attlee the pragmatist came to the fore.

The position of PPS to the opposition leader gave Attlee an important role. He had to keep the party leader informed of thinking on the back benches, no easy job given MacDonald's proverbial aloofness from the rank and file. Indeed it required two PPSs, and Attlee formed a good working relationship with Jack Lawson of the Durham miners. His parliamentary education proceeded apace. He also made an immediate impact in the House, with a maiden speech only three days after parliament met.

The Clydesiders had been monopolising the opposition's contribution to the debate on the King's speech, and the Speaker called Attlee to get an alternative point of view. He took as his theme one of the key issues in modern British politics, unemployment, and in particular the unacceptably high levels in areas like Stepney. The true wealth of a country, he insisted, beginning with first principles, is its citizens, and yet men capable of productive work were almost destitute. The cure for this evil had nothing to do with free trade or protection, as so many supposed: unemployment had existed under both dispensations. The only time unemployment had not existed was during the war, and Attlee therefore insisted that the cure lay with the sort of political action that had been taken then. 'As the nation was organised for war and death, so it can be organised for peace and life, if we have the will for it.' He advised that unemployed men, the very men who had saved Britain during the war, should be set to work tackling the problems of peace-time – and there were plenty of such problems. In London alone, he detailed, there were some 600,000 people occupying one-room tenements, in conditions which did not make for morality or sobriety. The government should therefore direct the manpower available to tackle the jobs that needed to be done. Otherwise there would be a tremendous waste of potential – for unmerited suffering and privation, despite naive convictions to the contrary, did not build character. Future generations would be wasted, and he predicted that if a war started in twenty years' time a large proportion of recruits would be C3 not A1.[13]

It was a good speech: clear, incisive, well-prepared and based on his own personal experience. Its attack on the Conservative administration pleased Labour ranks; its concern with national fitness won the ear of Tory imperialists; and its patent sincerity appealed to the public-spirited. Although continuing to find public speaking uncongenial, Attlee was already a practiced performer. No one, over the next years, found him a brilliant speaker or debater, and many found him dull; but he was generally a competent performer. He did not go on too long, did not ramble and generally got his point across.

Yet there could be little more practice at parliamentary oratory in his first parliament. Ill health forced the resignation of Bonar Law in May 1923, and at the end of the year his successor, the conciliatory Stanley Baldwin, blundered into an election on the issue of protection. Attlee increased his majority in Limehouse, and in total Labour won 191 seats, only 70 fewer than the Conservatives, in a hung parliament. The first Labour government was formed, and far sooner than MacDonald had thought possible. At any time the combined Conservative and Liberal forces could force his defeat, but MacDonald judged that experience of office would be valuable. He could show the electorate that Labour was respectable and fit to govern; and, furthermore, a minority administration would be the perfect alibi to refuse the claims of the Clydesiders. Attlee endorsed his decision, believing that acceptance of office was the right choice: refusal would only have fuelled the charge of irresponsibility, and moreover it might have helped to rejuvenate the moribund Liberals. Nor did Attlee object when MacDonald followed time-honoured procedures and chose the cabinet himself, instead, as some hoped, of allowing the party to do so.

Attlee himself now entered the government. This was an important step forward in his career, and he accepted office without hesitation, though with some private misgivings, as one of his poems shows.

> No more the old branch meeting
> Where I learnt and where I taught.
> The minutes, correspondence
> And delegate's report.
> I've got a government job now,
> My silence has been bought.
> I feel a sort of traitor.[14]

He knew that office inevitably meant compromise, so that advancement was also a kind of loss; and he retained a nostalgic respect for the 'romantic left' whose socialist vision, while unfulfilled, at least remained unsullied.

Attlee became part of the Labour team at the War Office. Stephen Walsh, who had been MP for Ince since 1906, became Secretary of State; Jack Lawson, who had served as a private in the army during the war, became Financial Secretary; and Clement Attlee became Under-Secretary. MacDonald's choice of the Major was understandable, on one level. Yet Attlee had recently put forward pacifist views. At the previous year's party conference he had spoken in favour of the motion – described by Arthur Henderson as absurd and futile – that the party should vote against all military and naval estimates; and in the Commons he had urged that all armies should be done away with. Probably MacDonald was simply unaware of this. At all events, Attlee's new found pacifism was short-lived.

In March 1924 Labour backbenchers moved that the army be reduced to 10,000 men, but Attlee, the dutiful Under-Secretary, did what was expected of him, staying silent during the debate. This passivity was in fact symbolic of his period at the War Office, and indeed of the first Labour government as a whole. The new men were gaining experience of office, under the guidance of the Civil Service, and there was consequently little scope for innovation. Only the radical John Wheatley, with his Housing Act, made a real impact, a success story which may perhaps have encouraged Attlee, in 1945, to chance his arm with the appointment of another radical, Aneurin Bevan. Admittedly Labour reduced the army estimates by £7 million, but in fact they were merely rubber-stamping cuts inaugurated by the outgoing Conservative administration. Something was done to encourage promotion from the ranks into the officer class, and Attlee was behind a training scheme to supply tradesmen for the army. He also tried to reduce the number of military offences punishable by death, efforts that bore fruit after he left office. Yet in total his influence was necessarily limited. He would have liked to proscribe the death sentence for courts martial altogether, but he toed the government line and voted against a parliamentary amendment to this effect. Only in opposition did he follow his conscience and vote for the ban.

It is true that in April 1924 one journalist predicted that he would eventually make a good Home Secretary; but very few people formed an opinion about him one way or the other. Perhaps the person in the best position to judge was Lawson, who later wrote of this period that Attlee

> worked hard and had his facts at his finger ends when necessary. He was a master of detail which means much in a department. He never used a word more than was necessary. Patient, sound in reasoning, clear in exposition of his views – now and then caustic – he

fitted the Department . . . There was steel in him, and the spirit of service and integrity which is far above ambition.[15]

There are many perceptive comments in this assessment. Certainly Attlee worked hard and determinedly. But there is also an element of reading back the later man into this period. The brief period of Labour administration provided a poor testing ground of Attlee's true worth.

Labour went out of office after nine months and did well at the general election of October 1924, gaining an extra million votes. Once again Attlee's majority in Limehouse increased. Many believed that the party was indeed fit to govern. The problem, however, was that many more did not. The publication of the Zinoviev Letter produced a 'red scare' during the election campaign, damning Labour by association with the Russian Communists. It undoubtedly magnified a shift of votes from the Liberals to the Conservatives which gave Baldwin a majority of over 200 seats. Attlee, minus his ministerial salary, was now on the Opposition front bench.

Many thought that MacDonald had handled the Zinoviev issue badly: he should have denounced the letter as an obvious forgery, instead of dithering and then appearing to accept its authenticity. Attlee also recalled having misgivings on this score. Nevertheless, he was still a MacDonald man in the party leader's subsequent clash with Ernest Bevin, founder of the Transport and General Workers' Union. Bevin had been disappointed with the first Labour government and had particularly disliked MacDonald's willingness to invoke the Emergency Powers Act against strikers. This was not what he expected of a Labour government, even one dependent on Liberal support. Hence in 1925 he moved a resolution at the annual conference that Labour should not form a minority government again. He was defeated, Attlee among others deciding that all options should be kept open. The alliance between Attlee and Bevin, so important in the 1940s, as yet showed no signs of being forged.

Similarly, Attlee shared MacDonald's attitude to the General Strike of 1926. Both men refused to give it support: the way forward for Labour was through parliamentary action not through massive industrial dislocation. Even so, Attlee was far more involved with the strike, as a Stepney alderman and chairman of the electricity committee, than his party leader. He helped cement a deal with the TUC that local power workers would continue at their jobs. They would provide power for all the needs of the borough's hospitals but only for lighting else-where: it was agreed that if any firms refused to accept this agreement, and used power to run machinery, then the fuses would be pulled on them. Stepney was the only London bor-ough to use this ingenious system, the remainder having power supplied by volunteers or naval ratings. It was a sensible attempt to minimise the inconvenience of the strike, while also showing some solidarity with the strikers by refusing to call on blackleg labour. Only one firm, Scammels, refused to toe the line, and their fuses were duly pulled. In fact, this action threat-ened Attlee's whole career. Scammels later brought an action against him and the other Labour members of the electricity committee, and he was ordered personally to pay £300 in dam-ages. He might have left politics altogether, and taken more lucrative employment, if on appeal the verdict had not been reversed.

For much of the 1924–29 parliament, Attlee's role was more humdrum. Perhaps its most valuable aspect was that he was made a temporary chairman of committees, a role which neces-sitated a valuable mastering of parliamentary procedure. He also made valuable contributions to two pieces of Conservative legislation, Neville Chamberlain's De-Rating bill and the act which set up the Central Electricity Board in 1926. On both of these issues he was Labour's expert, given that the only other knowledgeable figure, Herbert Morrison, who had won a par-liamentary seat in 1923, had lost it the following year; and on both of them Attlee made important and constructive contribu-tions. Indeed, on the report stage of the latter, a Conservative inadvertently paid him a compliment by complaining at the undue deference shown to his views. When the bill became law, he was asked to sit on the Joint Industrial Council of the elec-tricity industry.

Attlee was playing the sort of constructive role in the House of Commons of which his leader approved, though this is not to say that he did not clash on occasions with the Conservatives. In particular he and Chancellor of the Exchequer Winston Churchill clashed over the 1925 budget. This was the beginning of a long political love-hate relationship between the two men which was to continue for the rest of Churchill's life, and one moreover, together with the Attlee–Bevin partnership, equally important for Britain's future.

For the present, however, Ramsay MacDonald was the most important star in Attlee's firmament. In late 1927 Labour's leader recommended Attlee for membership of the Simon Commission, which was to investigate the constitutional future of India. Attlee was chosen because the issue of India's military future required someone on the commission with army experience. Stephen Walsh turned the post down, because of ill health, and so Attlee was chosen. This was no 'leg up' to a promising young politician, though in the long run it proved remarkably significant for Attlee's – and India's – future.

. . .

THE SIMON COMMISSION

The 1919 Montagu–Chelmsford constitution, which had allowed Indians to control some ministerial portfolios in the provincial governments, was due to be reviewed after ten years. Further steps might then be taken *en route* to the 'responsible government' which Montagu had announced in 1917 as the ultimate goal of India's political evolution. Yet several members of Baldwin's Conservative government disapproved of the constitutional advances which had been made in 1919, believing them responsible for the subsequent outbreak of nationalist campaigns. Certainly the Secretary of State, Lord Birkenhead, judged that India would never be fit to become a self-governing dominion. Hence he decided to set up a constitutional commission ahead of schedule so that he – rather than another, possibly Labour, secretary of state – could control its composition. As chairman he chose Sir John Simon, the Liberal lawyer who had so pleased the Conservatives in 1926 by insisting – erroneously – that a general strike was illegal. Four staunch Conservatives were also members, including the editor of the *Daily Telegraph*, and there had, in addition, to be two Labour men.

Whoever was chosen from Labour ranks could expect a difficult time. Many in the party believed that Britain should concede independence to India immediately and so disapproved of the commission. They therefore gave its participants a rough ride, while in India Simon and his fellow commissioners were given an even worse time. Local politicians decided to boycott them. The Commissioners arrived in Bombay on 3

February 1928, to a national *hartal*, in which shops and businesses shut down and children stayed away from school. The local press was on the attack, and Attlee was an easy target. According to the *Indian National Herald*,

> Major Attlee cut a very sorry figure when tackled by the press people . . . He was so hopelessly flabbergasted by the volley of questions that his hand began to shiver as he tried to light his pipe. The pressmen thought it cruel to bully him any more and as they were taking leave of him, the Major said 'Thank you'.[16]

Such hostility stemmed from the fact that the commission was all-white. The Viceroy Lord Irwin (the later Lord Halifax) had a reputation as a liberal, but this was undeserved. He had little sympathy with Indians in general (once commenting that his father could have no conception of the squalor in India – the local houses were arranged 'real pigsty fashion, and I have no doubt that the people who live in them are real pigs'),[17] or nationalists in particular. It was he who recommended that no Indian should be allowed on the commission. Admittedly it would have been difficult to select a small number of Indians to represent all shades of local opinion, but this racial exclusivity did make the job of Simon and his men much more difficult. Then, in November 1929, he made it impossible. He announced that 'the natural issue of India's constitutional progress . . . is the attainment of Dominion Status'. This was a vague formula, in that no time-scale was specified, and Irwin did not think that it could be implemented in the foreseeable future; but he hoped that it would satisfy the nationalists, and he called for round-table talks in Britain. The Simon Commission, which had still not reported, was effectively short-circuited. Attlee's efforts, it seemed, would be wasted.

Attlee was in India in February and March 1928, covering over 7,000 miles, and then again from October 1928 to April 1929, this time with his wife. It was a fascinating, but also a dreary time: the commissioners had to consider evidence, often repetitious, from witnesses in thirteen centres, including Rangoon in Burma. Since the popular Congress Party was refusing to co-operate, the Britons spent much of their time questioning representatives of minority communities and thus inevitably received an impression which stressed not only the variety but also the disunity of India.

Attlee was back in Britain for the general election in May, and in Limehouse his vote was 2,000 up on the previous election. Labour did better than ever before, winning 288 seats and 37 per cent of the total vote. It was now the largest single party in the House of Commons, and for a second time MacDonald agreed to form a minority government. Attlee endorsed this decision. He had accepted his role on the commission with some reluctance and had gone to considerable trouble to obtain a promise from Ramsay MacDonald that absence from Britain would not affect his chances of ministerial office in the next Labour government. He was clearly ambitious for further advancement; but there was no place for him in the government.

. . . .

LABOUR GOVERNMENT 1929–31

There was good reason for Attlee's absence, in that he was busy helping to write the Simon Report. In fact, Attlee found time to speak on only two occasions in the Commons between July 1929 and May 1930. Yet the Prime Minister made no effort to reassure him that a post would eventually be found and nor, to add insult to injury, did he ever consult him on Indian policy. Having written two books on India before the First World War, MacDonald judged himself to be an expert in this field. The younger man soon decided that MacDonald's greatest weakness was his unwillingness to consult experts and admit his own ignorance. The first breach – essentially on personal grounds – was developing between Attlee and MacDonald.

In June 1930 the Report was published. Attlee had written important sections in its two volumes, but now his labours were over. Nor was his career harmed, for in the previous month he had entered the government as Chancellor of the Duchy of Lancaster, after the resignation of Sir Oswald Mosley. Some had thought that Mosley had the ability to become Labour leader, though others disliked his upper-class style. Attlee himself once voiced his disapproval at Mosley's habit of speaking 'to us as though he were a feudal landlord abusing tenants who are in arrears with their rent'.[18] At all events, his unwillingness to bide his time had provided Attlee with a welcome opportunity to join the government.

Mosley had resigned because of the government's unwillingness to tackle unemployment, which had been mounting steadily since the end of 1929. Eventually to peak at about 3 million, it was standing at over 1.5 million in May 1930. Jimmy Thomas, heading a special cabinet committee, had no confidence in any solution, and he and Philip Snowden vetoed Mosley's pot-pourri of measures. Yet Attlee was not being offered any poisoned chalice as Mosley's successor, as unemployment policy was henceforth the Prime Minister's problem child. Attlee's role was downgraded from Mosley's, but at least it was relatively free of economic responsibility.

Attlee became a – typically silent – member of the Economic Advisory Council, a fifteen-man 'think tank' set up in the wake of Mosley's resignation, and so witnessed the clash between the traditional views of the economic establishment, symbolised by the Governor of the Bank of England, Montagu Norman, and those of the radical economist Maynard Keynes. He was also able to gain a greater appreciation of Bevin's undoubted intelligence and grasp of theoretical matters on this body. Furthermore he wrote a memorandum in July 1930 on 'The Problems of British Industry'.[19] Here he attacked government policies of *laissez-faire*, and government inaction in general, as being completely discredited. Instead, he called for the creation of a Ministry of Industry, 'to control the development of the nation's economic life', and a Board of National Development, to stimulate the growth of new industries and to guarantee loans to industries in return for a measure of public control.

Less specific than the ill-fated Mosley memorandum, Attlee's was nevertheless in tune with progressive ideas, and at least it was a positive alternative to the government's policy of drift. Yet it was not taken to cabinet: it was simply filed away for the benefit of historians. Attlee was certainly annoyed, and several times he refused to wind up debates on unemployment because absolutely nothing was being done to tackle the problem. Yet he did not contemplate resignation, and at the annual conference in October, when Mosley launched a scathing attack on the pusillanimity of the government, Attlee spoke in favour of MacDonald. Party unity had to be preserved. Instead, he devoted himself to other matters. He was, in his own words, 'a sort of tip-horse put on to pull various wagons'.[20] He helped MacDonald with the arrangements for the 1930 Imperial Conference, and he also worked with the Minister of Agriculture, the former Liberal, Christopher Addison. Attlee described Addison as 'the best and most vigorous minister we've got'; and Addison, in turn, praised Attlee to the Prime Minister as 'most useful and clear-headed'.[21] Together they charted the 1931 Marketing and Land Utilisation Bills through the Commons. The former set up marketing boards, but it was not the far-reaching measure it might have been. Snowden, at the Exchequer, vetoed calls for imposing quotas on imports: though not as bad, to his mind, as outright protection, they would nevertheless interfere with free trade. The latter was to provide smallholdings for unemployed men; but once again the Treasury interfered, limiting the amount of money available for the scheme and then resisting its operation. Perhaps their shared adversity helped to bring the two men together: certainly Chris and Clem began to forge one of Attlee's few genuine political friendships.

Attlee at this time was an easily-overlooked member of the government. No one dreamt that he might one day be a prime minister. Yet his worth was beginning to be appreciated. His PPS, for instance, described him as having 'a sanity and integrity absolutely to be relied on', and another colleague judged that Attlee, who was 'too fastidious for intrigue, too modest for overmuch ambition', was 'the ideal Minister without portfolio'.[22]

In March 1931 a cabinet reshuffle made Attlee Postmaster-General. Now, for the first time, he was in charge of a ministry, albeit a minor one, and he approached his duties very seriously, even going so far as to undertake a crash-course in departmental administration at Imperial Chemical Industries. He knew that he had first to master the existing system before improving it, though it turned out that he had little time to make a major impact at the Post Office. He did, however, improve its public relations and begin a publicity campaign to increase the use of the telephone. His successor, Kingsley Wood, was to pay tribute to his good work.

Yet perhaps the most important consequence of this period in office was Attlee's growing dislike of the direct political control which he, or rather the government, exercised. He particularly came to resent the way in which the Exchequer could help itself to Post Office profits, instead of allowing them to be ploughed back into improvements in services. Treasury control was, he came to believe, 'wholly incompatible with the flexibility necessary in the conduct of a business concern'. Indeed the responsibility of the Post Office to parliament had several disadvantages, not least that the holder of the office of Postmaster-General was subject to frequent political change. Attlee therefore recommended fundamental reforms. Parliament, through a minister, should have control over 'general policy' but should 'relinquish its right of constant interference in detailed administration'. Instead the Post Office should be administered either by a non-parliamentary Postmaster-General or a Board appointed by the minister.[23] This reasoning had no immediate impact, but it did bring Attlee much closer to Herbert Morrison who, as Minister of Transport, favoured the semi-autonomous public corporation as the means of running a nationalised London Transport. Their views were to be vital for the post-1945 nationalisation programme.

Attlee remained Postmaster-General only until August 1931, when the financial and economic crisis reached its peak. For some time Snowden at the Exchequer had been insisting that the budget must be balanced. Now publication of the alarmist May Report and the failure of continental banks fuelled a run on the pound which the Chancellor insisted required Britain to negotiate loans from the Americans and the French, a precondition for which was a balanced budget. Yet this required expenditure cuts, including a cut of 10 per cent in unemployment benefit. That was the rub which split the Labour cabinet virtually down the middle. The result was the formation of the National Government on 24 August 1931. Attlee never wavered in his judgement that MacDonald had perpetrated 'the greatest betrayal in the political history of this country'.[24]

By August the loyal Attlee had become increasingly critical of the government. His former hero, MacDonald, was less and less able to impress him. Not only had MacDonald failed to consult him over India and consigned his memorandum on industry to the political dustbin, but he had begun to criticise other ministers when he and Attlee, a junior member of the government, conferred privately. MacDonald had always had a low opinion of his colleagues but, according to Attlee's code, he should have kept such views to himself. In the autumn of 1930 Attlee had joined a small discussion group founded by Oxford's G.D.H. Cole which, early the following summer, became the 'loyal grousers' of the Society for Socialist Enquiry, under Bevin's chairmanship; and at the same time he joined forces with Cole to found the New Fabian Research Bureau, attempting to put new life into the old Fabian society. He became its first chairman.

Such discontents came to a head on 24 August 1931. At noon MacDonald informed the cabinet that a national government was to be set up to make the necessary cuts in expenditure and to save the pound. This was not a coalition, he insisted, only a temporary alignment: after the emergency was over, normal party politics would be resumed and he would return to Labour ranks. That afternoon he was to address his junior ministers, before officially tending the government's resignation to the king. Attlee had returned hastily from his family holiday in Frinton, and over lunch with Hugh Dalton, Under-Secretary at the Foreign Office, he revealed his anger. Dalton recorded that Attlee was 'hot against JRM for his indecision and his inferiority complex, especially in all economic questions, and hotter still against Snowden who, he says, has blocked every positive proposal for the past two years'.[25]

This is the first time, at least for which there is evidence, that Attlee had indulged in fierce criticisms of his Labour colleagues. Perhaps he had wind of what was to be announced later, so that MacDonald and Snowden were no longer colleagues in any real sense. Perhaps the bottle of Burgundy they drank with the meal loosened Attlee's tongue a little. At all events, that afternoon he felt willing to ask MacDonald a question, though in typically terse terms, after the Prime Minister had explained what was happening (a histrionic performance which Dalton described as Christ Crucified speaking from the Cross). MacDonald spoke about the need for equality of sacrifice, so that not even the unemployed could be exempt; and Attlee asked 'What about the rentiers?'[26] Those on the dole would suffer, so what about those who lived off another form of unearned income? MacDonald replied, weakly, that he could not anticipate the new government's first budget.

To Attlee, this showed the untenability of MacDonald's position. He might well have approved both MacDonald's concern to pursue the national interest and his courage in taking what seemed likely to be unpopular decisions. In addition, he too believed in the importance of balancing the budget and maintaining the gold standard. Hence the rentier point was vital. Unless there were equality of sacrifice, cutting the dole was merely capitalist exploitation. The man who had been one of

MacDonald's greatest supporters now became one of his most implacable critics.

Many Labour Party members were in fact relieved at what had happened. MacDonald, together with Snowden and Thomas, could take the responsibility for unpopular public expenditure cuts, while the bulk of Labour ministers could enjoy a well-earned rest from responsibility. Not a few party members were glad to have got rid of MacDonald. Venom for the former Labour leader only really developed when Labour did so badly in the general election of October 1931. Attlee, however, was much more consistent in his bitterness.

When asked why Labour did not split in 1931, as the Liberals had in 1916, Attlee replied that it was because the party had merely shed 'a few parasitic appendages'; and in late August, in MacDonald's earshot, he declaimed loudly, 'And Esau sold his inheritance for a few pieces of silver'. Years later he was still outspoken, describing MacDonald as a 'political nudist', a man who had shed every shred of political conviction he ever had; and in 1937 he pronounced that 'MacDonaldism' was 'essentially Fascist'.[27]

This virulence against MacDonald, partly accounted for by genuine disapproval, may have been compounded by Attlee's willingness to believe conspiracy theories. Rumours that MacDonald was about to form a government with the Tories and Liberals had been circulating for some time. Fenner Brockway, for instance, had written an article three months earlier predicting what had now come to pass. Many believed that MacDonald, corrupted by the aristocratic embrace of London's duchesses, had masterminded a successful coup against his own party, and in addition that the world's financiers had plotted to unseat a socialist government. Neither view seems to make much sense today. MacDonald had not the ability to mastermind events, while bankers had scant reason to fear Labour. But these views were sincerely held by many on the left. A saviour to some, MacDonald was the devil incarnate to others, especially after the general election of October 1931 reduced Labour in the Commons to a mere rump.

But there was probably also an element of self-interest in Attlee's unchanging and implacable criticisms. With every jibe against his former boss he was able to distance himself from MacDonald and from his own moderation, including his approval of much that the 1929–31 government had done. In fact he wrote personally to MacDonald of his certainty that his actions had been dictated solely by his conception of the public good.[28] But it would have been impolitic to say so publicly, and Attlee refrained from doing so. At all events, it soon became clear that the events of August–October 1931 had done Attlee nothing but good. Could such a self-effacing and uncharismatic man aspire to the leadership of his party? In normal times, certainly not; after the disaster of MacDonald, perhaps so.

. . .

REFERENCES

1. C.R. Attlee, *The Way and the Will to Socialism* (London, 1935), p. 82
2. C.R. Attlee, *As It Happened* (London, 1954), p. 22; C.R. Attlee, *The Social Worker* (London, 1920), pp. 133–4.
3. Quoted in Geoffrey Dellar (ed.), *Attlee As I Knew Him* (London, 1983), p. 54.
4. Ibid., p. 3.
5. Kenneth Harris, *Attlee* (London, 1984), p. 32.
6. Burridge, *Clement Attlee* (London, 1985), p. 47.
7. William Golant, 'The Political Development of C.R. Attlee to 1935', unpub. Oxford B.Litt. thesis, 1967, p. 18.
8. Stephen Brooke, *Labour's War* (Oxford, 1992), p. 26.
9. Harris, *Attlee*, p. 54.
10. Ibid., p. 550.
11. Snowden to C. Addison, 7 February 1928, Addison papers, Box 95, Bodleian library.
12. William Golant, 'The Early Political Thought of C.R. Attlee', *Political Quarterly*, vol. 40, 1969, p. 248.
13. *Parl. Debates* (Commons), vol. 159, cols. 92–6, 23 November 1922.
14. William Golant, 'C.R. Attlee in the First and Second Labour Governments', *Parliamentary Affairs*, vol. 26, 1972–73, p. 319.
15. Ibid., p. 320.
16. William Golant, *The Long Afternoon* (London, 1975), p. 117.
17. Ibid., p. 38.
18. Ben Pimlott (ed.), *The Political Diary of Hugh Dalton 1918–40, 1945–60* (London, 1986), 20 November 1930, p. 130.
19. Reproduced in Harris, *Attlee*, pp. 570–84.
20. Attlee to Tom Attlee, 16 July 1930, Attlee Papers, Bodleian Library.
21. Ibid., 15 November 1930; Golant, *Parliamentary Affairs*, vol. 26, p. 328.

22. Golant, *Parliamentary Affairs*, vol. 26, pp. 325–6.
23. C.R. Attlee, 'Post Office Reform', *New Statesman and Nation*, 7 November 1931, pp. 565–6.
24. Attlee, *As It Happened*, p. 74.
25. Harris, *Attlee*, p. 95.
26. Burridge, *Clement Attlee*, p. 77.
27. Attlee, *Labour Party in Perspective*, pp. 58, 60; William Golant, 'The Early Political Thought of C.R. Attlee – II', *Political Quarterly*, vol. 41, 1970, p. 309.
28. David Marquand, *Ramsay MacDonald* (London, 1977), p. 649.

Chapter 3

THE RISE TO THE LEADERSHIP, 1931–35

I have neither the personality nor the distinction to tempt me to think that I should have any value apart from the party which I serve.[1]

Attlee's progress within Labour ranks from 1931 to 1935 was rapid, spectacular and, to almost everybody, entirely unexpected: he was transformed from an obscure junior minister in 1931 to the leader of the party in 1935. The first stage had come with the setting up of the National Government in August 1931. Already the talented and ambitious Oswald Mosley had left Labour ranks, *en route* to fascism; and now the first tier of Labour leaders had also been removed – Ramsay MacDonald, Philip Snowden and J.H. Thomas, as well as several lesser figures. Four Labour men took their place in the new National cabinet, alongside four Conservatives and two Liberals. The loss might have been greater, but several promising junior figures declined to participate. The Solicitor-General, Sir Stafford Cripps, hesitated for over a week before turning down MacDonald's offer, and Herbert Morrison, undoubtedly a success as Minister of Transport, also came within an ace of joining. Attlee was not asked: he was not considered sufficiently important.

The PLP elected Arthur Henderson, Foreign Secretary in 1929–31, as the new leader and Willie Graham, former President of the Board of Trade, as his deputy, and at the end of September the former leaders were expelled from the party.

The new government increased taxation and reduced public expenditure, with a 10 per cent cut in the dole. Attlee
believed the economies were essentially false and attacked the
Chancellor, Philip Snowden, for penalising the poor more
than the rich rentiers, adding, for good measure, that he was
also failing to tackle the problems of Britain's debts. With this
bold performance, Attlee was staking his claim as one of the
leading figures in the new Labour team; but Snowden had the
better of the contest. He pointed out that though, in Attlee's
words, the opposition was 'wholly opposed' to the new budget,
a majority of the previous Labour cabinet had in fact favoured
similar cuts. Such revelations of the degree of support
MacDonald and Snowden had received from the previous cabinet were certainly embarrassing, and it was hard to rebut the
charge that Labour had run away from the crisis. The party's
woes increased as it became clear that Henderson was not
proving the solid leader many had anticipated. He had little
zest for the position and tried for some time to keep the door
open for MacDonald's return. Soon his moderation began to
anger the left of the party.

Labour could take heart from the fact that, despite the budget, Britain was forced off gold. The position of the
government was now anomalous, since it had been formed
with the specific, short-term purpose of balancing the budget
and maintaining the gold standard. Yet there was no return to
normal party politics. Instead MacDonald bowed to
Conservative pressure and called a general election for 27
October. This saw the second stage in Attlee's rise.

Most voters, in an atmosphere of impending doom, genuinely believed that the national government had put country
before party. As a result all the old fears of Labour revived. In
the past many had deemed Tory taunts of Labour's unfitness to
be exaggerated; but it was not so easy to laugh them off when
they were repeated by Philip Snowden, who described Labour's
programme as 'Bolshevism Run Mad'. The Labour manifesto
was indeed hastily thought out, and moreover the party organisation was not yet geared for an election. Most of the party
literature, for instance, still carried MacDonald's portrait.

Even so, many were shocked by the magnitude of the swing
against Labour. In Gateshead, for instance, which Ernie Bevin
decided to contest, a 17,000 Labour majority at the previous
election, was transformed into a National majority of 13,000.

Indeed National candidates won over thirty constituencies which, at the previous general election, had produced Labour majorities of over 10,000. Party leaders Henderson and Graham lost their seats, as indeed did all the former cabinet ministers except George Lansbury. In Hackney South, Morrison lost by over 3,000 votes. In Limehouse Attlee did not notice any major differences in atmosphere from 1929, but in fact the result was startlingly different. Labour lost in the other Stepney division, and there was speculation that if his young Tory opponent had been able to campaign with his wife, who was about to give birth, Attlee might have been beaten. As it was, he hung on by a mere 551 votes, a victory which led to his immediate elevation in the depleted ranks of the PLP.

Only 52 Labour MPs (including 6 ILP representatives, under Maxton) were returned to the new parliament. Of these, only three had had any experience of government – the 72-year-old George Lansbury, who was also the only member of the NEC to retain his seat, Attlee himself and Sir Stafford Cripps. Henderson stayed on for a time as party leader, but Lansbury was the obvious choice as Chairman of the PLP, and Attlee the equally obvious choice as his deputy. Everyone recognised the potential of Cripps, a brilliant barrister who had become the youngest King's Counsel in the country a few years earlier; but he had only recently joined the party and had sat in the Commons only since January 1931. He was too much the newcomer to challenge Attlee at this stage.

Exceptional circumstances had led to Attlee's appointment as deputy leader – the defection of Labour's biggest names and the decimation of their replacements in the 1931 general election. Attlee had undoubtedly been lucky, and his good fortune continued. It was expected that by-election victories would stiffen Labour's leadership in the Commons, but several of those defeated in 1931 distanced themselves, in one way or another, from the party. Margaret Bondfield returned to her union, for instance, and A.V. Alexander to the co-operative movement, while Willie Graham caught a chill at Christmas and was dead a fortnight later. Many thought that Henderson would soon be back; but he was appointed to chair the world disarmament conference in Geneva, a time-consuming and soul-destroying task, so that in 1932 he gave up his, increasingly nominal, leadership of the party. Lansbury then became leader both of the party and of the PLP. When Henderson did return to the Commons, in 1933, his health was failing and he had few remaining political ambitions. He died in 1935. Yet chance alone did not crown Attlee. He also showed his mettle in the new parliament.

. . .

THE LABOUR OPPOSITION, 1931–35

The parliament elected in 1931 had the largest government majority and the smallest opposition in modern British history. In the Commons Labour's David was outnumbered by the National Goliath eleven to one (while in the Lords the figure was a staggering sixty to one). A hopeful sign was that the tiny total of 52 Labour MPs had received a total of 6.6 million votes, or 30.6 per cent of all those polled, the second largest total in the party's history. Labour's poor showing in the Commons was due, above all else, to the 'first past the post' electoral system and to the united Conservative–Liberal front. Hence there was a substantial base from which recovery could stem. Yet there was, of course, no guarantee of recovery. Could Labour's rump function as an opposition at all? It was not pre-ordained that 1931 would be the nadir of Labour's fortunes. Several commentators envisaged the formation of a new centre-left alignment in British politics, and morale among many Labour supporters was certainly very low. It was 'bloody to be alive and to be young was very hell', misquoted one of these in 1931.[2] Furthermore, the party did very badly in the municipal elections in November and could not afford to put forward a single candidate in five of the earliest by-elections of the new parliament. Party subscriptions and membership numbers were down, and the staff at Transport House had all to accept 5 per cent cuts in their salaries. Labour under Lansbury and Attlee had to work very hard to ensure that the election debacle would not be merely a stage in the demise of the party.

The new parliament, containing so many new faces, presented a daunting prospect. Even the experienced Winston Churchill confided privately to Attlee that he had seldom been so nervous. For Labour's rump of an opposition there were daunting problems. Not only were their numbers so small that they could never hope to win a division or substantially affect government legislation, but they lacked financial, secretarial and other resources. They also recognised a tendency among many Conservatives to treat them with contempt. Conservative leader Stanley Baldwin was awake to this. Always a man to take the broad philosophical view, he believed that a government needed an opposition: unless Labour MPs were treated fairly and with courtesy, therefore, the normal procedures of parliamentary democracy might break down: indeed Labour might turn to extra-parliamentary action. Hence he went out of his way to spend time in the smoking room with trade unionists and to show that he valued their opinion, and he also rebuked Tories who insulted Labour MPs. Attlee was to recall in later years that Baldwin always seemed far friendlier to Labour than to the Conservatives; and he also praised him as, at times, a superb parliamentary performer with an essentially 'modern outlook'. Yet he also knew that he was generally 'undynamic and lazy'.[3] Baldwin undoubtedly meant well, but he meant well feebly, and in fact he did little of real substance to ease Labour's trials. Several times Attlee had to complain about needlessly late sessions: these were little disadvantage to the government benches, since so few of their MPs needed to attend, but a high turn-out for Labour was obligatory if they were to put up any sort of show.

Of the fifty or so Labour MPs, about a third were trade unionists who, whatever their other sterling qualities, tended to be silent and ineffectual in the Commons. Members of the press gallery could sometimes hear the loudly whispered coaching delivered by Lansbury to some of his inexperienced men: 'Speak up. Put your chin up.'[4] Some help was provided by by-election victories, especially with the return of Arthur Greenwood in 1932 and Christopher Addison in 1934; but there was a massive responsibility, and a corresponding workload, on Attlee's shoulders. Yet in retrospect, we can see that he was presented not only with a difficult situation, to which he reacted manfully, but with an ideal training ground.

Labour's leadership comprised a triumvirate: Lansbury, Attlee and Cripps, who all shared the leader of the opposition's room in the Commons and worked closely together. By the end of 1931 Attlee was writing in optimistic terms about the first few months of the new parliament. Cripps was 'a tower of strength and such a good fellow', while Lansbury was 'an excellent leader' with 'far more idea of team work than ever MacDonald had'. In total, 'we are quite a happy family'. He hoped that the recent 'shake up', together with a return to 'basic socialism', would 'ultimately prove the salvation of the party'. He also poured scorn on the National administration. MacDonald made 'a ghastly speech' on the Address – 'no grip at all' – and the government was without a coherent plan for dealing with economic problems.[5]

Over the next years Attlee's private letters to his brother continued to show robust criticisms of the government, and in particular of MacDonald. In February 1933 he penned a remarkable portrait, one-sided but also perceptive, of his former hero:

> It is difficult to get at MacDonald's mind at any time. It is, I think, mainly fog now. I think that while at the back of his mind he realises his own incompetence for the job which he has in hand, he sees himself in a series of images in the mirror . . . Now he is the Weary Titan or the good man struggling with adversity, anon he is the handsome and gallant leader of the nation or the cultural and travelled patron of the arts and letters. Whatever he does, he is the central figure keeping things going. Despite this, however, there is some leavening of shame.[6]

These letters also reveal confidence in the Labour MPs: Tom Williams and David Grenfell, two miners promoted to the front bench, had done extremely well, making themselves conversant with a range of new subjects, while 'Lansbury has been splendid all through and Stafford Cripps a tower of strength'.[7] Running through all such judgements was also a remarkable confidence in his own judgement, of which few observers were aware.

Perhaps he needed to maintain such an attitude to fortify himself for the struggle, which was hard, long and exhausting. In comparison with this period, his previous nine years in the Commons were as the Boer War compared with the First World War. Never before had he taken so prominent a role in the House of Commons. In the first session, in 1931, he spoke on multifarious matters almost every day, and in addition he was put on the Committee of Privileges. The following year he had to reply to the Chancellor's budget speech, 'rather an ordeal as I have never previously taken part in debates on financial matters and I do not move easily amid the arcana of exchanges, gold standards, etc.'.[8] Nevertheless he did realise that Neville Chamberlain's goal of free trade within the Empire, and protection against the outside world, was doomed to at least partial failure: the manufactured goods which Britain wanted to export to the Dominions were precisely the sort of goods the Dominions wished to manufacture for themselves, a fact which imperial sentiment was not strong enough to overcome. The Ottawa conference of 1932 showed Attlee's clear-sighted appreciation of the facts of imperial economic life. He also managed consistently to point out the government's fundamental unconcern with the social conditions of the poor, comparing the Minister of Health with a visitor to Limehouse who once showed local people how to make a baby's cradle out of an old banana crate.

Attlee filled more columns in Hansard than anyone else in 1932. He dealt with the big issues and the small, including foreign policy, civil liberties, licensing hours, proportional representation and the outbreak of poultry disease on a Yorkshire farm.[9]

Attlee was in fact the rock of the Labour opposition. Lansbury, a representative of the romantic left, was, as Beatrice Webb once noted, an evangelist rather than a parliamentary tactician. Moreover his age sometimes rendered him less than efficient. In July 1932 he wrote that life was getting more and more difficult for him: 'Everything gets so mixed; persons, causes, tumble into each other and form such a hotch-potch of ideas that truth or what seems like truth gets just smothered.'[10] In addition, Stafford Cripps was not only relatively inexperienced but was devoting a portion of his time to the law. Hence Attlee needed remarkably broad shoulders, and it was in large measure due to his efforts that the PLP acquitted itself as well as it did. Its attendance was 'exceptionally regular', and, though its performance seldom attracted much attention in the press, Baldwin acknowledged in 1935 that Labour MPs had 'equipped themselves for debate after debate and held their own'.[11] It certainly put up staunch opposition to the government's household means test. It was also remarkably united: in this embattled position, when everyone was working flat out to fight the government, there was little energy left for Labour MPs to squabble among themselves. There was a moral here that Attlee was to remember in 1945.

Attlee was lucky in that the issue which took up more parliamentary time than any other was one with which he was familiar, Indian constitutional progress. The Irwin declaration of October 1929, and the subsequent round-table conferences, may have rendered the Simon report redundant, but his time on the commission had ideally equipped Attlee to spearhead

Labour's attack on government policy. He was one of four Labour men on a thirty-two-man joint select committee which sat for a total of eighteen months examining the government's White Paper on Indian reform. The members then issued a report, which subsequently became the basis of the Government of India Bill and was debated extensively in the Commons. The proposals conceded virtual self-government in the Indian provinces, while at the centre of affairs, in Delhi, there was to be a federal government, with a number of Indian ministers, once the Indian princes had accepted participation. There was to be a complex arrangement of reserved seats for the different communities, a decision which the National Congress believed amounted to divide and rule. The whole scheme, embodied in the longest bill ever put before parliament, was in fact immensely complicated. Much of it was also immensely futile, for although the provincial arrangements came into force in the late-1930s, the princes were never to accept the federation.

The foremost critic of the bill was not in fact a Labour member at all but Winston Churchill, whose implacable – and, most people thought, totally unreasonable – opposition made the bill seem more liberal than it really was. Attlee judged that Churchill had somehow managed to convince himself that the dissolution of the Empire was imminent, but that Baldwin had the beating of him. All he had managed to do, in Attlee's view, was to cut his own throat.

Attlee himself, on the other hand, argued that the bill did not go far enough, especially since it failed to conciliate the nationalists, who were once again mounting civil disobedience campaigns. He judged that the essential problems of the subcontinent were social and economic rather than merely political but that only a government capable of evoking the support of the local people could hope to tackle them. In short, only a nationalist government could succeed, and therefore Britain should frame legislation which would win the support of the major nationalist body, the Indian National Congress of Gandhi and Nehru. The government should also 'state beyond all cavil that it is the intention of this country to grant full Dominion Status to India within a measurable period of years'.[12] Attlee's view of the required number of years would no doubt have differed significantly from that of the nationalists, and certainly he did not advocate immediate

British withdrawal. But, even so, he was now putting forward a policy more radical than that of government – and indeed more radical than any he himself had hitherto supported. There can be little doubt that the needs not of India but of party politics were uppermost in his mind. He wrote to Lansbury that in every question that arose Labour must stress that 'there is a different line of approach by Socialists even where we may in part approve of Government policy'.[13]

Yet it was not only in the House of Commons that Attlee was so busy. He undertook a good deal of journalistic work, and also speaking engagements elsewhere. In February 1933, for instance, he deputised for Aneurin Bevan in a debate with Mosley in the Cambridge Union: 'I laughed him to scorn pretty effectively and got a good majority.'[14] The next day he had to open a new telephone exchange in Mile End, before speaking in the House later that afternoon. On the following day he gave a broadcast in place of an ill Megan Lloyd George; and the day after he travelled to Catterick to give a talk to the officers.

It is not surprising that Attlee seemed indispensable or that his stock rose in the party. Harold Laski judged in mid-1932 that he had 'grown rapidly under grave responsibilities'.[15] The death of Lansbury's wife in March 1933 was a severe blow to the party leader, throwing greater burdens than ever on to Attlee; and no one was surprised, when Lansbury broke a hip in December1933, that it was Attlee who took over as acting leader. The accident was undoubtedly fortunate for Attlee, as was the fact that Lansbury was out of action for eight months, longer than anyone had expected. Cripps acquiesced in Attlee's appointment not because he was not an ambitious man but because a caretaker leadership would interfere with his thriving legal practice and so did not have sufficient appeal. There was good feeling between Attlee and Cripps, symbolised by the fact that in 1933 Cripps donated £500 to the party for Attlee's salary as acting leader; but there was also an inevitable rivalry between them, and both were expected to contest the leadership when the ageing Lansbury decided to step down. Cripps was in fact Lansbury's first choice to succeed him as permanent leader, especially since the two men shared similar Christian convictions; but Attlee's period as acting leader gave him a definite advantage: he could be seen as the candidate who had already led the party competently. It certainly helped his election to the National Executive

Committee (NEC), for the first time, in 1934. Yet ultimately the leadership hinged on policy.

. . .

THE POLICY DEBATE

The traumas of September–October 1931 provided Labour with a severe jolt. Until now most party members had believed in an almost automatic progress. History was seen to be on their side: the days of capitalism were surely numbered, and slowly but surely – 'with the inevitability of gradualness' – socialism would come to pass. At every election since 1918 Labour had increased its popular appeal, so that an absolute Commons majority could be foreseen just over the horizon. Then came the débâcle of 1931. After this, the last thing that seemed inevitable was gradualness. But perhaps the future still lay with Labour. Might capitalism be about to collapse?

Labour's reaction was certainly not monolithic. All agreed that there had to be changes in party policy, but there were some who managed to believe that the party had been intrigued out of office by a bankers' conspiracy: the blame, therefore, lay not in the party but in the machinations of the evil capitalists – in which case Labour would have to be better armed for the conflict next time. Others were more prone to soul-searching and to recognise that faults had lain within themselves.

The trade unionists, of whom TUC heavyweights Citrine and Bevin were the most important, tended to favour moderate but practical changes: the capitalist system would be modified to bring about higher standards of living, better social services and so on. Others called for structural changes in the economy, especially the nationalisation of the 'commanding heights', which should have priority over social reform. A third group, led by Stafford Cripps, called for revolutionary changes, including the nationalisation of virtually the whole economy and, moreover, for constitutional changes to prevent anticipated obstruction by the capitalists. It was on this last issue that there was most dissension. The sweeping changes demanded by the intellectual wing of the party were deemed entirely impracticable by others. The tiny PLP may have been harmonious in 1931–35, but the party was much larger and stronger outside the House of Commons and its voices did not sing in unison.

Many key bodies took part in the party's policy debate. The

most important of these was the NEC, which now contained only a small minority of MPs and so was not amenable to parliamentary control. It set up an important eight-man policy committee at the end of 1931; and this in turn had several sub-committees, including the finance and trade sub-committee, chaired by Hugh Dalton, and the local government and social services sub-committee, under Herbert Morrison. The TUC's economic committee, dominated by Bevin, was also important, as was a revitalised National Joint Council (renamed the National Council of Labour in 1934), containing representatives from the PLP and the NEC but on which the TUC had a majority. Also significant were the XYZ Club (founded by Labour sympathisers in the City), the New Fabian Research Bureau, of which Attlee was chairman in 1931–33, and the Society for Socialist Information and Propaganda. The last, merging with many former ILP members who disapproved of Maxton's disaffiliation from Labour in 1932, became the Socialist League in the same year, losing Bevin as chairman in the process. Labour was also beginning to attract a new generation of intellectuals, including promising young economists like Evan Durbin, Hugh Gaitskell and Douglas Jay. An intellectual efflorescence was beginning on the left; but there were too many conflicting ideas, and intra-party clashes, for comfort.

At the 1932 Leicester conference, a motion was passed in favour of the next Labour government introducing 'definite socialist legislation . . . immediately'. Members drew the moral from 1929–31 that Labour should not be content merely to administer the system while dreaming impractical dreams of a future socialist utopia. There should be no more MacDonaldite slush and word-spinning, or, as Attlee put it, 'blooming gradualism and palliatives'.[16] Instead, Labour must hammer out radical reform measures to introduce as soon as they could form a government. Yet while all agreed that *laissez-faire* economics equated with anarchy and that the Bank of England would have to be nationalised, a motion that all the joint stock banks should also be owned by the state was accepted only very narrowly.

The tide of radicalism continued into 1933, and at the Hastings conference several far-reaching reforms were accepted. For instance, delegates agreed on important changes in the way a future Labour government would be run. Henceforth, in order to prevent a dominant figure like

MacDonald from riding roughshod over his colleagues, a Labour Prime Minister was to consult members of the party over ministerial appointments and over the timing of a dissolution. Even more controversial were calls for constitutional changes. Given the perceived danger of obstruction from outside the government, Cripps, now chairman of the Socialist League, favoured not only the abolition of the House of Lords and, perhaps, a further curtailment of the monarchy's powers but an Enabling Act which would confer emergency powers. In fact this package of proposals was not accepted; but the conference did unanimously pass a Socialist League resolution pledging the party 'to take no part in war and to resist it with the whole force of the Labour Movement'. Direct action – a general strike – would be used to stop British participation in a war, regardless of the fact that the 1926 strike had lasted only nine days.

In 1934 Labour's theoretical stocktaking reached a degree of fruition. The Southport conference debated *For Socialism and Peace*, Labour's fullest policy statement of the interwar period, containing specific and precise proposals. It pledged the party to a far greater degree of economic planning, stemming from the nationalisation of key industries, than in the MacDonald era. Yet Socialist League supporters thought it too moderate. For them, it did not propose to nationalise a sufficiently large portion of the economy or intend to proceed swiftly enough, and nor did it endorse proper workers' control.

A key battle for Labour's future took place at Southport, and victory went to the NEC. Not only was *For Socialism and Peace* accepted as the manifesto for the next election, but on two other important issues Cripps and the League were defeated. Their call for communist affiliation was rejected, and in addition pacifism was repudiated. Labour henceforth stood for multilateral disarmament under the League of Nations (a body now strengthened by the Soviet Union's admission), but the party accepted that, in certain circumstances, it might be necessary to resist an aggressor. Events in Europe, and especially the destruction of the Austrian socialists, despite their attempted deployment of a general strike, had focused delegates' minds on realities. The young Richard Crossman described Labour's foreign policy succinctly: in office, the party would react 'as any rational creature who finds himself alone in the jungle. His first job is to defend himself'.[17]

Attlee's role

Attlee, a member of the Socialist League, had been fully behind the radicalism of the early 1930s, whose millennial atmosphere no doubt appealed to his latent romanticism. Indeed he was more to the left than at any time in his career. During the 1931 election he had insisted that the City of London was incompatible with socialism – 'as anomalous as would be the Pope in Moscow'[18] – and he had spoken strongly the following year in favour of committing a new Labour government to immediate measures of definite socialism. In his view, there could be no socialism without tears. At the start of 1933 he and Cripps had submitted a joint NEC paper – described as 'feverish' by Dalton[19]– calling for the nationalisation of all the joint stock banks, their aim being that a newly elected Labour government should not merely wound but strike an early and fatal blow at the capitalist enemy. Similarly, he had been in favour in 1933 of refusing to take part in war and – despite clashing with Bevin at Hastings – of constitutional change, especially the abolition of the Lords. In 1933 Bevin had judged, pragmatically, that instead of anticipating opposition Labour should go forward with its socialist proposals and only frame new constitutional amendments if the opposition acted unconstitutionally.

It was Cripps who led the way leftwards in 1932–33. Attlee seemed more a follower than an initiator, and some may indeed have judged that he was being carried along by a stronger personality. Yet in 1934 he distanced himself from Cripps: at Southport he was ranged against his PLP partner. In 1931–33, when radicalism was popular, Attlee had undoubtedly been a radical, flirting with revolutionary ideas. Now, in 1934–35, he daintily stepped to the right in line with the party as a whole, severing his connections with the Socialist League.

What can best explain the shift in his position? There are several possible explanations. First and foremost, there were the changing circumstances of the times. In the early 1930s it had seemed quite possible that the whole capitalist system might be breaking down, not only in Britain but in the whole world. By the middle of the decade, however, it was clear that this was not the case: stability had returned, with rising prosperity for many, and so gradualism was once more on the socialist agenda. Furthermore, developments in Europe, and especially Hitler's rise to power, were rendering pacifism naive. Only eight days after the 1933 conference dispersed, the Nazi leader withdrew from the disarmament conference and the League of Nations. Cripps was unmoved by this: a recent convert to socialism, he adopted absolute and doctrinaire views. He agreed that fascism seemed menacing but judged that in reality it was merely the latest guise of capitalism, and that therefore the only real hope lay not in the League of Nations, itself an alignment of capitalist powers, but in socialism. He believed that a war against the fascist powers would, essentially, be a war for profit, and so would be playing the capitalists' game: instead, the Labour party should refuse to prepare for war and should call for Britain to leave the League and adopt a common front with the USSR and other socialist governments. It was all remarkably clear-cut, and all remarkably unconvincing to many, who began to think that the most intellectual Labour figure of the 1930s had the least common sense.

Cripps was a undoubtedly a clever man but not a sensible one. In this he was unlike Attlee. Many doubted Clem's cleverness, but none doubted, at least not for long, that he was sensible. Attlee wrote privately that the situation on the continent was 'terribly serious': judging that social democracy in Germany was 'down and out' for a generation, he recognised the essential fluidity and unpredictability of events on the continent.[20] This was an intelligent pragmatism. It made little sense to lump together all the capitalist powers, the dictatorships and the democracies. As Gaitskell asked, were there not 'degrees of temperature even in hell'?[21]

Another difference between the early and the mid-1930s was that a general election was in the offing. Perhaps power could not be won next time, but Labour had to put up a better showing than in 1931, and that meant hammering out policies for which the electorate would vote. Herbert Morrison, very much a moderate but a zealous and efficient one, showed the way with a Labour victory in the 1934 London County Council elections. On the other hand, would Cripps's ideas attract wide support? The prospect of a Labour attack on the monarchy had drawn bad publicity from the press, so that Hugh Dalton insisted privately that the Tories regarded Cripps as their greatest electoral asset. Union leaders also thought that the Socialist League was becoming too much of a liability.

There were other reasons too for Attlee's change of stance.

He disliked the idea of a united front with the communists; and he was falling much more under the influence of the NEC, having been co-opted onto its policy committee before being elected as a member in his own right in 1934. He also came under trade union influence on the TUC–Labour party National Council. Perhaps, also, Attlee's clash with Bevin in 1933 had had a salutary effect.

Yet the key factor in Attlee's transformation may simply have been his perceived need to back majority positions. This was especially important at the 1934 conference, when he was acting leader of the party. As he once said, 'a leader must know when to follow'.[22] There was principle in his position but also a good measure of self-interest. He had a few years earlier analysed the qualities a party leader and prime minister needed, arguing that he should be neither a prima donna, 'strutting before the world', nor a politician with his eyes fixed so closely on the House of Commons that he saw 'all questions in the light of Parliamentary tactics'. In other words, he should be neither a MacDonald nor a Baldwin. Above all, he should be a good chairman, able to lead a team without dominating it and able to get others to work together.[23] Consciously or not, Attlee was describing a role which he thought he could fill – providing he was not isolated over policy.

Now, as acting leader, he had the chance to practice what he had preached. He followed the party, and was seen to do so. For instance, instead of arguing in favour in any particular foreign policy, he waited for a consensus to emerge. He had written philosophically to his brother in November 1933, after the Hastings conference, that the movement 'has not really made up its mind as to whether it wants to take up an extreme disarmament and isolationist attitude or whether it will take the risks of standing up for the enforcement of the decisions of a world organisation against individual aggressor states'.[24] Until Labour had made up its mind, Attlee's mind would also be undecided. Small wonder that insofar as there was a consensus in the Labour party Attlee embodied it.

This was not an heroic form of leadership, far from it, and it required a definite elasticity of policy convictions – or, ideally, no such convictions at all. Certainly it would be easier to respect Attlee's *volte-face* in 1934 if he had spoken out plainly against Socialist League ideas: but, instead, he let others take the lead, especially Dalton and Morrison. This was a form of leadership peculiarly Attlee's own, and one the party was to see on several occasions in the future.

By 1934–35 Attlee was in a good position in the party. Despite his gyrations, and his clash with Bevin, he had largely avoided making enemies. As the man who followed, rather than led, majority opinion, he had avoided confrontation. It was Cripps who earned the ire of the right of the party, not Attlee; and it was Bevin, Dalton and Morrison who displeased the left by opposing them so firmly. Not that there was much brotherhood on the right. In particular Morrison and Bevin, who seemed naturally to antagonise each other, had clashed on the programme of nationalisation. It was not the extent of the programme or the basic form which it should take which divided them, though these were contentious issues in the party: instead, they disagreed over the comparatively minor issue of workers' participation on the boards of future state-controlled industries. Morrison was all for giving the minister a free hand, so that members would be chosen solely for their ability, but Bevin believed that there should be a statutory obligation for union representatives to be included on these boards. Attlee agreed with Morrison, but he stood aside in the debate, and it was Bevin who received majority backing in the 1935 conference. There were definite advantages in being temperamentally inclined to take a back seat.

Powerful animosities were dividing the brothers in the Labour party, but no one felt very strongly about Attlee. Dalton described him as 'a small person, with no personality'.[25] Not many people would have gone this far in disparagement of him, and the judgement doubtless reflects Dalton's discontent that Attlee had outdone him several times in his career – in getting the post at the LSE in 1913, in getting into parliament first and in staying there. Most people, instead, thought that he was a little colourless and certainly uncharismatic, but also hard-working, loyal and trustworthy. He seemed to have an integrity which ruled out of order charges of time-serving.

In 1935, despite being phenomenally busy, Attlee found the time to write another book, *The Will and the Way to Socialism*. In this he attempted to compose his own statement of the party's purpose, one which would unite not divide its adherents. Hence he backed majority opinions, including those which he himself had opposed during earlier years. For instance, he endorsed two policies which Bevin, not he, had campaigned for over the previous few years. Labour would secure emergency powers to deal with obstructionism, but only if undemocratic elements first sought to thwart the will of the people. Secondly, he endorsed a degree of workers' control in industry. Yet despite specifying policies, including the nationalisation of key industries and redistributive taxation, Attlee insisted that there could be no 'fixed, unchangeable plan' to be implemented regardless of circumstances. He wished to see a flexibility of approach. Socialism, he insisted, was more than an exact formula of precise, fully-defined policies: it was a philosophy of life facilitating brotherhood, freedom and equality. To him, a socialist society would be not like a tidy mosaic pavement; instead, it would be organic, capable of growth and variety, like a garden. Seen from a distance, his garden would reveal 'a general plan and harmony, but viewed closely, every plant is unique. This general harmony is not fixed like a mosaic pattern. It is always changing. Each plant and the garden itself is in a state of becoming. When the pavement is finished the artisan has no more to do. The gardener's work is never done.'[26] Ramsay MacDonald himself might have been pleased with this image, at once impressively comprehensive and yet also reassuringly vague.

The book was not nearly as impressive intellectually as those of other key figures in the party. There was no profound economic analysis, no acceptance of Keynes' demand-management with a repudiation of his social values, such as can be seen in other works of the period. Dalton no doubt believed his own publication, *Practical Socialism for Britain*, to be far superior. Even so, Attlee's volume did embody several of his most characteristic ideas. It showed his confidence that governments could make a difference to the quality of life of people: where there was a will, there would be found to be a way. It was also a real plea for toleration within the party. There could be no final (or, as Nye Bevan later said, 'immaculate' conception of socialism; and therefore there was room for variety within the movement, just as there would be in a socialist state. What mattered to Attlee was the direction of change rather than the ultimate goals; and what mattered also was unifying socialist energies to fight the Conservatives in the 1935 election.

May the book have been Attlee's attempt to bolster his

claims as the next leader of the Labour party? Certainly there would soon have to be a new leader, if only because of Lansbury's age. But although Labour's leader had distanced himself even more than Attlee from the policy debate, focusing almost exclusively on his role in the House of Commons, there was one issue on which he was profoundly out of step with majority thinking – foreign policy.

THE ACTING LEADERSHIP

Lansbury was a devout Christian. As such, he felt that pacifism was the only policy he could follow, for whose who took the sword would perish by the sword. This outlook was quite in keeping with the Hastings resolution of 1933, and ideally almost all Labour supporters wanted to abolish war and armaments. Yet the new menacing international situation in the 1930s – with the Japanese invasion of Manchuria in 1931 and Hitler's rise to power in 1933 – seemed to require new policies. When Mussolini invaded Abyssinia in 1935, the latent divisions within Labour ranks were revealed. Lansbury's position was clear: he would not support Britain in any action that might lead to war. Cripps and the Socialist League had a similar position: they would not support any capitalist government in warlike actions, believing that such actions were bound to be dictated by the profit motive. Cripps resigned from the NEC on this issue in September 1935. The bulk of the party, however, while loath to contemplate war, believed that sanctions should be imposed against an aggressor state. These would comprise economic sanctions, which it was hoped would be an alternative to fighting: but, in the last analysis, war – a collective war by the League – could not be ruled out as a possibility. This was accepted by the 1934 conference. Labour was prepared to bear the stigma of being described by its enemies as 'bloody-minded pacifists who desire to make war to stop war'.[27]

Lansbury knew that his pacifist position put him in a minority, and he was intending to resign after the 1935 conference if, as anticipated, a resolution in favour of sanctions was passed. In a tactful speech, Attlee made very clear his own disagreement with his boss: where there is government, he insisted, 'there is force behind it in some way or other', and therefore non-resistance was a personal, not a political attitude. Whereas everyone was against capitalist or imperialist wars, 'we are in favour of the proper use of force for ensuring the rule of law'.[28] After this, Lansbury's resignation was certain. Ernie Bevin, however, could not resist twisting the knife. He insisted that it was Mussolini who had taken the sword and that he should perish from economic sanctions; and, in a ferocious personal attack, he complained that Lansbury was placing the executive and the movement in a false position by hawking his conscience round from body to body, asking what he ought to do with it. The party leader's resignation followed.

In the protracted process of theoretical stocktaking, which produced so many disagreements in Labour ranks, there was one thing on which all could agree. The party leader should be someone who was as unlike MacDonald as possible, a servant not the master of the party. Lansbury had seemed unlike MacDonald, simple and straightforward rather than devious and vain; and yet he too had harboured ideas at variance with the party. If Lansbury was nothing like MacDonald, there was someone who was even less like MacDonald – and that someone was Clement Attlee. It was he who took over the temporary leadership on Lansbury's resignation. As deputy leader, he was the inevitable choice. After all, who else was there? Cripps, another pacifist, was not in the running. Nor was there any time for a debate about Attlee's merits. Baldwin took advantage of Labour's fratricidal disarray to call a general election earlier than anticipated. After the election was over there would be time to consider the issue at greater length. The press noted patronisingly that Attlee 'deserves the success that is his momentarily'.[29]

. . . .

THE 1935 GENERAL ELECTION AND THE LEADERSHIP CONTEST

The National Government was in a strong position in 1935. It had few spectacular successes to its credit and unemployment remained high, but there had been a substantial economic improvement, and the government could boast that more people were employed than ever before in British history. Admittedly, there were foreign policy difficulties, and it was especially troublesome that public opinion seemed favourable to the League of Nations; but Baldwin, chameleon-like, now evinced a new-found enthusiasm for collective security under the League. Some said he had stolen Labour's policy, but he did call for rearmament, which Labour opposed, Attlee insisting that Beelzebub could not cast out Satan. Some feared a new arms race, but Baldwin wanted their votes too, giving his word that there would be no great build-up of armaments. Neville Chamberlain summed up the differences between the government and opposition with the epigram: 'Our policy is defence without defiance; their policy is defiance without defence.'[30] The Conservatives could also take heart from the fact that their propaganda machine, in terms of film units and mobile cinema vans, was far better funded than Labour's.

It is not surprising that the election results were generally disappointing to Labour. The government was returned with a reduced but still massive majority of almost 250 seats. Labour won 154 seats, a net increase of 94; and in terms of votes, it polled over 8 million, with a slightly higher proportion of the total vote than ever before in its history. The electoral system had worked against Labour: it took about 54,000 votes to elect a Labour MP, but only half that number to return a Tory. In all, therefore, the party under Attlee had done about as well as could be expected. He himself won a larger majority than ever before in Limehouse, and during the campaign he had spoken at fifty meetings, all over the country. But would the party retain his services as leader? Most pundits thought not. To them the leadership had been in cold storage not merely since Lansbury's resignation but since the 1931 election; and now that the party had returned to something like full strength there could be a proper election, in which the caretaker would give way to a real leader. Attlee was the fourth leader of the party since 1931: who would be the fifth?

Lansbury and Cripps were returned to the Commons, but their views on foreign policy ruled them out of the contest. Of the old triumvirate, only Attlee was a candidate. Another contender was Arthur Greenwood, Minister of Health in the second Labour government, who had returned to the Commons in 1932. A working-class intellectual, and head of Labour's research department since 1927, he was a good speaker with a ready wit, and he also had the support of the trade unionists in the party; but he nevertheless suffered several disadvantages. He had a reputation as a heavy drinker and was also thought to be a freemason, supported by the other freemasons within the party, a suspicion which led to a backlash. But the two figures who looked most likely to win were

Hugh Dalton and Herbert Morrison, both of whom had served in the second Labour government and both of whom were important figures on the NEC by 1935, having dominated the policy sub-committees for several years. Unlike Attlee, they had not flirted with revolutionary ideas in 1931–33; and it was their moderate, practical view which had won out in the party debates. Yet rather than split the vote, Dalton agreed to become Morrison's campaign manager.

Dalton was stepping down in favour of the likely winner. Morrison had become a borough mayor, and had entered parliament and government later than Attlee; but he had overleapt his rival during the second Labour government and had far more achievements to his credit. He had been a real success as Minister of Transport in 1929–31, he had been elected to the NEC as early as 1920 and had been re-elected continually since then: indeed he had not fallen below third place in the elections and had been first in 1934, when Attlee scraped home for the first time. In addition, he had virtually created the London Labour Party and had made it into a formidable political machine which had captured the capital for Labour the previous year. Hence he controlled easily the largest local authority in Britain – with 117 square miles, 4.5 million inhabitants and an annual budget of £4 million. Beatrice Webb gave him her supreme accolade, calling him a Fabian of Fabians. Another of his supporters referred to him as 'the rising hope of the Labour Party, one might almost say, its only hope'. Certainly he attracted a surprisingly wide mix of support, from, at one extreme, young right-wing intellectuals to, at the other, the far-left D.N. Pritt, who praised him for his 'drive and capacity'.[31] Cripps also was for Morrison, who was thought to have been Labour's outstanding performer at the 1935 election. He was a better speaker than Attlee and, despite the lack of a middle-class education, seemed a far more accomplished individual, as well as a 'man of the people'. He also seemed to have more drive, dedication and all-round ability.

On the first ballot of MPs, Attlee received 58 votes, Morrison 44 and Greenwood 33. Since no-one had a majority, Greenwood dropped out, and on a second ballot almost all of Greenwood's supporters switched to Attlee, so that he defeated Morrison by 88 votes to 48. Attlee was the first middle-class man to be elected as Labour's leader, but he was elected largely with the votes of working-class MPs. Several factors were involved in this result, not least the rancour between Morrison and Bevin. It is virtually certain that Bevin advised the trade union MPs, with a force which only he could muster, to switch from Greenwood to Attlee. It was not that Bevin had much admiration for Attlee, but he saw him as infinitely preferable to the hated Morrison. Bevin, and other trade unionists, wanted someone as leader whom they could trust, someone who would follow the party line, which they themselves would do much to determine: they could not build their hopes on the quicksands of the overtly ambitious. There is a story, almost certainly apocryphal, that Bevin once responded to the question of who should lead the Labour party with the assertion that it was not such a difficult job: 'Do you see that little man in the corner who smokes a pipe and says nothing? I don't know much about him. But he'd do.'[32]

Another factor in Morrison's defeat was Dalton's loud campaigning in his favour, which looked too much like intrigue. He also lacked real experience of the Commons, having been absent in 1925–29 and 1931–35. In retrospect, he could reckon it a mistake not to have fought the East Fulham by-election of 1933. In addition he was too closely associated with London, and moreover he had not made it clear that, if elected, he would devote himself full-time to parliament. Certainly he refused to accept the deputy leadership because of his LCC work. This must also be accounted an error. As Attlee's deputy he would have been in an ideal position to challenge for the leadership in the future. By default, therefore, the number two post went to Greenwood.

Some people looked upon Attlee as too moderate and too closely allied to MacDonaldism. To them, he had been too concerned to channel socialism into parliamentary realms, despite the impotence of the PLP in 1931–35, and too loath to contemplate extra-parliamentary socialism. He disapproved, for instance, of the hunger marches organised by the communist-led National Unemployed Workers' Movement. He was too much the evolutionary socialist. On the other hand, such critics were undoubtedly a minority. The majority in the party inevitably found Attlee's position acceptable because, by 1935, his position was theirs – or, rather, theirs was his. His determination to follow the majority position meant he was a very difficult target to hit. And if in his outlook he resembled MacDonald far more than he was ever prepared to admit, it remains true that in personality and political style, he was the opposite of 'The Lucifer of the Left'. He almost certainly had fewer enemies – if fewer real friends as well – than anyone else on Labour's front bench.

Dalton's comment after the leadership election was that 'a little mouse shall lead them' , while A.V. Alexander also considered Attlee 'negligible'. There was also 'deep gloom' among the bright young economists of the party: Jay, Gaitskell and Durbin looked upon Attlee as 'an unglamorous, routine member' of the PLP.[33] Most of the press also wrote disparagingly of the new leader. But this was by no means the full story. Attlee was not a modest little man who had the leadership unexpectedly thrust upon him, as some have insisted. He had worked very hard since 1931 and had earned the genuine respect of those who had seen him in action. The backbone of his support in 1935 came from those MPs who had survived the 1931 débâcle and so had known him longest. One of these, George Hicks, wrote of his 'capacity, persistence, quiet strength and quality of leadership'. With a leader like this, who in William Golant's phrase 'embodied leadership without vanity', the party's policies would spearhead its appeal to the public.[34]

Herbert Morrison wrote many years later that Attlee's apparent diffidence in 1935 was something of a ploy: in reality, he intended to hold on to the reins put into his 'ostensibly unwilling hands'.[35] To argue that Attlee was a Machiavellian, intriguing behind the scenes for the leadership, would be unconvincingly melodramatic. Here was no English Stalin, building his empire behind a blur of unthreatening mediocrity and using 'democratic centralism' to isolate opponents. Yet there was surely more than a grain of truth in Morrison's view. Attlee did not lobby or campaign for the leadership in 1935. To have done so would not only have been alien to his character: it would have destroyed the persona he had consistently cultivated of the loyal, trustworthy and hard-working stalwart who would always bow to majority opinion once that opinion had been firmly established – in other words, the antithesis of Ramsay MacDonald. He had worked hard for the leadership, deliberately subordinating his personal views in order to represent the party. His ambition was never paraded – it was as effectively disguised as his intellectual self-confidence – but it undoubtedly existed.

REFERENCES

1. Kingsley Martin, *Harold Laski* (London, 1953), p. 159.
2. Philip M. Williams, *Hugh Gaitskell* (London, 1979), p. 248.
3. Attlee to Tom Attlee, 3 April 1933, Attlee Papers, Bodleian Library.
4. Raymond Postgate, *The Life of George Lansbury* (London, 1951), p. 279.
5. Attlee to Tom, 16 November and 18 December 1931.
6. Ibid., 15 February 1933.
7. Ibid., 15 July 1932.
8. Ibid., 25 April 1932.
9. I am grateful to John Swift for the last piece of information.
10. Postgate, *Life of Lansbury*, p. 284.
11. Dean E. McHenry, *The Labour Party in Transition, 1931–1938* (London, 1938), p. 173; Keith Middlemas and John Barnes, *Baldwin* (London, 1969), p. 695.
12. William Golant, *The Long Afternoon* (London, 1975), p. 118.
13. William Golant, 'The Political Development of C.R. Attlee to 1935', unpublished Oxford B.Litt. Thesis, 1967, p. 262.
14. Attlee to Tom, 28 February 1933.
15. Golant, 'Political Development of C.R. Attlee', p. 251.
16. Attlee to Tom, 7 February 1933.
17. John F. Naylor, *Labour's International Policy: the Labour Party in the 1930s* (London, 1969), p. 79.
18. Elizabeth Durbin, *New Jerusalems: The Labour Party and the Economics of Democratic Socialism* (London, 1985), p. 74.
19. Ibid., p. 89
20. Attlee to Tom, 3 April 1933.
21. Philip M. Williams, *Hugh Gaitskell* (London, 1982 edn), p. 69.
22. W. Golant, 'C.R. Attlee in the First and Second Labour Governments', *Parliamentary Affairs*, vol. 26, 1972–73, p. 331.
23. Golant, 'Political Development of C.R. Attlee', pp. 239–40.
24. Attlee to Tom, 6 November 1933.
25. Ben Pimlott (ed.), *The Political Diary of Hugh Dalton, 1918–40, 1945–60* (London, 1986), 8 October 1932, p. 169.
26. C.R. Attlee, *The Will and the Way to Socialism* (London, 1935), p. 120.
27. Naylor, *Labour's International Policy*, p. 93.
28. Roy Jenkins, *Mr Attlee: An Interim Biography* (London, 1948), p. 160.
29. *Daily Mail*, 14 October 1935.
30. Naylor, *Labour's International Policy*, p. 116.
31. Bernard Donoughue and G.W. Jones, *Herbert Morrison: Portrait of a Politician* (London, 1973), pp. 190, 235, 237.

32. Jay, *Chance and Fortune* (London, 1980), p. 57.
33. Pimlott (ed.), *Political Diary*, 26 November 1935, p. 196; Ben Pimlott, *Labour and the Left in the 1930s* (London, 1977), p. 25; Jay, *Chance and Fortune*, p. 57.
34. Golant, 'Political Development of C.R. Attlee', pp. 280, 281.
35. Herbert Morrison, *An Autobiography* (London, 1960), p. 164.

Chapter 4

ATTLEE AND APPEASEMENT, 1935–40

The occasion does not, in my view, call for long and eloquent speeches. My words will be few and simple.[1]

.   .   .

ATTLEE AS LABOUR LEADER

Attlee's victory in November 1935 was not regarded as final. Most commentators believed that he was still a caretaker leader – 'a natural Adjutant, but not a General', 'a good enough Parliamentarian, but desperately uninspiring'.[2] He would therefore hold the position only until the PLP was ready to commit itself to a 'bigger' figure. Attlee gave the impression that he himself shared this view, insisting that he had been elected for only one session and that he would give way as soon as the parliamentary party wished. He made no attempt to rally personal support or to impose his personality on the party. Instead, much as before, he got on with the job, as leader of the party but also as its servant.

Yet, paradoxically, such modesty made his position as leader more, not less, secure. He wrote in 1937 that he was not prepared

to arrogate to myself a superiority to the rest of the movement. I am prepared to submit to their will, even if I disagree. I shall do all I can to get my views accepted, but, unless acquiescence in the views of the majority conflicts with my conscience, I shall fall into line, for I have great faith in the wisdom of the rank and file.[3]

This was a beguiling – and potentially misleading – modesty, for Attlee was in fact parading his humility as a political virtue. He had undoubtedly found his political persona as the humble servant of the party; and it would certainly not be possible to dislodge him as leader by outmanoeuvring him on policy issues. It requires superhuman skill to chop off the head of anyone who so meekly but resolutely refuses to stick his neck out.

Similarly, Attlee was hard to pin down to any precise ideological position. As in the past, he refused to support the hunger marches of Wal Hannington's National Unemployed Workers' Movement; but he did share a platform with Hannington. He also supported the Jarrow march of early 1936 and was also a prominent supporter of the National Council of Civil Liberties, which Special Branch believed to be a communist front. In addition, he wrote a volume, *The Labour Party in Perspective*, for the Left Book Club, being among a minority of non-communist contributors.

Life was easier for Attlee in parliament. From 1937 he was, as leader of the opposition, paid a ministerial salary of £2,000 a year. In addition, he was less frenetically busy than before the general election: the PLP had tripled in size and so he did not have to speak on every conceivable subject. He distributed the limited patronage at his disposal wisely. For instance, he gave Hugh Dalton the position which he coveted, as Labour spokesman on foreign affairs. Attlee was now a practiced performer in the House of Commons, and made several speeches of distinctive quality. In January 1936 he was called upon to speak on the death of George V after the Prime Minister, Stanley Baldwin, who spoke for twenty minutes with 'every word perfectly chosen, and perfectly balanced'. He was a hard act to follow. 'We on our side thought he [Attlee] would jar, and do badly', noted a Conservative; 'but on the contrary he was excellent . . . He too held the House.'[4] Several of his other speeches were similarly well received. Yet most people had got into a fixed way of denigrating Attlee's oratory, operating the sort of selective censorship which reduced all his efforts to his worst.

To most Labour supporters, Attlee was too reasonable and moderate. They wanted him to oppose at every opportunity, while he saw the need to operate responsibly. This can be seen during the Abdication Crisis, where his views were very close to Baldwin's. He too believed that Edward VIII's proposed marriage to Mrs Simpson could not be accepted and that, therefore, the king should be manoeuvred into abdicating. Hence he pledged that if Edward resisted, and Baldwin resigned, the Labour party would refuse to form a government. Such a promise was profoundly relieving to Baldwin, and the whole crisis was ended with remarkable ease. But some in the Labour party, including Nye Bevan and even Dalton at first, believed that Labour should cash in on the crisis instead of lending their efforts reverently to solve it.

· · ·

DOMESTIC AFFAIRS

Events in Europe inevitably overshadowed all else during this period. Nevertheless there was progress in hammering out economic and social policies for a future Labour government. In 1937 the annual conference, meeting at Bournemouth, accepted *Labour's Immediate Programme*, which had already sold a massive 300,000 copies. A concise, eight-page document, it promised 'four vital measures of reconstruction' (with finance, land, transport and energy being the industries to be rebuilt) and 'four great benefits' (abundant food, good wages, leisure and security). The Bank of England was to be nationalised but not, as Attlee himself had urged in 1932, the joint stock banks; and coal, gas, electricity and the railways were also to be taken into public ownership. In addition there was to be a national investment board. There would also be better pensions, more secondary education and holidays with pay for all, together with public works schemes and the location of new industry in the depressed areas. Hugh Dalton, party chairman in 1936–37, had a keen ear for the ideas of the younger economists in the party, and he – and they – had done far more to hammer out the document than Attlee. Indeed his biographer has judged that Dalton was the 'effective leader' of the party at this time.[5] Yet Attlee's contribution was important, and he helped to rewrite a first draft into what became the final version. Dalton acknowledged that Attlee was 'very helpful in providing a continuous thread of argument to hold the programme together', so that in the end it became 'much better than a bare list of items'. Attlee commended it to the conference for its 'practical idealism' which combined 'ameliorative measures with fundamental changes'.[6]

By the end of the 1930s, therefore, Labour had an effective set of domestic policies. One commentator believes that the party had 'travelled light-years' in the depth and sophistication of its economic ideas since 1931, and hence was much better equipped to deal with financial and economic issues, both in the nation as a whole and in the depressed areas in particular.[7] There were no panaceas, only slow and curative – but realistic – remedies. Many similar ideas were being put forward by non-socialist economists, and indeed Labour thinkers, as in MacDonald's day, judged that socialism would have to grow out of a thriving capitalism; but the emphasis on equality and on state control did give a distinctively socialist flavour to these schemes. Labour's programme in 1945 owes far more to the *Immediate Programme*, and the experiences of the 1930s, than many historians who stress the crucial importance of the war years would allow.

The other main domestic feature of this period was the challenge of Cripps. The Socialist League had started as a research and propaganda body within the Labour party; then it became more of a faction; and finally, in this stage, it was virtually an alternative to the party. Cripps, most Labour colleagues believed, had no conception of party loyalty, though his supporters responded that he had a higher loyalty, to ideas – rapidly changing ones, it must be said. His main belief was that the fascist challenge demanded a common front between all those on the left – the Labour Party, the Communist Party, the ILP and radical Liberals – and he founded the journal *Tribune* as part of his Unity Campaign. Nye Bevan judged that communist affiliation would lead to the 'spiritual reawakening' of the whole working-class movement,[8] and Soviet support for the Spanish republicans in the civil war gave fuel to the call. But too many important figures in the party remembered their previous clashes with the communists, and news from the Russian show trials was an added warning that they should keep their distance from the CP. Attlee regarded both fascism and communism as equally obnoxious variants of totalitarianism.

The NEC and the Bournemouth conference in 1937 ruled decisively against association with the communists. In order to pre-empt expulsion, Cripps then disbanded the League. Yet if he was down, he was not out. The conference also accepted that the number of places for the constituency parties on the NEC should be increased, and that candidates should be elected solely by constituency delegates, and Cripps and fellow left-winger Harold Laski were the first to be elected. He remained an important voice in Labour affairs and a thorn in the flesh of the leadership.

Henceforth calls for a political realignment centred on a Popular Front, an attempt to unite Labour men with Liberals and dissident Conservatives. Something had to be done to get rid of Chamberlain, its supporters reasoned, and at least the Popular Front was a positive proposal. At the start of 1939 Cripps threw his weight behind this new cause. But once again the party hierarchy was resistant, arguing that Labour was the only viable opposition to Chamberlain's government and that a spatchcocked alignment, even if united on foreign policy, would be divided over domestic issues . Even Attlee now criticised Cripps, writing that his 'instability' gave one 'little trust in his judgement. In a few months he may ask us all to change again.' (Later Attlee was to comment scathingly on intellectuals 'who can be trusted to take the wrong view on any subject'.)[9] These negative attitudes led Cripps to issue a memorandum against official party policy and then to begin a national petition. When the NEC gave him a stark choice between withdrawing the memorandum and expulsion, he chose the latter, taking with him some of his supporters – including Bevan – into the political wilderness. Popular Front agitation came to an end in March 1939.

The expulsions represented a victory for Hugh Dalton, who considered that Cripps had all 'the political judgement of a flea'.[10] Certainly Cripps had no real understanding of the nature of the Stalinist regime, which he openly proclaimed as properly socialist and democratic. It was Attlee who had the better understanding of the Soviet Union, despite a visit there in 1936 in which he had been shepherded around with Intourist care from one showcase to another. Yet, as so often, Attlee did not take the initiative. Indeed he found the expulsions distasteful and had done his best to retain the services of the dissidents within the party.

To many, Labour's leader was adopting too equivocal a position. They tacitly believed that if a leader must sometimes know when to follow, he must also, at times, know when to lead. Some believed that, by taking the initiative boldly, he might even engineer splits in the Conservative and Liberal ranks, thus reversing 1931 and whittling down Chamberlain's majority. The feasibility of this remains a moot issue. Admittedly there was no chance of doing a deal with Eden and his followers. Eden had resigned as Foreign Secretary in February 1938, but his resignation speech was apologetically mild, and he clearly aimed eventually to replace Chamberlain as premier, not split the Conservative party. Yet for a brief moment, in the aftermath of Munich, a significant realignment seemed at least possible. Churchill praised Labour's declaration of foreign policy, only to receive a brief 'I am glad you think so' from the Labour leader. Attlee would not sign a 'vehement letter of protest' against the betrayal of the Czechs, which Churchill was hoping would gather widespread support.[11] Perhaps more might have been achieved, and certainly more might have been attempted. Yet Attlee was not the man to provide bold leadership, especially when the trade unionists were against action. He himself had written in 1937 that some realignment might be possible 'in the event of the imminence of a world crisis',[12] but presumably the crisis was not yet critical enough. He waited for bolder initiatives from the Tories, and they waited for more from him. Hence he played it safe, in effect rejecting the possibility of removing Chamberlain before the next election.

At the same time, the Labour hierarchy might also have done more to scotch the Popular Front agitation. At a by-election in October 1938 the Oxford constituency party withdrew the Labour candidate, Patrick Gordon Walker, in favour of a Popular Front man. Gordon Walker felt aggrieved: he had stood for official party policy but had not been backed up by Transport House. Attlee believed that Gordon Walker was one of the best of Oxford's younger dons and that he had put up a 'splendid fight' in the 1935 general election. Yet he gave him no support. It is therefore not surprising that it took the younger man a long time to begin to respect Attlee.[13]

It is possible to see Attlee as an exponent of a new form of collective leadership in this period, but some thought that really he was just weak and should be replaced by someone stronger. There had been some talk of a new leader in 1936, and continually thereafter there were those who thought the little man not up to the job; but it was in 1939 that a movement got under way to replace him. Dalton noted in June that Bevin, Citrine and Francis Williams, editor of the *Daily Herald*, had been saying that Attlee should go. Bevin's inclusion in this list may seem surprising, in view of his later loyalty; but at this stage, as he himself put it, he was ploughing 'a lonely furrow', feeling that he could not discuss the fundamental issues with any of the parliamentary leaders. He often complained in the late-1930s that 'The Party's got no leadership'.[14]

The first move was made by 'Red Ellen' Wilkinson, MP for Jarrow, who wrote an article attacking Attlee and angling for his replacement by Morrison. Yet the beginning of the conspiracy, if such it was, was almost its end. The move to crown Morrison provoked the ire of Bevin, who had no wish to promote Morrison, and of Greenwood's supporters, who believed that if anyone was going to replace Attlee it should be the deputy leader. In addition, Morrison's image had become somewhat tarnished with the PLP: not only had he turned down the deputy leadership in 1935 but his attendance in the Commons – due to the pressure of LCC work – had been poor. The move also coincided with Attlee's ill health – as he awaited a prostate operation – and so won sympathy for him within the party. A meeting of the PLP in June 1939 saw a unanimous, if insincere, vote of sympathy with him in his illness and of personal confidence in him.

A second stage in the behind-the-scenes intrigue occurred when Dalton switched horses. Instead of calling for Morrison's elevation, he decided that Greenwood was the man to lead the party: as deputy, he was already doing the job far better than 'poor little Rabbit' had ever done . At the back of his mind was the notion that 'once we got the leadership moving', it would be relatively easy later on to replace Greenwood by Morrison – or perhaps by Dalton himself.[15] Yet Attlee was in hospital longer than envisaged, leading to continuing personal sympathy, and Morrison was no longer willing to lend a hand if the beneficiary might be someone other than himself. The move therefore petered out. Had there been one obvious candidate to take over, it might perhaps have been different; but, even so, Attlee's attitude towards the key issue of the day, foreign policy, meant that once more he was an exceptionally elusive target.

. . .

FOREIGN POLICY UP TO 1937

We have seen that Attlee had been anything but consistent in his attitude to foreign affairs. The man determined to fight for his country in the First World War had decided, by 1923, that his efforts had been in vain, for the Paris peace conference had betrayed the hopes of mankind. He, and many other

Labour figures, were particularly aggrieved that the Sudeten Germans had been placed under Czech rule and that the contrived Polish 'corridor' cut off east Prussia from the rest of Germany. The settlement seemed to be based on short-sighted emotions of sour revenge. At the 1923 Labour conference, Attlee came close to espousing pacifism. As Under-Secretary at the War Office in 1924 , he forgot about such idealism; but it returned in the early-1930s, under the influence of Cripps, only to disappear once more in 1934–35. Henceforth he favoured multilateral, but not unilateral, disarmament and was a supporter of the League of Nations. He stood not for the 'balance of power' and the division of Europe into armed camps, as before 1914, but for collective security. He told the annual conference in 1934 that Labour had abandoned mere national loyalty: 'We are definitely putting a world order before our loyalty towards our own country.'[16] From this perspective, patriotism was merely the last refuge of the arms manufacturer.

Attlee's tergiversations had mirrored those of the party, and as leader he continued to voice the uncertainties and ambiguities in Labour thinking.

At the 1935 election Labour policy was clear. Labour stood for collective security through the League of Nations, and it also stood for general disarmament. Had not the First World War been caused by the arms race, combined with international anarchy? Now similar causes must be eliminated. There should be no arms races, Attlee insisted, and international affairs must be regulated by the League of Nations, with the ultimate goal of the creation of a 'super-State'. In the meantime countries should be prepared to give up elements of their national sovereignty to make the League work, and in particular be prepared to scale down and subsequently abandon their private armed forces.

This was a policy which made eminently good sense in terms of party requirements: while not pacifist, it yet took account of pacifist feeling within the party. It also made sense in broad human terms, for no one doubted that another war would be far more destructive even than the last. Attlee shared with Baldwin a horror of mechanised warfare and several times cited the Conservative's speech in which he had shocked his audience with the stark warning that 'The bomber will always get through'. Civilisation would be wiped out, averred Attlee, unless air warfare were somehow restrained.

Yet these ideas did not make practical sense: indeed they ignored foreign policy realities. Again and again, Attlee spoke as though the National government was turning its back on the League of Nations and ruining a viable international organisation. Yet the fact was that the League of Nations had always been viewed with a mixture of indifference and disdain by successive British governments. Even MacDonald's Labour governments had failed to bring it fully to life, and Japan's unpunished aggression in Manchuria in 1931 had been a severe blow to its credibility. Attlee himself had judged that the Manchurian issue was the 'acid test . . . perhaps the last chance' for the League, for unless the blackmailer is punished, he comes back again and again, enlarging his claims.[17] Yet the League failed the test. There was therefore an undoubtedly large dose of wishful thinking in Attlee's continuing belief in the League, especially when he put it forward as an alternative to rearmament. This was the equivalent of trusting in God and failing to keep your powder dry. He continually spoke as though the League were greater than the sum of its parts, but in fact it could only work if its leading members supplied the muscle, which in the last analysis meant military muscle – and the only Powers to serve continuously as members of the League Council from its inception onwards were Britain and France. Attlee and the Labour party were therefore guilty of profoundly wishful thinking, willing the ends but not the means. Perhaps their impotent parliamentary position encouraged such an unrealistic approach: since there was little that Labour could do to influence government, there was a natural tendency to suit themselves and devise a policy to which the largest number of party members could subscribe.

Baldwin's government also had its foreign policy difficulties. Having won the 1935 election on the tide of League of Nations popularity, the government promptly attempted to bypass the League by doing a deal to buy off Mussolini with two-thirds of Abyssinia. The Hoare–Laval plan created a storm of disapproval, and led to Hoare's resignation as Foreign Secretary. The ensuing debates in the Commons were therefore a great opportunity for Labour, and Attlee attacked with real vigour. He spoke of the mad folly of the government's policy, stressing that what was at stake was 'the vindication of the rule of law against the rule of force'. The government was using the old method 'of buying off the aggressor': but this had never

worked before and would not work now. Instead, the government should have applied immediate sanctions under League
authority. Attlee admitted that the League of Nations was frail,
but it was the one thing standing between the world and
another world war – and now it was now being sacrificed by
this 'surrender to an aggressor of half an Empire in exchange
for a corridor for camels'. It was a good hard-hitting performance, and he insisted – with historical accuracy – that the
responsibility lay not merely with Hoare but with Baldwin himself. The reference to Baldwin may have been a tactical
mistake, since it allowed Conservative backbenchers to rally to
their leader's support; but Attlee had discomfited the Tories
and rallied his own party.

Yet while Attlee's criticisms were good, his positive recom-
mendations lacked real substance. His most constructive plea
was for the creation of a new Ministry of Defence to co-ordi-
nate the separate activities of the army, navy and air force.
Orderly planning, including the nationalisation of the muni-
tions industry, should replace chaotic competition. In short,
Attlee believed that if there had to be rearmament, it should
be efficiently organised. Yet his remarks on rearmament were
at best equivocal. Labour consistently voted against the military estimates; and while this did not mean that the party was
against all expenditure on defence, it could easily be twisted
by political opponents to imply this. While Attlee admitted,
in the Abyssinian debate, that Labour was prepared to consider British rearmament, he went on, more strongly, to insist
that the party was not prepared to give the government a
blank cheque ('an undertaker's mandate'), and that, anyway,
there was really no such thing any more as national defence.
If the League were made effective, disarmament rather than
rearmament would soon be the order of the day.[18] Hence he
was able to accuse the national government of putting guns
before butter.

Several key figures in the Labour movement believed that
the party had to grasp the nettle and support British rearmament, even under a Conservative government. Dalton believed
this: he had spent four days in Berlin in April 1933 and henceforth believed that a European war 'must be counted among
the probabilities of the next ten years'.[19] In 1934 he had suc-
cessfully obtained party approval of the need to resist
aggression, though leaving open the means of doing so. But

this was not enough, and he and Bevin were determined to impose clarity and a sense of reality on the party. It was they who led the way, and Attlee – and the party – who followed.

At the 1936 party conference in Edinburgh there was a full-scale row about foreign policy. Dalton tried hard to get the PLP to abstain rather than vote against the Service estimates, but in vain. In the end unity of a sort was preserved, but only at the cost of continuing ambiguity. A motion was passed acknowledging that 'The countries loyal to the League must be as strong in armaments as the potential aggressors.' But there was no agreement on the precise meaning of these words. Dalton introduced the motion as though it meant supporting the government's rearmament plans; Morrison contradicted him; Bevin attacked Morrison; and Attlee intervened to support Morrison, arguing that rearmament should be under collective League responsibility and that there was no suggestion that Labour 'would support the Government's rearmament policy'.[20] His reasoning was predicated on the notion that one could not oppose fascism by becoming fascist oneself. Bevin came close to despairing of the party, but Attlee judged that the acceptance of the Bevin–Dalton line might well split the Labour brethren, given members' pacifist feelings and also their widespread suspicions of the government's motives, which had been reinforced by the Hoare–Laval plan. Nye Bevan, for instance, believed that Labour support for rearmament would 'put a sword in the hands of our enemies that may be used to cut off our own heads'.[21] Fudging issues was therefore the lesser evil.

Further problems arose at Edinburgh over the civil war in Spain. Several months earlier Britain had been signatory to a 'non-intervention' agreement, along with France, the Soviet Union, Germany and Italy; and the NEC wished to endorse neutrality – which was, after all, the policy of the French socialist leader Leon Blum. The conference accepted this official recommendation. But after the impassioned pleas of Spanish fraternal delegates, and a hasty visit from Attlee and Greenwood to Neville Chamberlain, Attlee moved that if reliable evidence were forthcoming that Hitler and Mussolini were supplying arms and that therefore non-intervention was a farce, the republic should be able to buy arms. Here was another potentially divisive issue on which unambiguous statements were best avoided.

Greater clarity appeared the following year, when Dalton was Labour's chairman. The 1937 Bournemouth conference not only expelled the Socialist League and accepted *Labour's Immediate Programme* but called for the end of non-intervention in Spain and endorsed a policy of active rearmament, even under the existing government. What was the sense of urging arms for Spain but no arms for Britain? The key vote had been taken a few months earlier, in July, when the PLP decided by 45 votes to 29 to abstain rather than vote against the Service estimates. There was now a new realism to Labour's foreign policy, though this owed more to Dalton and Bevin than to Attlee.

. . .

FOREIGN POLICY, 1937-39

After the reversal of policy in 1937 Labour was able to hammer out a more realistic policy. One was certainly needed, given Hitler's actions – the *Anschluss* in March 1938, his determination to absorb the Sudetenland in September 1938, the invasion of the rump of Czechoslovakia in March 1939 and, finally, the invasion of Poland in September 1939. Attlee's response, for the Labour party, was a firm denunciation of Chamberlain and of appeasement.

There was undoubtedly personal animosity between Attlee and Chamberlain. The new Prime Minister had none of Baldwin's fellow-feeling with Labour MPs. Attlee later described him as 'absolutely useless for foreign affairs – ignorant and at the same time opinionated . . . He always treated us like dirt.' If Baldwin's antenna had been tuned in to the national wavelength, Chamberlain's 'never got beyond Midland Regional'.[22] In particular Attlee was critical of appeasement. Indeed he always had been, despite the fact that, intellectually, he had sympathy with Germany's grievances: he insisted that Britain should not give to Hitler and force what had been denied to Stresemann and reason. He complained of the ending of sanctions against Mussolini and indeed of the whole dishonourable meekness of Chamberlain's policy towards the dictators:

> I do not believe in throwing sops to Dictators . . . It is about time we ceased to accept the dictates of Berlin and Rome . . . We believe in democracy, but if democracy is to survive it must be prepared to stand up to the dictators.[23]

On another occasion he insisted that appeasement, which was making the Concert of Europe into a 'thieves' kitchen', was misguided because it depended on the 'piecrust promises' of the dictators. After the *Anschluss*, Attlee was highly critical, and after the Munich settlement he was positively scathing:

> This has not been a victory for reason and humanity. It has been a victory for brute force . . . We have seen to-day a gallant, civilised and democratic people betrayed and handed over to a ruthless despotism. We have seen something more. We have seen the cause of democracy, which is, in our view, the cause of civilisation and humanity, receive a terrible defeat . . . The events of the last few days constitute one of the greatest diplomatic defeats that this country and France have ever sustained. There can be no doubt that it is a tremendous victory for Herr Hitler. Without firing a shot, by the mere display of military force, he has achieved a dominating position in Europe which Germany failed to win after four years of war. He has overturned the balance of power in Europe. He has destroyed the last fortress of democracy in Eastern Europe which stood in the way of his ambition . . . The cause [of the crisis] was not the existence of minorities in Czechoslovakia; it was not that the position of the Sudeten Germans had become intolerable. It was not the wonderful principle of self-determination. It was because Herr Hitler had decided that the time was ripe for another step forward in his design to dominate Europe . . . Hitler has successfully asserted the law of the jungle.[24]

Labour's answer was that Britain should press ahead, faster than Chamberlain contemplated, with a realistic policy of rearmament – involving a real Minister of Defence and better air defences – and, at the same time, should foster collective security. Attlee still threw in an honourable mention to the League of Nations, but by collective security he meant alliances with key powers, in particular France and the USSR.

Many writers have insisted that the government were belated converts to Labour ideas of collective security; but in practice there was little difference between Labour's new stance and the 'balance of power' diplomacy which Attlee had previously criticised. He approved Chamberlain's guarantee to Poland, though he also insisted forcefully, despite the Poles' antipathy to both of their overmighty neighbours, that to make good the guarantee an alliance with Stalin was essential. Labour's policy was in fact very similar to that of Churchill, Amery and the other Conservative critics. Admittedly Labour opposed the introduction of conscription in the spring of 1939, and the government used the vote to argue that the party had still not shuffled off its pacifism; but there were good reasons to vote against conscription, as the military expert Liddell Hart argued at the time, not least in that there would be too little equipment for the men who were called up. Later some conscripted men, who had special skills required in civilian industry, had to be very hastily demobilised.

. . .

ATTLEE'S FOREIGN POLICY: AN ASSESSMENT

There is much that can be said in favour of Attlee's views. According to Burridge, he scarcely put a foot wrong after 1935.[25] In view of the difficult job of securing unity within the party, he has particularly praised Attlee's sense of timing. According to this view, Attlee had similar objectives to Dalton; but had he, like Dalton, pressed for changes in policy earlier, he might have failed to secure the degree of realism that was achieved by 1937. Indeed Dalton was, in comparison, a poor party tactician, failing, for instance, to realise the significance of Spain to the party. For him, it was simply a dangerous diversion; whereas Attlee knew its emotional importance for the left wing, and his visit there in December 1937 won their approval. In short, Dalton's boldness needed Attlee's caution. A year earlier, Dalton's views had not been acceptable, and even in 1937 the PLP vote was a close-run thing, with a large number of abstentions.

Also in Attlee's favour was his laying bare, with skill and insight, of the folly and self-deception of appeasement. Furthermore, had his support for the League become British policy earlier then perhaps the troubles would not have escalated so catastrophically. Finally, Attlee had the right attitude towards the Soviet Union in 1939. Admittedly there was an inconsistency between his call for a Soviet alliance and his refusal of a united front in Britain; but then it was entirely realistic, when supping with Stalin, to prefer a long spoon. Attlee had warned the government – quite correctly – that if they maintained the same lukewarm attitude to Russia they 'would be left to face the music with only France to help us'.[26]

A case can certainly be made out for Attlee as a far-sighted and skilful spokesman on foreign affairs. Yet such a view surely distorts the degree to which his mind was free from ambiguity and misconception. In fact several criticisms must be made of Attlee's thinking on foreign affairs. Defining fascism in 1933–34 as 'an expression of capitalism in decline', he had initially allowed his views to be obfuscated by the socialist theory that wars were engendered by capitalism, with the result that he, like other socialists, sometimes could not see what was in front of his nose. He was slow to spot the menace posed by the fascists, especially by Germany, and had for too long believed that if a war did arise, it might involve only the nations of central and eastern Europe. He had referred to 'irresponsible dictators, who are here to-day and gone tomorrow', while his judgement in 1935 that 'the peoples of the world are overwhelmingly in favour of peace' smacked of positively Baldwinian complacency. Similarly his oft-professed belief that real security lay in total disarmament was starkly irrelevant in the conditions of Europe in the mid-1930s. Certainly, as we have seen, he had made obeisance for too long before the shrine of the League, speculating that its members should pledge themselves to refuse allegiance to their own countries. He had spoken so glowingly of the League of Nations because this was one of the issues on which he felt strongly and was prepared to fight.[27] World government was a theme to which he returned in old age.

There is also evidence that, initially, he opposed rearmament not because of the party's wishful thinking but because of his own. At the end of 1936 he described rearmament as 'futile and wasteful', and early in 1937 he judged that 'the way to meet Fascism is not by force of arms, but by showing that with better co-operation in the economic sphere far better conditions are obtainable than by pursuing a policy of aggression'. Entry into an arms race, he added, would not give security: 'On the contrary, I think that it is leading straight to the disaster of another world war.'[28] It was around this time that the PLP had its crucial debate over whether to continue voting against the estimates. It is not absolutely impossible that Burridge is right and that Attlee did approve the new decision merely to abstain. With such an inscrutable figure, all things are possible. Perhaps this is why, against most people's expectations, he failed to support Greenwood and Morrison in speaking against Dalton. But such silence was habitual with Attlee not exceptional, and the fact is that he cast his vote against a change in policy. It therefore seems likely that he merely acquiesced in the decision, sinking his personal opinion in the interests of party unity. Clearly there were important differences between Attlee and Dalton. By obscuring them, and loyally accepting the new policy, Attlee managed to safe-guard his own position in the party; but to a large degree the new realism of Labour's foreign policy had been achieved against his considered judgement. Attlee did not bring the party into line; instead, it was he who fell into line. The tradi-tional view of an impassive, imperturbable Attlee gradually weaning his party from the old shibboleths is no longer accept-able. Certainly he was far more perturbed – and emotional – than most historians have allowed. He once shouted and swore at Walter Citrine, the ally of Dalton and Bevin in the call for rearmament, and on another occasion his eyes were observed to be red with weeping. He was also passionately against Chamberlain's introduction of conscription and was visibly shaking with rage when the issue was debated.[29]

Nor was Attlee's approach to foreign affairs as sure-footed in 1938–39 as his admirers have insisted. Before the Munich conference, Attlee had been worried that Chamberlain, whom he considered an old-fashioned imperialist, was leading the country into war; and after Munich he entertained his fair share of impractical views. On 3 October 1938 he was calling for a full-scale international conference: this would surely give substance to the 'utter hatred and detestation of war' that existed throughout the world and that was, he was sure, as strong in Germany and Italy as in Britain He even ventured the opinion – which has been stigmatised, quite correctly, as verging on the ridiculous – that Hitler might be induced to rejoin a resurrected League.[30] A few days later he urged that Britain should give a lead to the world – by promoting social justice at home. Given the circumstances of the time, this amounted to little more than navel-gazing. It is true that, after March 1939, he was urging a strong alliance between Britain, France and the Soviet Union, but this, he believed, would pre-vent war. In addition, many of his colleagues, like Citrine, felt that 'Clam Attlee' failed to give sufficient guidance on foreign policy. Furthermore, almost all of Attlee's speeches on foreign policy showed a blithe unawareness of Britain's relative eco-nomic decline. Britain was still 'the greatest Power in the world',[31] and so he was incredulous that the government was allowing the old standards to go by the board and trailing Britain's honour in the mud. Had he been better informed, he might have seen Chamberlain's efforts to avoid a major confrontation as realistic rather than cowardly.

Attlee was no far-sighted statesman before the Second World War. He was feeling his way, sometimes reluctantly, towards a more realistic foreign policy. Too often his frame of reference was not the world as it actually was but as he would have liked it to be. Yet this was surely only to be expected, given his inexperience of foreign affairs, the state of the Labour Party and the bewildering array of problems that faced Britain at the time, which probably had no solution. Nor could he have the full knowledge of Britain's economic and international position which membership of the government might have given him. The case against Attlee should not be pushed too far. Very few politicians in the 1930s come well out of the appeasement debate, and many emerge more tarnished than he.

In September 1939 Attlee was unwell, convalescing at Nevin after a bungled prostate operation. But he would have endorsed the policy of the PLP. On 1 September Hitler invaded Poland, but Chamberlain hesitated about making good his guarantee. The House of Commons, taking its lead from Labour Members, then threatened to become ungovernable unless war were declared. Acting leader Arthur Greenwood was urged to 'speak for England', and a declaration followed on 3 September. Labour policy had indeed been revolutionised since the earlier part of the decade.

. . .

LABOUR AND THE 'PHONEY WAR'

The Labour Party's position after the declaration of war was a curious one. It refused to serve in a coalition, not that Chamberlain particularly wanted it to: he preferred merely to bring in Tory rebels like Churchill and Eden instead. Yet Labour did accept an electoral truce, so that by-elections would not be contested by the major parties: instead the candidate of the incumbent party would be unopposed. Hence Labour was seen to support the war effort, and so could not be branded as irresponsible, while at the same remaining free to criticise the government – as it did over the clumsy declaration of war, without consulting local people, on India's behalf. There was thus no political truce.

There was soon much to criticise. Chamberlain failed to put the country on a proper war footing – so that the trade unions

were held at arm's length and unemployment remained high
– while at the same time he appeared unduly optimistic. Yet
Labour's leaders had no idea how to remove Chamberlain.
Attlee, back in harness by November, issued a statement, subsequently published, that 'practical socialism' had to replace
'economic anarchy'. Socialist measures – including control
over the economy and social reforms – were necessary to win
the war: planning for war would necessarily involve planning
for a better society. So far, so good. But he also insisted that if
the Germans repudiated Hitler and Nazism, and made full
restitution to their victims, a peace settlement could be drawn
up which would make the world safe for democracy. Attlee
called for the inauguration of the rule of law in international
affairs: in particular, armed forces were to be internation-
alised, while 'Europe must federate or perish'.[32] Such a
scheme, he asserted, quite erroneously, was not chimerical. In
February he was warning that Britons must not allow the evil
things against which they were fighting to overcome their own
souls. Hope still sprang eternal in the Labour, as in the government, breast: perhaps the war might be ended by the blockade
of Germany or by an uprising of the German people? Attlee
had been cannily quiet about the Soviet invasion of Poland, in
September 1939, but the party did back the government offer
to help the Finns against the Russians in December.

Many Labour backbenchers were becoming highly critical of
the electoral truce and of their leaders' passivity. In January
1940 Chamberlain believed that Labour, 'saturated with the
pettiness of party politics', were angry with Attlee for his common sense and moderation.[33] Yet in early May, when
dissatisfaction with the failure of the Norwegian campaigns
brought criticisms of the Chamberlain administration to a
head, Attlee was very much in tune with the feelings of the PLP.

The significance of the crucial two-day debate of 7 and 8
May 1940 for unseating Chamberlain is well known. Much less
appreciated is Attlee's role. In fact, he made the first opposition speech, skilfully widening the attack from the specific
campaign to cover Chamberlain's prewar record and the government's weakness on the economic front. He ended by
calling for Chamberlain's resignation and by urging the
Conservative backbenchers to overcome their party loyalty in
the interests of the nation. The speech may have lacked the
virulence later employed, among others, by Admiral Keyes and

Lloyd George; but at this stage more extravagant speeches might have fallen flat or even rallied Conservatives to Chamberlain's defence. Attlee appealed to reason not emotion. He had been 'pretty good', according to Amery, who delivered the Cromwellian peroration at the end of the day;[34] and next morning the party executive decided to divide the House at the end of the debate. Dalton was against, thinking it would only strengthen Chamberlain's hand, as Attlee had been earlier; but he and those of like mind were defeated. Attlee's role here is controversial. Morrison later insisted that it was he himself who convinced the reluctant committee; but Attlee, on the contrary, recalled that he took the lead while Morrison was the reluctant one. Dalton's diary supports Morrison's interpretation and fails to mention Attlee at all; but perhaps the answer is that Morrison took the initiative at the executive meeting, while Attlee presided over the subsequent full meeting of the PLP.[35]

What is not in doubt is the efficacy of Labour's decision to divide. Chamberlain's majority slumped to only eighty, as well over a hundred Conservatives either abstained or supported Labour. His only real hope lay with a proposal to Attlee and Greenwood that Labour should agree to serve under his leadership and enter a coalition. As German forces attacked westwards, adding momentous importance to the response, Attlee telephoned a typically terse reply from Bournemouth, where, of course, he had been punctilious in consulting the NEC: no, they would not serve under Chamberlain, but yes they would enter a coalition under someone else. Labour did not end Chamberlain's government on their own, but they had taken a leading role. Had they not done so, the subsequent course of British history might have been significantly different.

Chamberlain then recommended to the king that Churchill should form an administration. He received the job largely because Lord Halifax, Chamberlain's preferred successor, refused the position. Perhaps, as Andrew Roberts believes, Halifax thought he could do a better job of restraining Churchill if he were foreign secretary rather than prime minister;[36] more likely, he simply had not the stomach for war, especially as head of a democratic regime with which he had never wholly sympathised. ('What a bore democracy is to those who have to work it.')[37] At all events, Labour had little influence in the choice of Churchill.

Would Attlee have preferred Churchill or Halifax? This is an issue which has exercised most commentators, who have tended to give more confident judgements than the evidence allows. Harris and Burridge insist that he was for Churchill, as by far the best man for the job. Yet their views are drawn from Attlee's later memories, which were at least in part rationalisations. Dalton's diary for 9 May records Attlee's preference for Halifax, and others too – like Leo Amery and Lord Home – believed he favoured Halifax. Certainly he had a high, and perhaps exaggerated, view of him, recalling that he had been the most sympathetic of the viceroys. Attlee had told Harold Wilson and the other assembled Oxford guests at a dinner at University College during the early months of the war that Winston was too old to become premier: he apparently expected that, as a Churchill, his life-expectancy would not be great. Yet the fact is that neither Attlee, nor most of his colleagues, had strong feelings either way. The important thing was simply for Labour to enter government.

Attlee had no doubt where the party's patriotic duty lay – and there could be no shirking. He was also aware of political advantages: here was a real chance for Labour to gain valuable administrative experience. But he was careful that there should be no repetition of MacDonald's 'betrayal'. Hence on 13 May he reassured Labour's annual conference that the whole party was joining the coalition, not just individuals. We go in, he told them, 'as partners and not as hostages', and he was sure that the war effort needed 'the application of the Socialist principle of service before private property'. Their aim would be to win liberty 'on the sure foundation of social justice'.[38] To Churchill, he likewise insisted that he was entering the government as a representative of Labour, not as an individual. His words were pertinent. Clement Attlee as an individual had done little to earn a key position in Britain's wartime administration: Labour was not his party, he was the party's servant. He had been leader for over four years, but – to his critics – he had shown little capacity for real leadership. Dalton, Bevin and Morrison had taken the initiative more often. The 'caretaker leader' was still in office, but for how much longer? Would he sink or swim in the high office which had now come his way? What is certain is that he still had a reputation to make – and that here was a golden opportunity to make it.

. . .

REFERENCES

1. *Parliamentary Debates* (Commons), 3 December 1936.
2. Dean E. McHenry, *The Labour Party in Transition, 1931–1938* (London, 1938), p. 147.
3. C.R. Attlee, *The Labour Party in Perspective* (London, 1937), p. 136.
4. R.R. James (ed.), *Chips: The Diaries of Sir Henry Channon* (London, 1993 edn), 23 January 1936, p. 55.
5. Ben Pimlott, *Hugh Dalton* (London, 1985), p. 236.
6. Elizabeth Durbin, *New Jerusalems: The Labour Party and the Economics of Democratic Socialism* (London, 1985), p. 247.
7. Ibid., p. 261.
8. Ben Pimlott, *Labour and the Left in the 1930s* (London, 1977), p. 86.
9. Pimlott, *Labour and the Left*, p. 177; C.R. Attlee, *As It Happened* (London, 1954), p. 86.
10. Pimlott, *Hugh Dalton*, p. 256.
11. John Charmley, *Chamberlain and the Lost Peace* (London, 1989), p.146.
12. Attlee, *Labour Party in Perspective*, p. 124.
13. Attlee to Tom, 16 July 1936, Attlee Papers, Bodleian Library; Robert Pearce (ed.), *Patrick Gordon Walker: Political Diaries, 1932–1971* (London, 1991), pp. 8–11.
14. Stephen Brooke, *Labour's War: The Labour Party during the Second World War* (Oxford, 1992), p. 27; Francis Williams, *Nothing So Strange* (London, 1970), p. 135.
15. Ben Pimlott (ed.), *The Political Diary of Hugh Dalton, 1918–40, 1945–60* (London, 1986), 22 August 1939, p. 282; November 1939, p. 311.
16. *Labour Party Annual Conference Report* (1934), p. 174.
17. C.R. Attlee, *War Comes to Britain* (ed. J Dugdale) (London, 1940), pp. 22, 25, 37.
18. Ibid., p. 92.
19. Pimlott, *Hugh Dalton*, p. 227.
20. Alan Bullock, *The Life and Times of Ernest Bevin*, vol. 1 (London, 1960), p. 584.
21. Kenneth Harris, *Attlee* (London, 1984), p. 136.
22. *Clem Attlee: Granada Historical Records Interview* (London, 1967), p.17; Cyril Clemens, *The Man from Limehouse: Clement Richard Attlee* (Missouri, USA), p. 29.
23. Attlee, *War Comes to Britain*, pp. 128–31.
24. Ibid., pp. 163, 167, 184–5, 188–9.
25. Trevor Burridge: *Clement Attlee: A Political Biography* (London, 1985), pp. 96–137.

26. Attlee to Tom, 19 September 1939; John F. Naylor, *Labour's International Policy* (London, 1969), p.251.
27. Attlee to Tom, 18 August 1933; C.R. Attlee, *The Will and the Way to Socialism* (London, 1935), esp. pp. 2, 91, 93; Attlee, *War Comes to Britain*, p. 75.
28. Attlee to Tom, 26 October 1936; Attlee, *Labour Party in Perspective*, pp. 224, 270–1.
29. Pimlott (ed.), *Political Diary of Dalton*, 11 April 1938, p. 228. James (ed.), *Chips*, 20 October 1938, p. 174; 26 April 1939, p. 194.
30. Attlee, *War Comes to Britain*, pp. 199–200; Naylor, *Labour's International Policy*, p. 252.
31. Attlee, *War Comes to Britain*, p.165.
32. Ibid., p. 246.
33. John Colville, *The Fringes of Power: Downing Street Diaries, 1939–1955* (London, 1985), p. 72.
34. John Barnes and David Nicholson (eds), *The Empire at Bay: The Leo Amery Diaries, 1929–1945* (London, 1988), p. 592.
35. Bernard Donoughue and G.W. Jones, *Herbert Morrison: Portrait of a Politician* (London, 1973), p. 272.
36. Andrew Roberts, *'The Holy Fox': A Life of Lord Halifax* (London, 1991), p. 199.
37. Ibid., p. 307.
38. Harris, *Attlee*, p. 178.

Chapter 5

ATTLEE'S WAR

Those who belong to a great Party such as ours, which aspires to power so that we may bring about great changes, cannot tread the primrose path of independence.[1]

Winston Churchill became Prime Minister on 10 May 1940. Immediately he saw Attlee and Greenwood to negotiate about the composition of a new, all-party government. He offered Labour a good deal. Small wonder, then, that when he first entered the Commons as Prime Minister on 13 May, promising nothing but 'blood, toil, tears and sweat', it was the Labour MPs who cheered him, while the Conservatives – who had had no say in the elevation of this renegade – remained stony-faced, reserving their warmth for Chamberlain, who was still their party leader.

The party's two leaders were to enter the five-man War Cabinet and, in addition, Labour was to have one of the three service ministers. Churchill mentioned Bevin, Morrison, A.V. Alexander and Dalton as men he particularly wanted to include in the government. Attlee then compiled a list of people for particular offices. He strove to achieve a balanced representation of the party, from right (Sir William Jowitt) to left (Ellen Wilkinson). Dispensing patronage gave his standing a fillip within the party. For instance, when he told Hugh Dalton that Labour needed 'tough guys' in prominent positions and that therefore he would have a department of his own, he automatically rose in Dalton's estimation. Attlee, he wrote, paying him a compliment for almost the first time, had 'rather an engaging smile'![2]

The main bone of contention, in fact, was the role to be assigned to Neville Chamberlain. Churchill spoke of him as a possible Leader of the House of Commons, but Attlee argued very strongly that this would be unacceptable to the party, and instead he became Lord President of the Council. Labour would have preferred to see Chamberlain – together with other appeasers like Sir John Simon – out of office altogether; but Attlee noted philosophically that there were no doubt several Labour figures whom the Tories would not want to see in government. He knew that coalition inevitably meant compromise, so that no one group could possibly achieve all that it wanted. As it was, Churchill was able to call the new administration the most broadly-based in British history.

Attlee himself was appointed Lord Privy Seal and Greenwood Minister without Portfolio, both with seats in the War Cabinet, alongside Chamberlain, Halifax and Churchill himself, who doubled up as Prime Minister and Minister of Defence. There were rumours that Ernest Bevin was to be in the War Cabinet instead of Attlee, but these lacked foundation, merely reflecting the speculation to which Attlee's supposed weakness often gave rise. In fact, Bevin became Minister of Labour and National Service, outside the War Cabinet initially; Alexander took over from Churchill as First Lord of the Admiralty; Morrison became Minister of Supply and Dalton Minister of Economic Warfare. In total, there were sixteen Labour members of the new government, and in the course of the war their numbers increased, to twenty-two by March 1942 and twenty-seven by 1945. They had greater representation than the party's strength in the Commons warranted, and it is generally agreed by historians that their influence on the government – especially on the home front – was disproportionate to their ministerial strength. Churchill laid down the ground rules for the parties with the dictum: 'Everything for the war, whether controversial or not, and nothing controversial that is not *bona fide* needed for the war.'[3] He hoped that no party would gain politically from the war, but the ethos of this People's War was on equality of sacrifice, on fair shares and state control, and this inevitably favoured Labour.

Two men, both of whom had been spoken of before the war

as alternatives to Attlee as party leader, were particularly successful. After an unhappy but brief spell at Supply, Herbert Morrison was made Home Secretary during the blitz. Here his unrivalled knowledge of London stood him in good stead and he proved remarkably successful. In November 1942 he was promoted to the War Cabinet. At the end of 1943 Lord Beaverbrook referred to him as 'the biggest figure in the country' apart from Churchill, and Churchill himself judged that Morrison had the best mind of the Labour men in the government. The other undoubted success was Ernest Bevin. He had not sat at Westminster before 1940, and indeed was never really at home in the Commons, but he reorganised the Ministry of Labour with real administrative flair to serve the manpower needs of the country, in the process improving conditions for many groups of workers. He entered the War Cabinet in October 1940. The *Manchester Guardian* later judged that he came out of the war 'second only to Churchill in courage and insight', and the popular novelist and broadcaster J.B. Priestley also compared this 'fine lump of England . . . an oak tree' to Churchill as representing 'the other half of the English people'.[4] But what of Clem Attlee's war?

In his first appearance on the government front bench, dwarfed by Churchill and Bevin, Attlee did not cut an impressive figure. A hostile witness described him as a 'little gad-fly' looking smaller and more insignificant than ever.[5] Here was a man who, according to his critics, owed his position in the War Cabinet not to his personal strengths but to the 'accident' of his election as a stopgap Labour leader in 1935. His detractors believed that this explained Churchill's choice of office for him: everyone knew that the Lord Privy Seal was neither a lord, nor a privy, nor a seal, but no one knew his real function. There were some who hoped, and others who expected, that Attlee would fail.

· · ·

ATTLEE AS MINISTER

The deputy leader of the Labour party, Arthur Greenwood, proved to be little more than a passenger in the coalition and was shuffled onto the back benches in February 1942. But Attlee was made of sterner stuff and stayed the full course. He was the only minister besides Churchill to serve in the War Cabinet for its full duration. In 1942 a cabinet reshuffle led him to become Dominions Secretary, but his other multifarious duties were recognised by official appointment as Deputy Prime Minister; and in 1943 he took on the role of Lord President of the Council, the key position in organising the home front. Furthermore, he was the only member of the government to sit on the three key wartime committees – the War Cabinet itself, the Defence Committee and the Lord President's Committee. This was a committee structure which Attlee himself had done much to determine when he undertook an early review of governmental machinery. Trevor Burridge has acknowledged that Attlee often seemed unobtrusive, if not downright invisible, during the war – but only because was he virtually ubiquitous: having few specific departmental duties, he was free to range over the full range of foreign and domestic issues.[6] Attlee was everywhere, and thus it was hard to see him in any one particular place.

As soon as he entered government in May 1940 Attlee, who took up residence at 11 Downing Street, was catapulted into important war work. It was he who introduced all the government's early legislation, including the vital Emergency Powers Bill, which gave the government almost complete powers over all citizens and their property. Britain's ancient liberties, he said, were being placed in pawn, to be redeemed by the destruction of Hitlerism. It passed in a single day. His was also an important voice in the key decision to reject Hitler's offer of a compromise peace at the end of May. There is little doubt that Churchill wanted to fight on, despite the fact that France seemed certain to fall and Italy to enter the war on Germany's side; but there is equally no doubt that his position was still insecure or that Chamberlain and Halifax were in favour of pulling out of the war while Britain's independence was still intact. To them, Churchill's defiant speeches were so much histrionic hot air. If only, lamented Halifax, who was threatening to resign, Churchill would use his brain instead of working himself up into passions of emotion. The fact that Attlee sided with Churchill was therefore crucial. On 26 May the French premier Reynaud proposed that the allies should call on Mussolini to persuade Hitler to negotiate a European settlement. Attlee had broadcast in April that any attempt to negotiate peace with Hitler would be like trying to bargain with a criminal lunatic. Now he was much more reticent, and indeed according to Neville Chamberlain he 'said hardly anything'; but it was clear that he was 'with Winston'.[7] The two old soldiers were determined on either liberty or death. Without Attlee's support, and that provided shortly afterwards by Greenwood, Churchill might well have been overruled. A few days later, Attlee warned that public morale would be gravely compromised if Britain agreed to negotiations, thus providing support which enabled Churchill to proclaim to the cabinet that 'we must . . . fight on'.[8] The Prime Minister insisted that no word of the discussions should ever be leaked, and Attlee continued to observe this self-denying ordinance for the rest of his life.

Yet Attlee is often seen merely as an adjunct of Churchill during the war, with only a supporting role to the man who, according to an American observer, '*is* the government in every sense of the word'. He was often put in the shade by his more flamboyant and oratorical boss. Beaverbrook likened the two men to a sparrow and a glittering bird of paradise, and another observer believed that, after Churchill's oratory, Attlee seemed like 'a village fiddler after Paganini'. When the Australian premier Sir Robert Menzies first met Attlee in 1941 he wrote in his diary that he was the sort of man who should be 'a Sunday School superintendent', and Canadian leader Mackenzie King believed that Churchill bullied Attlee. The first time Churchill's doctor spent some time with the little man he noticed his lack of self-confidence and his quick, nervous manner. Beaverbrook noted that in the Defence Committee, which Churchill chaired, Attlee's major contribution was the hasty and constant refrain 'I agree' to all of Churchill's proposals.[9] What truth is there in these charges?

Several points must be made in Attlee's defence. First, Beaverbrook was certainly a hostile witness. Attlee got on well with almost all his cabinet colleagues. The parlous nature of Britain's position by the end of June 1940, when France had fallen and Britons stood alone, helped individuals overcome previous difficulties, which were now rendered petty; and even with Chamberlain the Labour leader established a working relationship of 'complete harmony'.[10] Attlee did not attract many enemies, but Beaverbrook was certainly one. For his part, the Labour man considered the unscrupulous newspaper magnate the only evil person he had ever met, a judgement with which others concurred. Lord Reith, for instance, thought Beaverbrook 'dreadful' and 'evil': 'to no one is the vulgar designation shit more appropriately applied'.[11] Attlee was certainly taciturn in committee, and men who respected his opinion, like Anthony Eden, wished that he would say more; but there was an undoubted virtue in saying 'I agree' in only two words, a feat not many politicians have been known to manage. Furthermore, Beaverbrook's criticisms were made in 1940, while there is plenty of evidence that Attlee grew in stature and confidence as his experience of government grew. In the later stages of the war he was quite prepared to 'bark' at colleagues; and although Leo Amery sometimes found him to be 'rather a tiresome little man in many ways' and occasionally a mouse, he also knew that he could be 'a perfect lion brow-beating me'.[12] To use the terminology of the Permanent Secretary at the Foreign Office, Sir Alexander Cadogan, the dormouse could become a 'rabid rabbit . . . sour and argumentative'.[13] (Most people, if described as sour and argumentative, could not also be considered as mouse-like, but Attlee seemed to combine the uncombinable.) Indeed Attlee was emerging as a decisive and bold executive, not merely a follower of majority opinions.

Admittedly Attlee was no orator as Churchill was – 'Don't get rattled', he broadcast prosaically to the nation in May 1940, in complete contrast to Churchill's grandiloquent and inspiring offerings – but at least he wisely recognised the fact and was content to be a plain blunt man. He undoubtedly felt patriotic emotions, but he was never the man to try to express them openly: to do so would be too embarrassing. In his own words, he decided to eschew embroidery and stick to plain fact, seeking 'a mean between dignity of language and dullness'.[14] There were times, no doubt, when he missed the mark, but there were others when he was undoubtedly successful. Often, in the early years of the war, he had to announce defeats, but he did so with considerable dignity. In June 1942, for instance, he had to announce the fall of Tobruk. By this time, a full six months after the entry of the United States, the war should have reached its turning point, but in fact it was obstinately refusing to turn. Everyone's natural instinct, therefore, was to blame the messenger. Yet an observer judged that, though Attlee's statement was made 'in his usual colourless style', he 'really handled the House well'.[15] Certainly Attlee showed no want of courage when a motion of no confidence in the central direction of the war was subsequently debated.

Critics were bent on removing Churchill, or at least on securing the appointment of an alternative minister of defence, but Attlee insisted at a meeting of the PLP that he himself had been effective head of government when Tobruk fell. He thus shielded Churchill with exemplary bravery.

Attlee was often singularly – but deceptively – unimpressive at first sight. Menzies, therefore, was not the only one to revise his early, disparaging judgement. He decided that the undemonstrative Attlee had hidden depths: indeed he was 'a very great Englishman and a most astute manager of men'. Many others also decided that Attlee's performance during the war merited high praise. 'Pug' Ismay, Churchill's wartime chief of staff, believed that he made 'an immense and self-effacing contribution to the victory', and Alan Brooke, chairman of the chiefs of staff committee, noted in his diary that when Attlee first deputised for Churchill, who was in the United States, cabinet business was conducted 'very efficiently and quickly'. Similarly, he wrote in August 1944 that life was quiet and peaceful with Winston abroad: 'Everything gets done twice as quickly'. Attlee had a reputation as a man who 'never wasted time or uttered an unnecessary word'.[16]

During the war Attlee was in many ways the civil servant's perfect prime minister, and he established excellent relations with his official staff. Ministers also noticed the improvement when Churchill was away. Winston insisted on holding meetings at inconvenient times, generally very late at night, where he would treat those assembled to brilliant but interminable monologues. He rarely collected opinions, much preferring to talk rather than consult, and he certainly did not like anyone to argue with him. 'All I wanted', he later recalled, 'was compliance with my wishes after reasonable discussion'[17] – and he was prepared to do all the discussing himself. Our agenda, complained one minister, never had 'any other business' at the end: instead Winston would ramble on about whatever 'happy thought' happened to occur to him, however long it took and however many ministers were waiting in an adjoining ante-room to be called in. Attlee was the complete contrast. Churchill's understudy had his own, much briefer, text. He was far more businesslike and expeditious, and yet he allowed ministers to have their say. 'Attlee took the Chair,' noted Amery, 'and consequently we got through the business in no time.'[18] Under Attlee, a cabinet's agenda could often be completed in forty-five minutes. The great enemy of government, he observed, was inertia, 'the habit of putting off decisions on critical matters from week to week and month to month'.[19] He would tolerate none of it. The efficiency of the government was boosted considerably when Attlee took over the important Lord President's Committee in 1943. From this time onwards, during Churchill's absences abroad, Attlee chaired all three major wartime committees, as well as several lesser ones.

. . .

ATTLEE AND CHURCHILL

Nor was Attlee afraid to stand up to the great man, at least as his experience and confidence grew. When a critical back-bencher insisted that Attlee should tell Churchill to go to hell, he received the response that on occasions he did exactly this.

One area of disagreement between the two men was over policy towards India. Attlee's previous involvement on the Simon Commission had made him something of an expert, and indeed he was spoken of during the war – much to his own consternation – as a possible future viceroy. India's future was now vitally important: not only was it a divisive issue between Britain and the anti-imperialist United States, but, after Japan's entry into the war at the end of 1941, it seemed all too possible that the sub-continent might be invaded. It was essential, therefore, to try to produce some sort of agreement with Gandhi, Nehru and the Congress party. Attlee became chairman of the cabinet's India Committee, set up in February 1942, and soon decided that the main obstacle was Churchill. He recalled that his attitude to India was 'both obstinate and ignorant', and that as a result he had a good many 'stiff con-tests' with him. This was no retrospective rereading of history: Alan Brooke wrote in his diary of 'a real good row' between them. Attlee was keen to break the deadlock in India, and it was partly due to his pressure that in 1942 the Cripps mission to India went ahead, with its promise to the nationalists of independence after the war.[20] Its failure, however, and the sub-sequent 'Quit India' campaign, meant that he had to bear the stigma of sanctioning the arrest of the Congress leaders.

On other issues too Attlee was Churchill's critic. He did much to temper the criticisms of Montgomery's strategy which Churchill had wished to make before the victory at El Alamein. The following year Attlee teamed up with Anthony

Eden to pressurise Churchill into retaining the policy of unconditional surrender for Italy as well as Germany. Similarly, when Churchill was abroad in 1944, Attlee informed him that the War Cabinet intended to publish new rates of pay for those serving in the Japanese war, despite the fact that Churchill was known to disapprove of them. The Prime Minister was described as being livid and as calling Attlee a rat (instead of the usual mouse), but his violent reply was never sent.

They clashed also over the need to declare war aims and over whether to repeal the Trade Disputes Act, which had been introduced in the aftermath of the General Strike and was still hotly resented by Labour. But perhaps the key issue that divided them, and on which they had a long-running battle, was their attitude to social and economic reforms. Attlee thought Winston far too unimaginative over the need for both immediate changes and plans for future, postwar reforms. Churchill ruled out of order controversial items which were likely to detract attention from the war effort and, moreover, divide the coalition partners; but Attlee insisted that some measures of nationalisation, for instance of the railways, were needed to increase wartime efficiency. Similarly, he adopted a much more positive approach than the Prime Minister to the Beveridge Report, published after the victory at El Alamein in November 1942, which even Churchill admitted was perhaps the 'end of the beginning' of the war. When Churchill circulated a memorandum urging caution, Attlee countered with one of his own, arguing that 'unless the government is prepared to be as courageous in planning for peace as it has been in carrying on the war, there is extreme danger of disaster when the war ends': in particular the fighting men would not forgive them if they failed to take decisions.[21] It was largely due to the pressure of Attlee and the other Labour ministers that Churchill decided to accept Beveridge in principle, instead of giving a flat negative. In addition, Labour had an important impact on schemes to set up a national health service. The White Paper of 1944 did not satisfy Labour, but at least its proposals envisaged universal provision; and when Churchill insisted that the scheme went too far and should be jettisoned, Attlee responded with the threat that, in that case, Labour would press for a full-time salaried medical service and other measures which Conservatives would dislike. Furthermore, Labour ministers secured the appointment of a

Minister of Reconstruction at the end of 1943, vetoing Churchill's initial suggestion that the post should go to Beaverbrook, and by the end of the war they were dominating the Reconstruction Committee.

Victory in the war seemed assured long before VE Day (8 May 1945). The inexorable progress of the Red Army in the East and the Anglo-American invasion of France in June 1944 inevitably focused the minds of the politicians not merely on the end of the war but on the type of postwar world which they could help to bring about. As a result, the differences in political outlook between the members of Churchill's coalition came increasingly to the fore.

During one meeting of ministers, after Churchill had talked at length and concluded with the words 'Well, gentlemen, I think we can all agree on this course', Attlee responded: 'Well, you know, Prime Minister, a monologue by you does not necessarily spell agreement.'[22] Now, early in 1945, his criticisms of Churchill came to a head. He decided to send the Prime Minister a stinging rebuke on his conduct in cabinet, complaining that he had often not read the necessary papers:

> Often half an hour and more is wasted in explaining what could have been grasped by two or three minutes reading of the documents. Not infrequently a phrase catches your eye which gives rise to a disquisition on an interesting point only slightly connected with the subject matter. The result is long delays and unnecessarily long Cabinets imposed on Ministers who have already done a full day's work and who will have more to deal with before they get to bed.

He also insisted that too much time was wasted listening to the – often ignorant – views of the Lord Privy Seal and the Minister of Information (Beaverbrook and Bracken). In short, Churchill's working methods were imposing a strain inimical to the successful performance of the government and therefore injurious to the war effort. For good measure, Attlee added that though he was writing only for himself, he was expressing the minds of many colleagues, a judgement borne out by Leo Amery's diary. He finished by urging Churchill 'to put yourself in the position of your colleagues' – an exercise in humility which, it must be said, the egotistical Churchill was likely to find very difficult, having had so little practice.

Predictably, Churchill exploded. He immediately drafted a furious and sarcastic reply. Yet his secretary, John Colville, could not help admiring Attlee's courage, and Mrs Churchill insisted that Attlee's criticisms were justified. Even Bracken and Beaverbrook admitted that there was some justice in his case. Eventually Churchill bowed to the pressure, substituting a sweetly reasonable letter for his earlier diatribe: 'I shall endeavour to profit by your counsels.' Consoling his wounded ego, he decided to go to a film-show and not bother about either 'Atler or Hitlee.'[23] Small wonder that Churchill never knew quite what to make of 'Poor Clem'. No one in his experience had been quite like him.

On many issues, including foreign policy, there had been little difference between the Prime Minister and his deputy. They agreed to rebut early calls for a second front and, despite private doubts on Attlee's part, they approved the policy of attempting to bomb Germany into submission. They also had similar ideas about the future of Germany, and Attlee, no less than Churchill, wanted to see Nazism extirpated from the country, an end which led him to extend lists of war criminals to include German generals who had committed atrocities. In addition, they both began to fear the might of the Soviet Union as the war drew to its close and, as a consequence, saw the need to associate the United States with the defence of Europe in the future. Attlee, who was chairman of the committee on postwar Europe from July 1943, was the first to reject the Morgenthau plan to destroy all German industry and thus pastoralise the country, partly because of his suspicions of Stalin. In addition, he had more faith in de Gaulle than Churchill. Furthermore, Attlee disliked Churchill's support of the Italian government of Marshal Badoglio and persuaded him to switch allegiance to a broader government under the man Churchill described as 'this wretched old Bonomi'.[24]

Yet perhaps the most divisive issue was Greece. Again and again, after Nazi occupation ended in the autumn of 1944, Churchill spoke against the appointment of Archbishop Damaskinos as regent, pleading that he would turn out to be a left-wing dictator, but Attlee retorted that he had not produced a 'scintilla of evidence in support of your thesis'.[25] Churchill bowed before Attlee's view, which commanded majority support in the cabinet, and the archbishop was appointed at the end of 1944. But when civil war broke out in Greece, Churchill ordered British support for the king, despite his former ambivalent relationship with the Nazis, against the left-wing partisans who had fought against Hitler. Opinion within the Labour party was divided, many on the left believing that Britain was fighting not communists but democrats, and Attlee's loyalty to the Prime Minister was put under severe strain.

Attlee and Churchill had ambivalent views about each other. Yet they were partners – albeit sometimes sparring partners – and as such they always kept their disagreements within bounds. In short, they were a good team, a combination of opposites who complemented each other. For five years from May 1940 they stood together, and they seemed likely, if the government failed, to fall together. Outside observers may have believed that the wartime coalition was a one-man show, but this was a simplistic judgement.

Yet while Churchill became the hero of the nation and the darling of the Conservatives, Attlee's stock did not seem to rise significantly. The explanation for this lies partly in Churchill's showmanship and Attlee's ingrained shyness. Attlee worked extremely hard during the war. Generally he rose at 7.30 and was not in bed before midnight; but, when he was not working, he preferred to relax well away from the public gaze, with his family or his beloved books. His reading had to be curtailed, but even so he reported to his brother Tom that he had enjoyed *Fame is the Spur* (based on MacDonald's career), *Straight and Crooked Thinking* (which ridiculed some of MacDonald's 'more ridiculous effusions'), David Cecil's study of Thomas Hardy, Milton and the 'more sonorous Elizabethans', Trevelyan's *Social History* and a good deal of American history.[26] In addition, he managed to take regular exercise each day and avoid Churchillian excesses with food and drink, factors which no doubt contributed to his reputation for being always spry and energetic. Furthermore, his wartime duties tended to limit his exposure to the nation. His expertise on committees, however important, could be appreciated only by the select few. It was therefore all too easy for the press to underestimate his worth. In December 1941 one journalist professed to be incredulous that in this 'war of wars' and 'struggle of struggles' men like Attlee and Greenwood were in the war cabinet: 'It is enough to make one turn one's face to the wall and give up the ghost. Can you tell me that no better men can be found than these?' Another referred in April 1942 to Attlee's 'two outstanding qualities', one being calm and even judgement and the other modesty,[27] neither of which was likely to win him much publicity. On 2 October 1943 *The Economist* judged that, after more than three years in office, Attlee had still a ministerial reputation to make. If he was to be considered a wartime wonder, therefore, it would only be to the wisest of wise men.

Churchill did not have a disparaging view of Attlee. Yet when he spoke of him as 'this honourable and gallant gentleman and a faithful colleague who served his country well at the time of her greatest need',[28] such rhetoric seemed – at least to outsiders – impossibly incongruous. But what of insiders – how did Attlee's standing in the Labour party change during the war?

. . .

ATTLEE AND LABOUR

A.J.P. Taylor once said that Attlee 'grows on you'. Certainly he grew on Bevin during the war. The two men worked closely together for the first time, as they sat in the War Cabinet from October 1940 onwards, and Bevin began to appreciate Attlee's qualities and to see him not as a middle-class interloper but as a brother worthy of respect. Indeed a real friendship slowly began to grow up between the two contrasting figures. One bond between them was a mutual antipathy to Beaverbrook. When Bevin and Beaverbrook clashed early in 1942 over the control of manpower, and it seemed that one or the other would have to resign, Attlee threw his weight behind Ernie and it was Beaverbrook who stepped down, blaming Attlee for what had happened. Attlee had acquired an ally of immense stature in the labour movement. His position was strengthened even more by the fact that the wartime association reinforced the antipathy Bevin felt for Morrison. Several times Bevin embarrassed colleagues by scornful, and highly audible, asides when the Home Secretary was addressing the War Cabinet. He believed that Morrison, unlike Attlee, was simply not 'straight', and he constantly suspected him of intriguing for the party leadership. In 1943 he said that Morrison would be a Tory within five years. Attlee had little success pouring oil on the troubled waters of this relationship, though he did manage to assuage a potential quarrel between Bevin and Citrine over conscription in 1941.

Dalton's view of Attlee also improved. This was a result of consistent support from his party chief. It was largely due to

Attlee that Dalton, the Minister of Economic Warfare, gained control of the Special Operations Executive, with its mission to 'set Europe ablaze', in 1940. Attlee also massaged Dalton's troubled ego during his tussles with the Minister of Information, Brendan Bracken, over the control of propaganda: he agreed that Bracken was simply not fit to be a minister in the middle of a war. He was also his ally when he was moved to the Board of Trade in 1942, supporting his efforts to rationalise – and if possible nationalise – the coal industry. This was not just blind party loyalty on Attlee's part – he was, after all, quite prepared to acquiesce in the sacking of Greenwood – and was therefore all the more appreciated by Dalton, who noted that 'whenever the pressure in the pipe gets too great, I see this little man, who is always most loyal, unruffled and understanding of my affairs'.[29] Yet this is not to say that Dalton considered Attlee the best man to lead the party after the war.

The war cemented Attlee's leadership of the party, in that it would have been virtually impossible to replace him during the conflict; but he had to survive a chorus of disapproval. The constituency parties had been unhappy about the electoral truce during Chamberlain's premiership, and it continued to be a bone of contention. During the emergency of 1940 there was little trouble, but in May 1941 the Kings Norton party was disaffiliated when its leaders urged members not to vote for any candidate in a by-election. Here was a potential cause of friction which, if inflamed, could harm the unity of the coalition. Therefore Attlee responded firmly, initiating the practice whereby government by-election candidates were endorsed by each of the three party leaders. But this did nothing to stop the anti-Conservative trend in by-elections from March 1942 onwards, and nor did his proposal that henceforth Labour speakers should support all coalition nominees, a measure which only narrowly secured NEC approval. Many active party workers would simply not agree to support the old Tory enemy; and some feared that unless Labour put up its own candidates, socialist fervour would be mobilised by other groups, especially the new Common Wealth party. At the 1942 annual conference there was a determined call for Labour to abandon the electoral truce, and a motion to this effect was defeated by a mere 66,000 votes (out of 2.5 million). This was a crucial, if narrow, victory for the NEC: defeat might have meant the end of the coalition. Yet the man who had led the counter-attack against the divisional parties was not Attlee but Herbert Morrison. 'Attlee did not shine at the conference,' observed a journalist, 'Morrison did.'[30]

At bottom, the discontent – exacerbated by poor war news – stemmed from the fear that Labour's leaders were not standing up for socialism. Attlee had said during the phoney war that socialism would be needed to win the war, a message he reiterated in May 1940. But was he really doing enough to justify the party's involvement, or – as George Orwell complained – were Labour's leaders the 'tame cats' of the Conservatives?[31] If so, perhaps that was why the war was not being won. Attlee argued that he was doing the maximum possible within the confines of an all-party coalition which meant that no single group could possibly get all it wanted. At the 1943 conference he insisted that

> The British never know when they are beaten, and British socialists never know when they have won. . . . The people of this country will not forget that some of the most onerous posts in government have been held by Labour men who have shown great ability, ability to administer and courage to take unpopular decisions. . . . We have a body of men and women who are experienced in administration and have proved themselves fit to govern. Had we remained merely a body of critics who left others to do the work, the Party would not have gained the respect and confidence of the country which I know it has today.[32]

Convinced that the course of constructive compromise was the right one, Attlee insisted that beneficial changes – like the abolition of the household means test and the provision of free or subsidised milk for children – had come about because of Labour's influence, and that further reforms could be expected in the future. In short, he and his colleagues had gone to the limit in pressing for socialism. It was an argument which may be corroborated to a large extent by Churchill's worries about a socialist conspiracy among the coalition's Labour men and by Tory backbench grouses at Labour dominance.

To Conservatives Attlee was being too socialist, while to socialists he was being too conservative. His was an unenviable, Janus-faced position, as Labour's spokesman to the coalition and as the coalition's spokesman to Labour. Hence to the government he put forward Labour's claims, including calls for nationalisation, while to Labour ranks he pleaded the government case in favour of avoiding divisive issues, for instance warning the NEC in March 1942 that Labour ministers should not try to get socialist measures implemented under 'the guise of war'.[33] Did he get the balance about right? Two implacable critics thought not.

One of these was Harold Laski, professor of political science at London University and a member of Labour's NEC since 1936. There was 'thrust and parry' between him and the party leader for virtually the whole of the war. In June 1941, in *Tribune*, Laski issued a broadside: the party under its existing leaders was becoming ossified and might soon cease to be an effective political force: 'pygmies have taken the place of giants'. The following year he singled out Attlee by name as the man who was destroying the party and urged him to make way for another leader. His insistence that Bevin should take over, however, showed considerable naiveté. Not only was Bevin a loyal supporter of Attlee and jointly responsible with him and the other members of the government for the policies which they produced, but he had an undisguised, irascible contempt for critics, especially intellectual ones. Laski's campaign culminated in a long letter in June 1945 'proving' the urgency of Attlee's withdrawal. Being on the receiving end of Laski's lengthy epistles of tortuous prose – once described by Orwell as a model of how not to write – cannot have been pleasant. How would Attlee react? Most people would have stayed up half the night composing equally lengthy and tortuous essays in self-justification. But Attlee sent the perfect riposte: 'Thank your for your letter, the contents of which have been noted.' A few weeks later, when Laski continued with unwanted advice, Attlee devised another perfect put-down: 'a period of silence on your part would be welcome'.[34]

Attlee's second assailant was probably his most important wartime critic, the Labour MP for Ebbw Vale since 1929, Aneurin Bevan. Not that he confined his criticisms to Attlee. Churchill was also the butt of his rhetoric (though the Prime Minister responded in kind, calling him a 'merchant of discourtesy . . . a squalid nuisance . . . the most mischievous mouth in wartime'), and Citrine and Pethick-Lawrence from Labour ranks were also his victims. He described Citrine as a 'drab and colourless personality' whose opinions were those of a political illiterate and who as a bureaucrat suffered – not from piles but – from files, while Pethick-Lawrence was 'the crusted old Tory who still remains a member of this Party'! He also clashed with Morrison over his threat to suppress the *Daily Mirror*, insisting that he was 'deeply ashamed' of the intolerant Morrison, who was the wrong man to be Home Secretary.[35]

The burden of his charge against Attlee was similar to Laski's. In February 1941 he insisted that Labour ministers were doing no more than defend Tory policies and that the government was really a one-man show. From then onwards he was consistently calling for the end of the coalition and for an early second front. In his view, the rank and file members of the party were being betrayed by their leaders. Attlee was thus a latter-day Ramsay MacDonald:

> Mr Attlee is no longer the spokesman of the Movement which carried him from obscurity into the second position in the land. This is a political fact, not a personal issue. . . . He remains loyal, but only to Mr Churchill. If Mr Attlee has gained some of the toughness which comes with high position in politics it has been reserved for the members and policies of his own Party.[36]

The reforms for which Labour ministers were trying to take credit were to Bevan's mind scarcely improvements at all. When Dalton, with the support of Attlee, proposed the dual control of the mines between the existing owners and the state, Bevan called the new system 'economic Fascism in all its elements'. He was also scornful of the 1944 White Paper on Employment, believing that full employment could not possibly be assured without substantial nationalisation. Bevan proclaimed starkly that Labour would have to abandon 'either its leaders or its principles'.[37]

In fact, Bevan came very close to being expelled from the party (for the second time) after clashing with Bevin over Regulation 1AA in 1944. Bevin believed that Trotskyites were fomenting wildcat strikes in the pits, and the new regulation provided for up to five years' imprisonment for this offence. Bevan insisted, however, that the miners were not so easily led astray. To his mind, the government was simply looking for scapegoats as an alternative to grasping the nettle of nationalisation, and therefore the Minister of Labour was betraying the workers – a charge Bevin was never to forget or forgive. When Bevan voted against the Regulation, there were many voices in favour of his expulsion, though in the end a compromise was reached. He was given seven days to promise to abide by Labour's standing orders in future – an undertaking he accepted, but only, he insisted, so as not to leave the field free for those who would work the ruin of the whole Labour movement. On issues such as this Attlee had, in the past, invariably been in favour of compromise; but this time he had spoken out clearly in favour of expulsion. The compromise was therefore a definite rebuff for him.

Nye's was not a voice crying alone in the wilderness. Many MPs seemed discontented with their leaders. In 1943 almost a hundred Labour backbenchers voted against the government's lukewarm response to the Beveridge report. In retrospect, we can see that this did Labour considerable good: they were, in a sense, both government and opposition, gaining valuable experience of office and finally putting to rest doubts about their fitness to govern, and yet at the same time gaining credit for being more progressive than the Conservatives. But at the time many were worried about party discipline. After all, Labour backbenchers had voted against their leaders. All seemed far from well with the state of the party. Labour's junior minister at the Board of Education, James Chuter Ede, lamented that Attlee was not doing enough to stem backbench revolts: the leader's constant refrain, when the issue was put to him, was that 'the position is very difficult'. The party's national agent, G.R. Shepherd, was also worried about the blurring of the party's identity within the coalition: he insisted in 1943 that 'Attlee must become a distinctive leader, identified with the Party as much as he is with the Government'.[38]

There was undoubted unease within Labour ranks. Could it have been cured? Attlee thought not. He made some attempt to minimise it, as when he threatened to resign in March 1944 if the rank and file did not support him. But on the whole he believed that the tension within wartime politics – between Labour and Conservative in the coalition, and between Labour ministers and the rest of the movement – had simply to be accepted and lived through. Perhaps he was right. Certainly he seemed to be justified by success. There was no repetition of 1931, when Labour's leaders were detached from the party, or even of 1918, when several ministerial figures carried on in government after the war. When, in later life, he was asked to name his greatest single achievement, Attlee replied that it was 'Taking the Party into coalition for the war and bringing them out without losing anybody'.[39]

Nevertheless, it did at least seem possible that Attlee himself might be a casualty of the war. Several people were dissatisfied with his performance, and many believed that a more charismatic leader was needed to put up a good show against Churchill in the next general election. Who might succeed him? Greenwood had disappeared as a serious contender, while Bevin's stock had risen considerably, and in addition Cripps was a contender. Despite his expulsion from the party in 1939 he rejoined in 1945, and in the meantime he had hit the political headlines: on returning from the Soviet Union in 1942 he had secured a place in the War Cabinet. Some had even thought, briefly, that he might replace Churchill, but his star faded as quickly as it had risen. The position of Leader of the House of Commons, to which Churchill had shrewdly assigned him, was ill-suited to his talents, and his mission to India also failed. Victory at El Alamein then cemented Churchill's position and within a few months Cripps had resigned from the War Cabinet and accepted a more lowly office, as Minister of Aircraft Production. In 1945 he saw a need for a new party leader; and though his own ambitions still existed, he believed that Morrison was the most realistic successor to Attlee, a judgement with which Dalton concurred. Party rivalry in 1945 was remarkably similar to that of 1935 and 1939.

In February it was announced that Attlee was to go to San Francisco for the founding of the United Nations. His left-wing critics disliked intensely the way Attlee was allowing himself, and the party, to be identified with the coalition's foreign policy: already he had failed pitifully to represent the socialist view on Greece, Italy and Germany, and this was the 'crowning glory'. Furthermore, Anthony Eden, the Foreign Secretary, was to lead the delegation. To go at all was bad, but to go as Eden's lieutenant was even worse. Nye Bevan wrote in *Tribune* that the whole affair was 'painful, humiliating and hurtful to the Labour Party. At no time has Mr Attlee stood so low in the estimate of his followers.'[40]

Yet Attlee still had his supporters, and far more of them than Bevan liked to acknowledge. When one backbencher insisted that Labour simply could not win a general election with Attlee as leader and that someone more brilliant was needed, another reminded him that the recent crop of 'brilliant men' – including Mosley, MacDonald and Cripps – had all been unreliable. Chuter Ede, who certainly had his criticisms of Attlee, insisted that the existing party leader was 'perfectly straight. He stood by a man even to his own hurt. I asked no more than that from my leader.' This was no exaggerated praise, and indeed it even implied certain deficiencies in Attlee's leadership armoury; but Ede reminded his friends that the Liberals had won their greatest victory, in 1906, under a 'plain, steadfast man', Henry Campbell-Bannerman. Nor was he the only one to draw this comparison: Bevin also called Attlee 'our Campbell-Bannerman'.[41] By this Bevin implied that he was far to be preferred to any ambitious intriguer like Morrison. The Home Secretary of course disagreed, as did his supporters, but a blow had come to his hopes when in 1943 Greenwood, not he, was elected as the party Treasurer. Bevin's control of the Transport and General Workers' vote had been decisive. The *Manchester Guardian* commented that the party wanted no more MacDonalds: 'They prefer the milder leadership of Attlee and Greenwood to the purposefulness of Mr Morrison.'[42]

. . .

THE END OF THE COALITION

Almost all of Labour's leaders, including Attlee, flirted with the idea of carrying on the coalition into peacetime. After all, Churchill's immense national popularity seemed to guarantee victory for the Conservative party, and so the alternative to continued collaboration was almost certain to be a return to opposition. Attlee also realised that there was a degree of common ground between the major parties. In his view, both would inevitably work within a 'mixed economy', though Labour would favour more public, and the Conservatives more private, enterprise. Yet the closer came the end of the war, the more difficult was it to secure agreement between the parties in the government and the more pronounced became the ground swell of feeling in favour of Labour pulling out. Towards the end of 1944 the life of the 1935 parliament was once more extended, but both the Conservative and Labour parties accepted that an election would follow the end of the war against Germany. Then, just after VE Day, 8 May, Churchill called upon his Labour colleagues to continue the government until Japan had been defeated, which might well be a year hence. The alternative, he warned, would have to be an immediate dissolution and election. Morrison's plea for an election in the autumn, after new registers had been compiled, was turned down flat.

On 18 May 1945 the NEC met at Blackpool, prior to the annual conference. Bevan, Shinwell and finally Morrison spoke strongly in favour of immediate withdrawal from the government, while Bevin and Dalton were ranged on the other side. Attlee was in favour of carrying on until Japan was defeated and had secured Churchill's agreement that a prolonged coalition would implement proposals for social security and full employment. Yet, true to his usual style, he failed to speak out strongly or unequivocally – and wisely so, for when the vote went in favour of ending the government and holding an immediate general election, Attlee did not lose face. Too many Labour supporters felt frustrated by the coalition, with the brake it imposed on social legislation and with its support of reactionaries abroad, for continued collaboration. Labour thus unmade the coalition which it had made in 1940.

The war had provided Attlee with a marvellous opportunity. Had peace been maintained and had Labour lost an election in 1940, as seemed likely, he might well have been replaced as party leader. Now he had been given a chance to show his worth, and he had seized it. Attlee had been at the very centre of affairs from May 1940 to May 1945, steadily becoming more and more valuable to the government. He had acted as prime minister on several occasions, between them totalling around six months, and always with great efficiency. He had shown beyond doubt he could take the strain of high office. True to his own advice, he did not get rattled. Despite being a loner in politics and often a somewhat distant colleague, he had also proved to be a good team man. In addition, he had been the key mediator between Labour and the government, and thus the linchpin of the coalition. Trevor Burridge believes no one ever had a better apprenticeship for the premiership than Attlee during the war, so that by 1945 he had unrivalled experience, proven executive ability and complete self-confidence.[43] We may well judge that Attlee, on his wartime record, had fully deserved his position as Labour leader. Yet political life is rarely fair, and it seemed quite possible that he would soon be replaced as leader.

Attlee had not pleased all the people all the time. It would, of course, have been quite impossible to do so; but his reverses over Bevan's expulsion in 1944 and over the decision to end the coalition in May 1945, instead of carrying on till the defeat of Japan, were undoubtedly setbacks. Nor had his generally low profile during the war given him the publicity which several of his more charismatic colleagues received. To most members of the public Attlee was still a little known, somewhat shadowy figure. His position as party leader was thus not unassailable.

Immediately the news of the coalition's end became known, Ellen Wilkinson, then chair of the NEC, began a campaign, as in 1939, to unseat Attlee in favour of Morrison. According to the press, Morrison was 'the present idol of delegates and the undoubted leader of the Party today', while Attlee was 'overshadowed by his colleagues'.[44] Yet it would have been an act of remarkable ingratitude to replace Attlee at this stage: he had led the party for ten years and had now brought them securely through the war. In addition, there was no time to achieve much. Churchill took an emotional farewell of coalition ministers, decided to make Attlee a Companion of Honour, an award which he also offered to an unwilling Bevin, and on 23 May he dissolved parliament and set up an interim, caretaker government until the electorate's verdict could be known. If Labour lost the election in 1945 it was extremely probable that a new leader would subsequently be elected. The alternative, Attlee's elevation to the premiership, seemed to most pundits far more implausible, if not downright bizarre.

. . .

REFERENCES

1. Kenneth Harris, *Attlee* (London, 1984), p. 229.
2. Ben Pimlott (ed.), *The Political Diary of Hugh Dalton, 1918–40, 1945–60* (London, 1986), 10 May 1940, p. 345.
3. Harris, *Attlee*, p. 179.
4. Bernard Donoughue and G.W. Jones, *Herbert Morrison: Portrait of a Politician* (London, 1973), p. 313; Alan Bullock, *The Life and Times of Ernest Bevin*, II (London, 1967), p. 365; J.B. Priestley, *Postscripts* (London, 1940), p. 27.
5. R.R. James (ed.), *Chips: The Diaries of Sir Henry Channon* (London, 1993 edn), 13 May 1940, p. 252.
6. Trevor Burridge, *Clement Attlee: A Political Biography* (London, 1985), pp. 141–2.
7. Neville Chamberlain's diary, 26 May 1940, Birmingham University Library.

8. Martin Gilbert, *Finest Hour: Winston S. Churchill 1939–41* (London, 1983), p. 419.
9. Henry Pelling, *Winston Churchill* (London, 1974), p. 46; A.J.P. Taylor, *Beaverbrook* (Harmondsworth, 1974), pp 576–7, 605; Harold Nicolson, *Diaries and Letters, 1945–62* (London, 1968), p. 105; Sir Robert Menzies, *Afternoon Light* (Harmondsworth, 1969), p. 45; Lord Moran, *Churchill: The Struggle for Survival* (London, 1968 edn), pp. 188, 201.
10. Chamberlain's diary, 5 June 1940.
11. Charles Stuart (ed.), *The Reith Diaries* (London, 1975), pp. 239, 281.
12. John Barnes and David Nicholson (eds), *The Empire at Bay: The Leo Amery Diaries* (London, 1988), pp. 747–8, 781.
13. David Dilks (ed.), *The Diaries of Alexander Cadogan, 1938–1945* (London, 1971), pp. 334, 459.
14. Attlee to Tom, 9 August 1941, 19 May 1943, Attlee Papers, Bodleian Library.
15. James, (ed.), *Chips*, 23 June 1942, p. 332.
16. Menzies, *Afternoon Light*, p. 45; Arthur Bryant (ed.), *Triumph in the West 1943–46* (London, 1959), pp. 252, 428, 483; *The Memoirs of General the Lord Ismay* (London, 1960), p. 404; James Stuart, *Within the Fringe* (London, 1967), p. 142.
17. Winston S. Churchill *The Second World War*, IV (London, 1951), p.78.
18. Barnes and Nicholson (eds), *The Empire at Bay*, pp. 981, 1031.
19. *The Listener*, 3 January 1980, p. 3.
20. Bryant (ed.), *Triumph in the West*, p. 230; Harris, *Attlee*, p. 201.
21. Harris, *Attlee*, pp. 220–1.
22. Stuart, *Within the Fringe*, p. 119.
23. Harris, *Attlee*, pp. 242–4; John Colville, *The Fringes of Power: Downing Street Diaries, 1939–1955* (London, 1985), p. 554.
24. Burridge, *Clement Attlee*, p. 173; Martin Gilbert, *Road to Victory* (London, 1986), p. 803.
25. Dilks, (ed.), *Diaries of Cadogan*, p. 689.
26. Attlee to Tom, 15 October 1940, 15 August 1941, 21 April 1943, 19 May 1943, 16 October 1944.
27. Harris, *Attlee*, p. 193; *Daily Telegraph*, 17 April 1942.
28. Harris, *Attlee*, p. 244.
29. Ben Pimlott (ed.), *The Second World War Diary of Hugh Dalton 1940–45* (London, 1987), 8 May 1941.
30. Donoughue and Jones, *Herbert Morrison*, p. 323.
31. *The Collected Essays, Journalism and Letters of George Orwell*, II (Harmondsworth, 1970), pp. 68, 245.
32. Harris, *Attlee*, p. 224.
33. Burridge, *Clement Attlee*, p. 140.

34. Stephen Brooke, *Labour's War: The Labour Party during the Second World War* (Oxford, 1992), pp. 93–101.
35. Michael Foot, *Aneurin Bevan*, vol. 1 (London, 1962), pp. 319–21, 354, 495.
36. *Tribune*, 2 October 1942.
37. Foot, *Bevan*, vol. 1, p. 276.
38. Jefferys (ed.), *Labour and the Wartime Coalition*, p. 89; Brooke, *Labour's War*, p. 310.
39. *Clem Attlee: Granada Historical Records Interview* (London, 1967), p. 54.
40. *Tribune*, 30 March 1945.
41. Jefferys (ed.), *Labour and the Wartime Coalition*, pp. 145, 166; K.O. Morgan, *Labour People* (Oxford, 1987), p. 146.
42. Donoughue and Jones, *Herbert Morrison*, p. 328.
43. Burridge, *Clement Attlee*, pp. 142, 183.
44. Harris, *Attlee*, p. 251.

Chapter 6

ELECTIONS AND THE PREMIERSHIPS

We went to a Victory Rally at Westminster Central Hall where I announced that I had been charged with the task of forming a Government, looked in at a Fabian Society gathering and then returned to Stanmore after an exciting day.

Herbert's a good all-rounder, a professional. Stafford on the other hand has not got many strokes, but he can score a century on his day. So can Ernie. He hasn't much style, but he can lift them out of the ground when his blood's up. Dalton's a bit erratic but he's got great zest. Loves having a knock . . . There's no one to touch Nye when he's got his length. Doesn't always find it though . . . Very safe pair of hands, Chuter. And Addison. Wise old bird. Very steady . . . Nothing so dangerous as a Ministry of all the talents.[1]

. . .

THE 1945 GENERAL ELECTION

There is absolutely no doubt that Attlee expected to lose the election held on 5 July 1945, just as most Conservatives expected to win. In this he was typical of Labour's leading figures, who were so absorbed in their work that they had become out of touch with popular feeling. Attlee told the 1943 Labour conference that by-elections, which were showing a distinct leftward trend, were a poor indicator of mass opinion; and nor did he have any greater faith in opinion polls, which predicted a clear Labour victory. He believed that Churchill's immense popularity would far outweigh any swing of the political pendulum. History was expected to repeat itself: just as Lloyd George, the 'man who won the war', had been victorious in 1918, so Winston Churchill would surely triumph in 1945. Attlee's most optimistic prediction was that the Conservatives would win only a small majority.

Yet there were significant differences between 1918 and 1945. Churchill did not enjoy Lloyd George's reputation as a social reformer, and indeed many looked upon him as a reactionary. Opinion polls indicated that the majority of those who approved his wartime leadership did not think he would make a good peacetime premier. The Prime Minister was unwise to brush aside 'this brave-new-world business' as being far less universal in Britain than the other dominant emotion of the time, gratitude to himself.[2] Furthermore, there was no coalition in 1945, as there had been in 1918. The Conservatives had to fight alone, and with the handicap of being associated with appeasement and the high unemployment of the 1930s. In consequence, 'Never Again' and 'You Can't Trust the Tories' were very difficult charges for them to rebut. Labour, on the other hand, now had a powerful team of popular and experienced ministers, as well as a manifesto whose commitments to full employment and the creation of a welfare state were highly popular. *Let Us Face the Future* sold a massive 1.5 million copies during the campaign. Admittedly it covered up the ideological fissure between the fundamentalists, who championed nationalisation, and the revisionists, who favoured a combination of other physical economic controls and demand management; but it did so very effectively. Labour also gained, paradoxically, from an issue which, in the past had harmed their cause – the supposed similarity between British socialism and Soviet communism. Stalin was still an ally, Uncle Joe rather than an inhuman tyrant, and the success of the Red Army against the Nazis was widely thought to reflect the inherent efficiency of his regime. Nor did Labour lose from being considered the party of the trade unions, especially since wartime strikes had often been censored from the press.

Attlee threw himself into the campaign with total commitment, speaking at around seventy venues. Despite his lack of flamboyance, many found him an acceptable symbol of the better postwar world Labour was pledged to achieve. Indeed at the British victory parade in Berlin on 21 July 1945 he was cheered more loudly than Churchill by the assembled troops. He also had the toughness needed to survive a bruising contest, in which the excesses of both of the major parties resulted in over fifty writs for libel.

Churchill set the tone for the contest in his infamous first election broadcast, on 4 June, in which he insisted that socialism was 'inseparably interwoven' with totalitarianism and that a Labour government would end up by introducing some form of Gestapo. Many Conservatives approved these scare tactics. In the House of Commons next day, the Tories were 'cock-a-hoop' and talking about a victory on the scale of that of 1931, while Attlee seemed 'shrunken and terrified'.[3] Yet the Labour leader's radio response was a very professional performance. While insisting that it had been a privilege to serve under Churchill during the war, he thanked him for showing the electors, by his irresponsible words, 'how great was the difference between Winston Churchill the great leader in war of a united nation and Mr Churchill, the Party Leader of the Conservatives'. He went on to damn the Conservatives' blind faith in private enterprise; but, above all, he stressed the virtues of Labour, the party which best represented the whole of the British nation and which was putting forward positive, progressive policies.[4] Dalton was not impressed: 'no flame, no flair'. But most people considered it the perfect reply, making a nonsense of Churchill's unscrupulous attempt to deck the sheep in wolf's clothing. Amery described it as 'a very adroit quiet reply to Winston's rodomontage [*sic*]'.[5] He was also generally considered to have the better of the tussle with Churchill over a clumsy intervention by Harold Laski. When Churchill invited Attlee to accompany him to Potsdam, Laski told the press that Attlee could go only as an observer, since neither Labour nor its leader could be bound by Conservative agreements. Churchill then seized on this to argue that real power in the Labour party lay not with its leader at all: a Labour government would be dominated by a party caucus, so that state secrets would be revealed to the NEC. But Attlee skilfully obscured the extent to which, in theory at least, a Labour leader was subject to the majority decisions of the party executive.

According to the major study of the election campaign, Attlee seemed like a tolerant schoolmaster and had 'the air of a sound and steady batsman, keeping up his wicket with ease against a demon bowler who was losing both pace and length'.[6] It was a description of which he was proud. Attlee certainly did not win the election for Labour. Yet insofar as the vote was a protest against the Fuehrer principle, as some believed, he did seem a far more democratic, and far less domineering, personality than Churchill. In addition, he was no vote-loser. He allowed the emphasis of the campaign to centre on policy not personality, while at the same time emerging with an enhanced personal reputation.

When the results were announced on 26 July, it was found that Labour had won 393 seats, making 209 gains, including 79 in seats which they had never previously held. They won Manchester and Leeds for the first time and ended the tradition of Unionism in Birmingham which Joe Chamberlain had begun in the 1880s. The party polled more votes than ever before and did so across the entire political spectrum.

'Bliss was it in that dawn to be alive': Wordsworth's exalted words about another revolutionary era came automatically to the lips of many Labour supporters, some of whom felt that they would surely be in power for the next generation. Yet no single mood can be said to epitomise the political nation in 1945, and the electorate as a whole was, almost certainly, less radical than was once thought. There were some revolutionaries, it is true, but similarly there were some reactionaries and cynics, as well as ignoramuses who did not realise that a vote for Labour was a vote against Churchill. Many people wanted not 'socialism', whatever the term be taken to mean, but merely a world stripped of its worst interwar features. The political 'sea change' of 1945 was really a matter of relatively minor swings in voting behaviour. Despite Labour's overall majority of 146 seats, the party had in fact polled less than half (47.8 per cent) of the total vote.

On 24 July, two days before the results were announced, Morrison had written to Attlee declaring that he would be standing for the party leadership when the new PLP assembled. He was, he insisted, animated solely by the party's interests and not by any personal unfriendliness to Attlee.[7] It was a statement which had the support of several key figures in the party, including Cripps and Bevan. Nor did news of Labour's victory deter Morrison: indeed it spurred him on, for now the premiership as well as the party leadership was at stake. When the invitation for Attlee to form a government duly came through to Transport House, Morrison insisted that

Attlee should not accept the invitation until the PLP had met to elect its leader. Party Secretary Morgan Phillips thought Morrison would probably win such a vote, but Attlee – with Bevin's support – decided not to keep the king waiting. Churchill had driven to the Palace to resign in his chauffeured Rolls Royce; now, in contrast, Clem turned up driven by his wife in the family Standard Ten.

Morrison and the others who thought the little man inadequate to the premiership were presented with a *fait accompli* and had to make the best of it. Returning from the palace, Attlee spoke at a victory rally, where he was given a great reception. According to a journalist, who was certainly not immune from the emotion of the occasion, he spoke 'with the assured simplicity of a Lincoln'.[8] At the first meeting of the PLP the following day, Bevin moved a vote of confidence in Attlee, which was passed by acclamation. Morrison kept tactfully silent. The caretaker was finally acknowledged as Labour's leader, though a minority of critics was still to be convinced.

. . .

ATTLEE AND CABINET MAKING

Attlee is generally thought to have been extremely shrewd in choosing his cabinet. Certainly he was wise to include MPs who, if excluded, might have been dangerous critics. There was a place for Ellen Wilkinson, at Education, and even for Aneurin Bevan. Attlee's most outspoken critic had doubted that he would be given a job, but in fact the Prime Minister gave him exactly the post he wanted, as Minister of Health. It was also realistic of Attlee to keep Bevin (Foreign Secretary) and Morrison (Lord President of the Council and Leader of the House) as far apart as possible. Yet the degree to which Attlee's cabinet-making was improvised is seldom recognised.

Despite his image as the humble servant of the party, Attlee ignored the consultation procedures laid down by the 1933 conference to guide a Labour prime minister in selecting ministers. He chose his cabinet in very much the same way as Ramsay MacDonald had done, relying above all on his own instincts. Yet, having confidently expected to lose the election, he had made no preliminary plans. There was thus a degree of muddle and hesitancy in his appointments. An illegibly scribbled note meant that instead of Joe Binns, MP for Rochester, becoming a junior whip, the post went to left-wing critic Geoffrey Bing. It was apparently impossible to admit the mistake, and Bing remained until he resigned in late-1946. Attlee also reversed an initial judgement that Dalton should go to the Foreign Office and Bevin to the Treasury. The reasons for this somewhat hasty change are controversial. Attlee's plea that he had to keep Bevin and Morrison as far from each other's throats as possible was eminently sensible reasoning – to keep a team together one sometimes has to keep them apart – but their antagonism was hardly a new factor of which he had just become aware. Perhaps, despite Attlee's later denials, George VI's dislike of Dalton, or the advice of the Civil Service, was a factor.

Other appointments were made without much real knowledge of the individuals involved. George Hall, for instance, was made Secretary of State for the Colonies because he was thought to be good at administration and because he had served as Under-Secretary for a time during the war. He was preferred to Arthur Creech Jones, who specialised in colonial affairs and who became the junior minister. Yet Hall confided privately that he was 'right out of his depth' at the Colonial Office. Ill health meant that he had to be moved the following year. Attlee then promoted Creech Jones, but with patent reluctance; and despite the fact that the new man made a constructive impact on colonial affairs, his Prime Minister never appreciated his worth.[9] Many have credited Attlee with an uncanny ability to understand the individual characters and foibles of all his ministers, but this is certainly an exaggeration. Attlee viewed his colleagues dispassionately but not always knowledgeably. Nor was he the proverbially good butcher he has seemed in retrospect. He allowed Creech Jones to continue despite thinking him not up to the job, and many people thought that he kept Shinwell at Fuel and Power for too long.

. . .

ATTLEE AS PRIME MINISTER

As premier, Attlee set an example to his colleagues of hard work and dedication. Often he was on duty from 8 a.m. to midnight. Yet he took it all very much in his stride and rarely seemed overworked. Generally he managed to take one issue at a time, finding each day's work sufficient unto that day and not worrying fruitlessly. As earlier in his career, he still found time to relax. During his visits to Chequers, he read a three-volume work on George III and reread the whole of Gibbon –

though complaining that in volume seven the great historian had failed to do sufficient justice to the achievements of Justinian. He found Wisden 'always good for settling the mind', and he was also a 'diligent student' of the *Dictionary of National Biography*.[10] On Saturdays in June 1949 he was to be seen at Lords and at Wimbledon.

Partly because of his ability to switch off, and to sleep well, he was able to survive the strains of high office better than most of his colleagues, several of whom had been continuously in government since 1940. Dalton, who was taking benzedrine tablets and suffering from chronic constipation and painful boils, wrote in August 1947 of his amazement that many of his colleagues did not simply drop dead in their tracks (adding, mischievously, that it would be a good thing if some of them did).[11] It was certainly amazing that for a time, in the middle of 1949, due to colleagues' ill health, Attlee was not only Prime Minister but acting Foreign Secretary and Chancellor of the Exchequer as well. His own health was not always good, especially as the 1940s drew to a close. In the summer of 1948 he had to go into hospital for treatment to a duodenal ulcer, and in 1951, when he was 68, he had to have an operation for the same complaint. Around the same time he was having trouble with his teeth, so that part of his gum had to be cut away; and later that year he was in pain with lumbago and sciatica. But by this time several of his colleagues had one foot, or two, in the grave.

He was very much the same man as in previous years: modest, laconic, a loner and a bad mixer. No one found Attlee vain or given to political gossip, and in this he was quite unlike Ramsay MacDonald. Yet it must be admitted that the second Labour Prime Minister did share with the first the quality of appearing remote. He tended to treat his colleagues, and his civil servants, impersonally. He was no automaton – only an extremely hard-working and efficient man who was so shy that, it was said, he had to positively screw himself up in order to say good morning – and so human feelings did come through on occasions. He was, for instance, very solicitous of the health of the young George Thomas, arranging for him to go on holiday to Switzerland for three months in 1951. He also wrote, in friendly fashion, to congratulate Harold Wilson on the birth of a second son in May 1948. Clem and Vi subsequently accepted Wilson's invitation to become godparents, as they did Roy Jenkins's. Attlee also wrote personally to congratulate Patrick

Gordon Walker on his success in reconciling India to continued Commonwealth membership in 1949. Nevertheless, Attlee was generally reticent and – a new quality discernible for the first time – also formidable. The longest phrase Douglas Jay, his personal assistant in 1945–46, could elicit from him was: 'Wouldn't serve any useful purpose.'[12] Patrick Gordon Walker did his best to break through Attlee's famous reserve, and he believed that he came close, as one night they talked of public schools, Attlee's favourite theme besides cricket; but the next morning the barriers were securely in place. Attlee was less the team captain of his Labour government than the umpire, less the colleague than the headmaster. Even when a cabinet minister, Gordon Walker always went to see Attlee as though summoned to the housemaster's study, and Nye Bevan once ended an argument with the dire threat: 'Say that again and I shall take you to see Attlee.'[13] Though personally quite unassuming and humble, urging backbenchers to call him Clem not Sir, he often seemed the distant autocrat to younger men. They would get no easy, ungrudged praise from him: they were far more likely to receive a sharp rap over the knuckles.

It was Morrison and Dalton who went out of their way to encourage and establish good relations with younger men, not Attlee. The Prime Minister might also have done more to promote the rising generation. The average age of the cabinet in 1945 was 60, whereas in the PLP as a whole it was significantly lower. Wilson, Gaitskell and Gordon Walker owed their advancement to Attlee, but there were others – including Richard Crossman and James Callaghan – whose talent he failed to spot.

Attlee in Parliament

In the House of Commons, Attlee made no brilliant oratorical speeches. Nevertheless, he was by now a practiced and accomplished performer. Before the war it was said that he applied himself diligently and with good humour – to the parliamentary tasks 'for which Nature has failed properly to equip him';[14] but no one said this now. One Conservative judged that Attlee 'gave the same impression of unruffled tranquillity and equanimity as did Mr Baldwin when he was Prime Minister. Neither man evinced, by the expression on his face, either interest or resentment when an attack was made upon the Government he led.' It was partly for this reason that he was liked and respected by the House as a whole.[15]

Churchill found it difficult to accept the new dispensation and could rarely keep a mixture of disbelief and scorn out of his voice when he referred to Attlee as Prime Minister. When told in 1947 how much better Attlee was now doing in the House, he quipped that if you feed a grub on royal jelly 'it turns into a Queen Bee':[16] in short, Attlee had benefited from his association with the master. Yet his skills were very different from Churchill's, as the Tory leader learned to his cost during debates. Attlee may have been weak on rhetoric, but as a debater he was strong on common sense, always well briefed and capable of delivering a short, sharp and very painful sting. He trounced Churchill in the House of Commons in November 1945, showing that the demobilisation plan which the opposition leader was criticising was the one he had accepted while in office. Similarly he adroitly turned the tables on his adversary the following month. Churchill introduced a motion of no confidence, arguing that Labour were 'deliberately trying to exalt their partisan and factional interests at the cost not only of the national unity but of our recovery and of our vital interest'. Attlee rephrased this charge, to devastating effect, as 'Why, when you were elected to carry out a Socialist programme, did you not carry out a Conservative programme?' According to Macmillan, the whole Churchillian fabric often 'began to waver and collapse' before Attlee's matter-of-fact approach.[17]

Attlee in Cabinet

'Anything to add to what is in the paper. No? Cabinet agree? Next business.'[18] Harold Wilson's vignette of Attlee as the efficient, masterful cabinet chairman does not tell the whole truth. Admittedly Attlee could silence over-talkative colleagues and even admonish ill-prepared ministers – including heavyweights like Bevin – in a magisterial fashion, surpassing any rebukes Churchill ever gave. Yet he was not always perfectly calm, as legend would have it, and sometimes cabinets were unruly or fruitless or over-long. On one occasion, when according to Dalton the Prime Minister showed no power of guiding discussions, Morrison walked out complaining of Bevin's 'drunken monologue'.[19] Nor were civil servants always particularly impressed. According to one of them, Attlee was a very efficient chairman, introducing each topic in sensible terms and asking the right ministers to express their views. But when the discussion was finished,

> his summing-up was often blurred or incomplete, and he rarely produced any constructive ideas of his own or seemed to give a powerful lead. His chairmanship was only a negative success. He was like a schoolmaster who kept order very well but did not really teach you very much.[20]

Furthermore, the meetings were not leak-proof. Indeed Massingham's diaries in the *Observer* were so accurate that security and intelligence experts were called in to track down the source of the leaks. Only much later was it found that the journalist had a movable rendezvous with Lady Cripps every Friday afternoon.

Another fundamental flaw was that the structure of cabinet and subordinate committees in the Attlee administration did not make for efficiency. Wanting a small cabinet, Attlee favoured delegating work to sub-committees of ministers directly concerned with an issue, his reason being that, in a large cabinet, those with least knowledge would probably speak the most. But the result was a proliferation of time-consuming meetings. As early as May 1946 Dalton complained that the 'greatest curse' of ministerial life was 'the mass and multiplicity' of committees, and over the following years the situation deteriorated. Correlli Barnett has calculated that, in all, the Labour cabinet created 148 standing committees and 306 *ad hoc* ones.[21]

Yet, despite these problems, Attlee managed to get things done, and with a minimum of fuss and a maximum of practicality. Knowing that democracy means government by discussion, but can easily degenerate into discussion without government, he was adept at getting consensus in the cabinet. He never needed to take a vote. Patrick Gordon Walker, in one of his first appearances in cabinet, observed that Attlee did not rush the meeting and indeed that he allowed 'stupid and repetitive discussion': but the argument moved steadily forward and gradually a policy emerged. In all, he found Attlee in cabinet 'most impressive'.[22] In general he was merely the referee, generally doodling and going along with majority decisions, but sometimes he would intervene decisively and occasionally, in Morrison's words, delivering 'pontifical judgments which would have been more in character from a vain and pompous man'.[23] He was not the faultless cabinet chairman of political legend, but he was broadly successful nevertheless: the sheer volume of work which he and his cabinet ministers dispatched – which is reviewed in the next chapters – testifies to this.

Attlee and his Colleagues

Attlee was a loner in politics, as he had been throughout his career. Nevertheless, he was a good team player in that he harnessed a very talented but contrasting set of ministers into an effective unit. It is often said, especially by left-wing historians, that Labour's leading political figures – Bevin, Morrison, Dalton, Cripps and Bevan – were as talented a group of ministers as any in the history of parliament; but they were also one of the most potentially divided. Attlee's role as the disinterested umpire was therefore a vital one.

There is plenty of evidence of the degree to which the brothers in the Labour party disliked each other. Dalton, for instance, once wrote that Shinwell was 'a coarse-grained shit and low cur'; and Bevin referred to Morrison as a 'little bugger', a 'scheming little bastard' and 'nothing better than a policeman's nark'.[24] Examples like this could be multiplied at great length. Nor is there any reason to suppose that Attlee was immune from such human – all too human – emotions. Almost certainly he disliked some of his colleagues, who, after all, had over the years given him good reasons for antagonism. Only later, when he was out of office, did he reveal at any rate some of his true opinions, and then in guarded language: Cripps, for instance, was 'rather a silly ass' and Dalton a 'perfect ass' whose trouble was that he would talk.[25] Of Morrison, he maintained a generally guarded and judicious silence. Yet in office he kept his mouth shut, avoiding gossip and camouflaging his feelings so well that many thought he did not have any. He seemed to have no favourites and no adversaries.

Attlee remarked of his pleasure that, during his first administration, even the press was hard put to invent dissension and splits in Labour ranks. This degree of unity was, of course, not solely due to Attlee: it also reflected the degree to which ministers, charged with a sense of mission, were busy getting on with their work. Nevertheless, there were potentially divisive issues in plenty, especially from 1947 onwards, as economic, financial and other problems beset an increasingly beleaguered government. Almost certainly, no one but Attlee could have kept disunity at bay for so long or to such an extent.

Was Attlee the best man to preside over the prima donnas, the strong and talented but contrasting figures, in his cabinet? Probably so. Bevin as Prime Minister would have found it hard to work with Morrison. There was a touch of genius about Ernie, but, despite his imagination and flair, he lacked Attlee's reliability. He was given to rages and sulks, and his speeches often rambled rather incoherently. Once, during a conference of foreign ministers at Lancaster House, the translator found that the only way to produce coherence from Bevin's ramblings and repetitions was by reducing the length of his speech by a half. Attlee was fond of telling a joke about Bevin's style. He recalled that at a meeting with Hugh Dalton and Dai Grenfell, Bevin concluded with the words 'We'll leave it all to YEWANDYE' – but did he mean 'you and I', 'you and Dai, 'Hugh and I' or 'Hugh and Dai'?[26] Bevin also drank far too much. According to one of his secretaries, he used alcohol as a car uses petrol, and the Conservative Chief Whip was told that Bevin had consumed one and a quarter bottles of whisky between 6.30 p.m. and 7.45 p.m. Small wonder that towards the end of his life, according to his doctor, there was no sound organ in his eighteen-stone body apart from his feet.

With his love of intrigue, and his capacity for making enemies, Dalton would almost certainly have made a poor premier. It was said that he had the loudest whispers of anyone in Westminster, and colleagues joked that if he had become Foreign Secretary secret diplomacy would have ended overnight. His foolish budget leak in November 1947, which led to his resignation, was in many ways symptomatic of his approach to politics. Nor was Cripps, who succeeded Dalton as Chancellor, likely to do well. Many were impressed at his amazingly keen intelligence. He was also extremely hard-working, normally putting in three hours' work before breakfast. Attlee enjoyed telling the story of someone turning up in Downing Street at 5 a.m. to see the Chancellor: of course the policeman on duty turned him away, thinking he must be a lunatic, but Cripps had indeed arranged the appointment for that hour. Some also thought him saintly because of his puritanical lifestyle (though he did smoke and drink, and his vegetarianism was largely due to the state of his gastric juices); but many more found him sanctimonious and a little inhuman. There but for the grace of God, quipped Churchill, goes God. Bevin referred to him once as 'that whited sepulchre'.[27] There were also some who thought him unbalanced. In the late-1940s he favoured economic austerity with the same fervour which he had reserved, in the 1930s, for a united front. He even came up with the astounding notion that those who worked harder should not be given more pay but should, instead, receive a medal.

Morrison's qualifications for the premiership were much more substantial. Few doubted that he had earned his position as Deputy Prime Minister. He was as hard-working as Cripps but far more accessible, and when deputising for Attlee he gave a much firmer lead in cabinet. Although his handling of economic affairs was generally considered weak, he undoubtedly did a good job as Leader of the House, and in addition he managed the party conferences well and handled the PLP with definite expertise, setting up liaison committees between the party and the government. Anthony Eden called him 'the linchpin of the post-war Labour Government . . . a formidable man'. He knew how things worked, and he liked to make them work better.[28] On the other hand, he did suffer two heart attacks in 1947. He was also too associated with the moderate, consolidationist wing to have any credence as an impartial mediator between opposing factions within the party. This, in itself, did not disqualify him as leader; but many felt it a grave handicap that Bevin would probably not have worked under him. He seemed far too ambitious to several of his colleagues. Dalton said that Morrison's ambition was 'so plain that it is indecent' and that he would not die happy unless he had been prime minister.[29]

Ernie Bevin, reviewing the 1945–50 government, once told a journalist that 'Clem's never put forward a single constructive idea, but by God, he's the only man who could have kept us together'.[30] Similarly, the Conservative Brendan Bracken wrote in June 1948 that Attlee was 'the only really perky minister; so long as his colleagues are fighting each other he is certain to maintain his leadership'.[31]

Further evidence of Attlee's key – and perhaps indispensable – role is provided, paradoxically, by the attempts to replace him. The way his rivals cancelled each other out shows their disunity and provides fairly convincing evidence that no one else could have done his job. The most important intrigue occurred in September 1947. Morrison, Cripps and Dalton –

three senior and influential figures within the party – all agreed that Attlee should go. But Morrison distanced himself when the other two proposed that Bevin should be promoted: Morrison felt that he himself should replace Clem, who had never really led the party and was 'no good now'. Cripps then went ahead without Morrison's support – and indeed without Bevin's either, for the Foreign Secretary had no wish to succeed the leader he often referred to as 'my little man'. The episode finally came to an end when, confronted by the rebel, Attlee – shrewdly, adroitly and without any noticeable embarrassment whatsoever – promoted him. Cripps was made Minister for Economic Affairs. To all outward appearances, Attlee did not resent the machinations of his colleagues, though inwardly he cannot have been indifferent, and hence he was able to work with them fruitfully. Cripps continued to think Attlee should go – and in September 1948 said it would be a disaster if he led Labour into the next election – but the two men worked well together.

Attlee's apparent lack of ego was undoubtedly one of his strengths. So was his very traditional image – with his love of cricket, his sober way of dressing, and his veneration for the old school tie (which some said led him to promote junior colleagues from Haileybury, like Geoffrey de Freitas, and also from University College, Oxford, like Harold Wilson). He also revered the monarchy, and was to shed tears at the death of George VI, and took a special interest in obscure, anachronistic ceremonies, like 'pricking the Sheriffs'. He was thus a very reassuring figure during a time of substantial changes. In addition, his image tended to minimise opposition from the Conservatives. He had only to be himself – the least dramatic of politicians, 'a man circumspect and moderate' in all things[32] – to make Tory criticisms of socialist dogma seem unconvincingly melodramatic. When he announced great changes he did so in a deadpan, throw-away style which minimised their significance. He seemed an eminently practical man, impatient of theory and interested only in making tangible improvements in the British way of life. Civil servants found him oddly apolitical in the way in which he put the interests of the nation above those of his party, and indeed many people considered him above the ruck of politics. He thus made Labour's socialism seem dull and banal, and thus almost by definition eminently respectable.

By the end of his first government, the 'little mouse' was more popular than the party he led. An *Observer* profile in 1949 judged that Attlee, of whom most of his colleagues were somewhat in awe, was 'the complete master of his Cabinet', that he was a man of great integrity and that he was 'completely self-sustained', with moreover great tactical skill and instinctive awareness of the reactions not only of Labour people but of the British people at large.[33]

. . .

THE 1950 ELECTION

By the late-1940s, when Labour had substantially completed the programme laid down in *Let Us Face the Future*, it was clear that another general election could not be long delayed. It was also clear that the party would find it much more difficult to agree on another set of proposals. Nye Bevan and others wanted a radical manifesto, with a commitment to nationalising a second tranche of industries; but the majority in the PLP – and probably in the party as a whole – favoured Morrison's cautious approach, with its emphasis on consolidation. Attlee, as in the past, seemed to stand aloof from the fray.

The Prime Minister would have preferred to hold an election in May 1950, but the Chancellor of the Exchequer, Stafford Cripps, threatened to resign rather than have a pre-election budget in April. Hence Attlee gave way and the election was held in February 1950. Attlee's own position was much more secure than ever before. He was much better known than in 1945 and was perceived much more as Churchill's equal. Hence satirists (like Sagittarius and Vicky in *Up The Poll!*) were able to personalise the 1950 election, as essentially Attlee versus Churchill, in a way which would have been impossible in 1945. The Prime Minister, with Vi at the wheel, conducted a 1,300-mile campaign tour. Gaitskell, among others, was impressed, believing that Attlee's political stature and confidence had increased.

In general Labour fought a low-key campaign, stressing their substantial achievements, especially full employment and 'fair shares', rather than any new plans. Labour under Attlee would not lose the election; instead the Conservatives would have to win it. Most members of the government expected a small but workable majority, whereas in fact a 2.8 per cent swing to the Conservatives meant that Labour won an overall majority of only five. In particular Labour lost ground in constituencies with a large number of middle-class voters, as in the home counties. In general, the more prosperous the constituency, the less likely was a Labour victory – a depressing outcome for the government, since further success on their part would surely be their undoing. Boundary changes in many constituencies had also worked to the Conservatives' advantage. The implementation of these alterations might have been delayed, but Attlee did not think twice about this: with his highly developed sense of right and wrong, he knew the importance of keeping a straight bat, come what may. A more substantial criticism concerned his timing of the election. If only, many a Labour supporter was to lament subsequently, and with good reason, Attlee had held the election in May, after the de-rationing of petrol, when opinion polls suggested that he would have secured a comfortable majority of 40–50 seats.

. . .

ATTLEE'S SECOND ADMINISTRATION

A Conservative wrote delightedly that now Attlee looked 'like a wasp that has lost its sting'.[34] The Prime Minister had good reason to feel discomfited. He had always insisted that Labour should never merely administer the system (à la Ramsay MacDonald): in retrospect, he had argued that in 1929 MacDonald should have ridden for a fall, introducing socialist legislation and challenging the opposition parties to turn him out. But now he felt it unwise to pursue such bold tactics himself. He told reporters that Labour would be carrying on, but his strategy was simply to try to stay in office for a reasonable amount of time, and in the meanwhile to try to cope with crises as they arose. Dalton lamented that the election result had been the worst possible for Labour, condemning the party to office without authority or power, and he judged that all the ministers were 'stale and uninspired and uninventive'. Soon he decided that they were indeed suffering from 'pernicious inertia'.[35] Bevan wanted bold action, but he was in a minority of one in the cabinet. Small wonder, then, that one left-winger professed to see the ghost of Ramsay MacDonald smiling over the shoulder of party secretary Morgan Phillips or that the Conservatives saw a good opportunity to harass the government. Macmillan, in retrospect, believed that Tory tactics had been effective, though he doubted whether they had added much to the dignity of parliament: nor did they manage to make Attlee lose a characteristic self-control 'sometimes amounting almost to nonchalance'.[36]

According to a Gallup Poll in May 1950 Attlee was significantly ahead of his party in popularity, but this must have been cold comfort as troubles multiplied for his second administration. Several colleagues proved signally unsuccessful in their offices. Morrison, for instance, who succeeded Bevin in March 1951, had a torrid time at the Foreign Office. Attlee had hesitated before making him Foreign Secretary and only gave him the post because he thought, mistakenly, that he wanted it. Later he admitted that he had made a definite error. But in fact the multiplication of problems – including the nationalisation of the Anglo-Iranian Oil Company by Iran's Dr Mossadegh, which might have prompted hasty retaliatory action had Attlee himself not exercised a restraining influence, and the start of the Korean war – meant that whoever occupied the Foreign Office was bound to have severe problems. Indeed this was an unfortunate time for any party to be in office, let alone a government with a tiny majority and with ministers – several of whom, like Bevin and Cripps, were patently dying – exhausted from ten years' continuous and demanding work.

The lack of a full legislative programme, and moreover doctrinal differences about Labour's fundamental purposes, allowed dissension in the ranks to increase. Brendan Bracken judged gleefully that there was no way of uniting Labour, except perhaps by declaring war on the United States.

Bevan's Resignation

On 21 April 1951 Nye Bevan resigned over the imposition of charges for National Health Service spectacles and false teeth by the new Chancellor of the Exchequer, Hugh Gaitskell. Bevan insisted that these charges destroyed the vital principle of a health service free at the point of need. He insisted, moreover, that the revenue saved was only going towards defence estimates which were already so bloated that it would prove impossible to spend the excessive sums involved. The following day resignations followed also from Harold Wilson, the President of the Board of Trade, and John Freeman, parliamentary secretary at the Ministry of Supply. This is an episode which has been studied intensely by historians, and blame has been apportioned in almost every possible way to the individuals concerned. Was Gaitskell the clear-sighted realist who saw the need to behave responsibly or was he a latter-day Philip Snowden, angular, dogmatic and determined to cut the escalating NHS bill even if there had been no urgent demand for it? Was Bevan the heroic advocate of socialist principles, the blinkered dogmatist who confused sensible compromise with the abandonment of principle or simply the frustrated and ambitious careerist, a working-class Oswald Mosley? And what responsibility should be assigned to Morrison, who was deputising for the hospitalised Attlee when the resignations took place? Colleagues felt that his handling of the key cabinet meetings was more authoritarian than usual. Was he trying to push Bevan out? It is difficult to believe that any of these three men can be completely exonerated. But what of Clement Attlee?

Admittedly Attlee was in St Mary's Hospital, Paddington, when the budget crisis raged, but he was not completely out of action. His doctor advised that he should work on official papers for only half an hour, every morning, and that visitors should be restricted to two hours in the afternoon. During this time he was consulted extensively (though he asked the ward sister on at least one occasion to tell Morrison that he was asleep and could not be disturbed). True to his usual style, however, he failed himself to put forward any compromise solution. He left that to others, and sensible suggestions were forthcoming. Perhaps the cuts might be suspended for a brief period to see whether the sums allotted to defence could actually be spent? Nor did Attlee champion such possible solutions with any enthusiasm. As ever, he was the impartial judge not an advocate. In the end, mindful of the pre-eminent importance of defence, and reacting against Labour's poor record in the 1930s, he reluctantly supported majority opinion in the cabinet and came down in favour of Gaitskell.

Attlee believed that there was 'too much ego' in Nye's cosmos.[37] This was a perceptive comment; but the fact is that Attlee had done very little to massage this ego and to ensure that the individualistic Welshman remained a member of the Labour team. This is surprising because Attlee judged, privately, that Bevan might well turn out to be his successor as Labour leader. Bevan's oratorical brilliance and his sincere passion for social improvements and equality undoubtedly appealed to Attlee's latent romanticism. He recognised his good features – that, in Jennie Lee's phrase, there was 'a kind of Rabelaisian Jesus Christ quality' in him.[38] Perhaps for this reason he treated him indulgently at times. For instance, when Bevan insisted in April 1948 that the Tories were 'lower than vermin', he received a rebuke from Attlee which was characteristically short but uncharacteristically lenient: 'Please, be a bit more careful in your own interest.'[39] But, even so, Nye had no inkling that he was Attlee's favourite to succeed him.

Attlee's treatment of Bevan, since 1945, revealed a lack of genuine understanding. Certainly he seems to have failed to take account of Nye's ambition. That he should be ambitious was quite natural. After all, his youth stood out in the 1945 cabinet. Photographs reveal that he was not only obviously the youngest person, at forty-seven, but that he was the only minister, apart from Ellen Wilkinson, with a full head of hair. He must have hoped and even expected to succeed to the party leadership in due course, especially when he was such an outstanding success in founding the NHS, certainly the most popular and probably the most beneficial of Labour's reforms. Yet in January 1951 Attlee moved Bevan to the Ministry of Labour. This could hardly be considered promotion, whatever Attlee protested to his later interviewers. Furthermore, a few months earlier Attlee had sent to the Treasury Hugh Gaitskell, Bevan's junior at only forty-four and moreover a man who had been elected to the Commons as recently as 1945. Gaitskell had the financial expertise for the job, but his elevation definitely upset the ministerial pecking order. It was not so much that Bevan wanted to become Chancellor himself – though in September 1949 he had defended government economic policy brilliantly in the Commons and launched a devastating attack against Churchill – as that he was aggrieved at this leapfrogging by someone with so little standing in the party. Harold Wilson was also resentful. To his detractors, Gaitskell lacked imaginative sympathy with socialist aspirations. Hence, in private Bevan poured forth 'a torrent of vitriolic abuse' on Attlee's head.[40] Yet Clem – as aloof as ever – had little inkling of Bevan's frustration. He had considered him for the post of Chancellor but decided that international reaction would be adverse. The office Bevan really coveted was the Foreign Office, but he was passed over in favour of Morrison in March 1951. Bevin would have preferred Bevan to Morrison as his successor; but though Attlee asked Nye his opinion as to who should get the post, he did not realise that he wanted it for himself. The Ministry of Labour was hardly an acceptable alternative from his point of view, and at the end of September 1950 it was rumoured that Nye wanted a defeat in an early election, which would boost his own chances for the leadership later on.

A more pro-active (or simply human) style from Attlee might possibly have made all the difference and prevented Bevan's resignation. Instead, Attlee simply hoped that the squabbles in his cabinet would blow over. Yet they were more than little local difficulties. Many considered that the battle between left and right was a contest for the soul of the party, but Attlee refused to see things in these grandiose terms or to give an unambiguous ideological lead himself. He was the distant arbiter not the passionate player. Such a stance had served him well in the past and could not be changed now, when the situation demanded greater involvement. In short, Attlee had the defects of his virtues.

. . .

THE 1951 ELECTION

With the resignations, on top of other problems, Attlee's administration virtually self-destructed. Many constituency parties were highly critical of the government, and Bevan came top of the 1951 NEC elections. He was far from being a spent force in the party. He had known that his resignation would harm the government; but his aim, he said, was not simply the return of a Labour government, but the return of a government which would make Britain into a socialist country.

A general election could not be long delayed, and Attlee timed his dissolution to suit the king, who was expected to make a trip to Australia in the spring of 1952. He thought it unfair to let George VI, who was apt to worry, go away with the possibility of a political crisis hanging over him. No matter that the date of the election, 25 October 1951, went against the wishes of several key colleagues, including Gaitskell and Morrison, or that opinion polls gave the Conservatives a 7 per cent lead. Douglas Jay and George Brown tried to change Attlee's mind, but they made no impression him. He could have hung on longer, and had he done so the party would have benefited from an upturn in the economy the following spring.

Attlee embarked on the election with his customary commitment, making over fifty campaign speeches and a single radio broadcast. On several occasions he stressed the importance of idealism – of what people could give, not what they could get. This had undoubted appeal for a section of the press. One journalist commented that Attlee was like 'a great headmaster, controlled, efficient, and, above all, good', and another judged that he never cheapened himself to gain applause, so that the tour was undoubtedly enhancing the personal respect in which he was held.[41] All the same, it was a message that for most people was wearing thin after years of austerity. Nor was it easy to paper over the cracks of party disunity. All seemed to be *bonhomie* at the October annual conference, but *The Times* correspondent was not the only observer to judge that this desperate attempt to present a united front had not succeeded: the 'struggle at the very heart of the party, where power resides', was still continuing.[42] Several journalists, and not a few subsequent historians, believed that the government's capacity for creative thinking had come to an end. It was Labour's turn to raise election scares – as with the charge that Churchill was warmongering – and this seemed to some a measure of the party's bankruptcy.

Nevertheless Labour won a higher number of votes than any political party had ever polled in British history, and its proportion of votes beat even its 1945 total. The Conservative victory by seventeen seats was therefore a psephological anomaly, caused mainly by the fact that the Liberals put up only 109 candidates, as against 475 the previous year. Even so, most observers sensed far less enthusiasm for Labour than in 1945, and it is probable that some Labour voters supported the party merely as a lesser evil to the Conservatives. The ardour and enthusiasm of 1945 had certainly ebbed away. Indeed many Labour politicians positively welcomed the chance of a restful spell in opposition. It was the Tories' turn to bat, and on what seemed like a very sticky wicket. No one guessed that their innings would last until 1964 and far outlast Attlee's career.

. . .

REFERENCES

1. C.R. Attlee, *As It Happened* (London, 1954), p. 148; Francis Williams, *Nothing So Strange* (London, 1970), p. 233.
2. Lord Moran, *Winston Churchill: The Struggle for Survival, 1940–1965* (London, 1968 edn), pp. 273–4.

3. R.R. James (ed.), *Chips: The Diaries of Sir Henry Channon* (London, 1993 edn), 5 June 1945, p. 408.

4. Roy Jenkins (ed.), *Purpose and Policy: Selected Speeches* (London, n.d.), pp. 3–12.

5. Douglas Jay, *Change and Fortune* (London, 1980), p. 72; John Barnes and David Nicholson (eds), *The Empire at Bay: The Leo Amery Diaries, 1929–1945* (London, 1988), 5 June 1945, p. 1046.

6. R.B. McCallum and A. Readman, *The British General Election of 1945* (London, 1947), p. 175.

7. Morrison to Attlee, 24 July 1945, Attlee Papers, dep 18, Bodleian Library.

8. *Daily Herald*, 27 July 1945.

9. R.D Pearce, *The Turning Point in Africa: British Colonial Policy, 1938–48* (London, 1982), pp. 91–2, 118–27, 121.

10. Francis Williams, *A Prime Minister Remembers* (London, 1961), p. 103; Attlee to Winterton, 6 January 1950, Earl Winterton Papers, Bodleian Library.

11. Ben Pimlott (ed.), *The Political Diary of Hugh Dalton 1918–40, 1945–60* (London, 1986), 8 August 1947, p. 406.

12. Jay, *Change and Fortune*, p. 132.

13. Roy Hattersley, *Between Ourselves* (London, 1994), p. 331.

14. 'Watchman', *Right Honourable Gentlemen* (London, 1940), p. 177.

15. Earl Winterton, *Orders of the Day* (London, 1953), pp. 340–1.

16. Moran, *Winston Churchill*, p. 795.

17. Jenkins (ed.), *Policy and Purpose*, pp. 27–8; Harold Macmillan, *Tides of Fortune, 1945–1955* (London, 1969), p. 42.

18. Geoffrey Dellar (ed.), *Attlee As I Knew Him* (London, 1983), p. 43.

19. Pimlott (ed.), *Political Diary*, 30 July 1947, p. 405.

20. George Mallaby, *From My Level* (London, 1965), p. 58.

21. Pimlott (ed.), *Political Diary*, 15 May 1946, p. 372; Correlli Barnett, *The Lost Victory: British Dreams, British Realities, 1945–1950* (London, 1995), p. 190.

22. Robert Pearce (ed.), *Patrick Gordon Walker: Political Diaries 1932–1971* (London, 1991), 10 February 1949, p. 184.

23. Lord Morrison, *Herbert Morrison: An Autobiography* (London, 1960), p. 295.

24. Pimlott (ed.), *Political Diary*, 12 April 1951, p. 529; Bernard Donoughue and G.W. Jones, *Herbert Morrison: Portrait of a Politician* (London, 1973), p. 346; Janet Morgan (ed.), *The Backbench Diaries of Richard Crossman* (London, 1981), p. 197.

25. Williams, *Prime Minister Remembers*, p. 227; *Clem Attlee: Granada Historical Records Interview* (London, 1967), p. 45.

26. Dellar (ed.), *Attlee As I Knew Him*, p. 33.
27. Morgan (ed.), *Backbench Diaries*, p. 197.
28. Donoughue and Jones, *Herbert Morrison*, p. 371.
29. Philip M. Williams (ed.), *The Diary of Hugh Gaitskell 1945–1956* (London, 1983), 12 August 1947, p. 26.
30. Leslie Hunter, *The Road to Brighton Pier* (London, 1959), p. 26.
31. Richard Cockett (ed.), *My Dear Max: The Letters of Brendan Bracken to Lord Beaverbrook, 1925–1958* (London, 1990), p. 94.
32. *News Chronicle*, 20 September 1951.
33. Kenneth Harris, *Attlee* (London, 1984), pp. 427–8.
34. James (ed.), *Chips*, 20 February 1951, p. 454.
35. Pimlott (ed.), *Political Diary*, 11 June 1950, p. 474; 21 June 1951, p. 546.
36. Macmillan, *Tides of Fortune*, pp. 322–3.
37. Attlee to Tom, 25 September 1950.
38. Michael Foot, *Loyalists and Loners* (London, 1986), p. 36.
39. Harris, *Attlee*, p. 425.
40. Jay, *Change and Fortune*, p. 202.
41. Harris, *Attlee*, pp. 490–1.
42. *The Times*, 4 October 1951.

Chapter 7

ATTLEE'S GOVERNMENTS, 1945–51: DOMESTIC AFFAIRS

*It has always been our practice, in accord with the natural genius of
the British people, to work empirically. We were not afraid of compromises and partial solutions. We knew that mistakes would be made
and that advance would be often by trial and error.*[1]

The work of the Attlee governments in home affairs is remarkably controversial. To some, especially on the political left,
1945 was a historic lost opportunity: the possibility of revolutionary changes was tossed aside by a government – led by a
middle-class moderate and committed to class collaboration –
that was too timid to grasp the socialist nettle. This is a view
which is complemented by Paul Addison's thesis that it was the
period of war which saw the important changes: Attlee and his
ministers merely implemented the all-party consensus, stemming from the work of two Liberals, Keynes and Beveridge,
which fell like ripe fruit into their laps. There is no doubt,
however, of the sheer size of Labour's legislative programme.
Certainly the Conservative Chief Whip was amazed that the
government managed to pass so much contentious legislation.
Others, therefore, have stressed the fundamental nature of the
changes wrought in 1945–51. Historians like Morgan and
Hennessy have insisted that the Labour administration
brought about important and beneficial changes, which were
all the more praiseworthy in view of the adverse economic climate which might well have led less committed reformers to

tear up their plans and concentrate merely on survival. Yet according to Correlli Barnett and others of a right-wing persuasion, Labour should have done precisely this and put economic revival first; but instead they sacrificed Britain's long-term prosperity by self-indulgent and profligate spending on social reforms and on foreign policy.

Estimations of Attlee's political stature inevitably hinge on interpretations of his governments. Whether deserved or not, prime ministers are judged to a large extent by the success or failure of their administrations. But what was Attlee's personal involvement with the work of the postwar Labour governments? This is a difficult issue to unravel. Was he merely a figurehead, gaining credit for the work of more talented ministers and at most harnessing their energies, or did he have a more positive and creative function? He is not easy to pigeonhole. Certainly he was no MacDonald, keeping a close and suspicious eye on colleagues and being unable or unwilling to delegate. Nor, on the other hand, was he a Baldwin, sitting back and surveying the scene, letting colleagues do their work almost entirely undisturbed. Admittedly he had no wish to intervene unless it was necessary. He aspired to be the sort of leader of whom colleagues would say, in the words of an old Chinese proverb: 'We did it all ourselves.' But he knew that at times it was necessary to take the lead and to do so boldly.

. . .

THE ECONOMY

Neville Chamberlain had always believed that another world war would be catastrophic for the economy, and he was right. Britain was dependent on American aid after only a few years of war, and by 1945 a quarter of the country's prewar wealth had been lost. Indeed at the end of the war Britain had larger debts than any nation in history. Furthermore, she had mobilised so high a proportion of her economy and workforce for war purposes that the reorientation of industry to meet peacetime needs was a correspondingly difficult problem. Overseas markets had been lost and only 2 per cent of the workforce were engaged in manufacturing for export. Attlee's administration therefore inherited a very difficult set of problems, and throughout the 1945–51 period economic and financial difficulties refused to go away.

An immediate crisis erupted when the Americans cancelled Lend-Lease in August 1945 without notice or discussion. Total economic ruin seemed to stare the country in the face. It was averted by a US loan of $3,750 million, to be repaid at 2 per cent interest from 1951, which Keynes helped to negotiate. No one could have secured a better deal, but even so the sum was less than the government had wanted, and nor was it the free gift for which they had hoped. Furthermore, there were strings attached, and in particular the Americans insisted that the pound should be made convertible into dollars in 1947. When this duly came to pass there was a run on the pound which dangerously depleted Britain's reserves. A month later, in August 1947, the government saw no choice but to renege on its agreement with the Americans by reimposing convertibility restrictions. To the Chancellor of the Exchequer, Hugh Dalton, this was not only a personal humiliation but a turning point in the history of the postwar government: never would it be glad confident morning again. What could go wrong, did go wrong. Even nature seemed to conspire against Labour in this 'annus horrendus'. February 1947 had seen the longest period without sunshine in British meteorological history, and temperatures were the lowest for a hundred years. The resulting fuel shortages saw industrial production fall by 50 per cent in the month, and unemployment briefly touched 2.5 million. A thaw then produced floods which played havoc with agriculture. It was calculated that the average shopper spent over an hour a day in food queues, and both bread and potatoes were rationed for the first time. Housewives were urged to buy the South African fish snoek (as inedible as it was unpronounceable), which soon had to be sold off as cat food.

There was a respite from problems in 1948, and indeed Britain now received the tremendous economic boost of Marshall Aid. The US government had turned a deaf ear to Keynes's plea in 1945 that a free gift would ultimately rebound to the advantage of the American economy, which needed customers; but now – in the Cold War era – they offered a lifeline to Western Europe. In total, Britain received almost $3,000 million. Yet this was certainly not the end of Britain's problems. In September 1949, in view of an under-valued dollar, the pound was devalued by a massive 30 per cent, from $4.03 to $2.80, and the onset of the Korean War in 1950 produced fresh problems. Not only did the government have to increase defence spending, but the terms of trade turned decisively against Britain, increasing the cost of imports and helping to fuel inflation. From one perspective, therefore, the government lurched ignominiously from crisis to crisis.

Yet a case can be made for Attlee's administration. Certainly severe problems were inevitable in the postwar period. The fundamental weakness of the economy was a large balance of payments deficit, particularly with North America. In 1945 the value of American goods coming into Britain exceeded the cost of British exports to the USA by ten times. Labour had therefore to try to rectify the situation by keeping imports as low as possible, even at the cost of austerity at home, while encouraging increases in exports. In this they had a good measure of success. Industrial production increased by one third in 1946–51, and by 1948 there was actually a trade balance, followed by a surplus in the next two years. Admittedly there was a renewed deficit in 1951, caused by the Korean War, but this was only temporary. Britain's share of world exports, which plummeted during the war, not only reached but exceeded 1938 totals. On the whole, therefore, this can be seen as a good economic record. In addition, there was – apart from in the bleak midwinter of 1947 – high employment. Levels of unemployment averaged only 1.6 per cent in 1948–50. Perhaps, therefore, Labour and its Prime Minister should be praised for their stewardship of the economy.

Attlee made no boasts about his personal contribution. Economics was not his field, and he did not take the initiative in economic or financial affairs. Dalton had warned him in January 1947 that the cabinet was failing 'to face unpleasant facts' and that, unless realistic actions were taken, the result might be 'worse . . . than in 1931'.[2] He subsequently criticised Attlee's role during the convertibility crisis in the summer of 1947. But at least the Prime Minister was always willing to consider advice in an open-minded manner, unlike Ramsay MacDonald during the second Labour government. Nor was he prepared to take risks. He insisted that bread rationing would have to go ahead, even when, at the last minute, the Minister of Food thought it could be avoided. It is true that, in 1949, relatively junior officials, like Robert Hall, were converted to devaluation first, followed by junior ministers. But at least Attlee was not last: he saw the need for devaluation before Cripps, the Chancellor of the Exchequer. Cripps thought devaluation would be dishonourable – at least Attlee wasn't as priggish as that.

Nevertheless there are grounds for criticising Labour, and its leader. The party did not plan the economy to anything like the extent implied in the 1945 manifesto. In reality, the government tended to rely on demand management, and wartime physical controls were dismantled after 1947. In addition, Labour was at least partly responsible for the fuel crisis of February 1947. The weather, an act of God, was not solely to blame: in addition, we must take account of the 'inactivity of Emanuel'. Manny Shinwell, as Minister of Fuel and Power, had failed to take steps to meet an anticipated coal shortage. Most important of all, Britain's successful production record, especially in exports, was due not so much to the government as to the pent-up demand that existed after the war, and which so few countries could possibly fulfil because of wartime devastation. Britain had escaped relatively lightly compared with prewar rivals like Germany and Japan, and therefore was ideally placed to do well. Even so, as the 1940s came to an end, and rivals began to revive, Britain's export lead began to tail off. There were clearly major industrial problems in Labour's Britain, including overmanning and underinvestment. It can also be seen that full employment was not so much the result of government policies as of world conditions. All the government did, taking its lead from Dalton, was ensure that a significant amount of new employment was channelled into the former depressed areas.

Correlli Barnett has indicted the Labour governments for failing to intervene to modernise the economy. In his view, much more could and should have been done to revitalise the country's economic infrastructure. New roads were needed; railways and ports were in crying need of improvement; coal-extraction and electricity-generation demanded large-scale investment; and extra resources were needed for technical training. But little was done. Instead, the government was, in his view, obsessed with welfare and the prestige of Great Power status. Houses were preferred to factories, and development in the former depressed areas was fostered even at the cost of discouraging some employers from expanding their activities. Even Marshall Aid was largely wasted: Britain had the largest share of any European nation, but the government 'botched' the opportunity to remake the country as an economic power.[3]

To criticise the economic record of the government is easy. But it must be recognised that the administration had to grapple with almost impossible problems from the first. Never in peacetime had there been so much need for massive expenditure. It was, surely, a 'no-win situation' for the government, as colleagues competed for scarce resources. It was also necessary to spend money feeding inhabitants in the British zone in Germany and in British India. No one was fully satisfied at the time at this deployment of resources, and no historian since has fully approved the balance. But Barnett overstates his case: he ignores not only the austerity which Labour imposed but contemporary political and psychological reality. At bottom he is, like Churchill in his motion of censure in December 1945, charging Labour with trying to implement the programme on which they had been elected.

No doubt Barnett is right in judging that if Labour had dismissed public opinion and concentrated on reinvigorating the economy (which, to his mind, meant ensuring a sizeable level of unemployment as well as abandoning plans for social reform), standards at a later date would have been higher. But Attlee, for one, did not want just to put the economy back on its feet. He had not waited for political power for almost a quarter of a century, since entering parliament in 1922, to perpetuate the existing order, at whatever level of prosperity. Instead, he wanted social improvements, and he was determined to have them if at all possible. Despite his well-earned reputation as a seeker after consensus and compromise, Attlee was, to this extent, undoubtedly a conviction politician.

Attlee remained philosophical: the economy would improve in time, and meanwhile the government must do what it could to promote the wealth of the country – in both economic and social terms. There would have to be undesirable – and electorally unpopular – austerity, especially after the convertibility crisis of 1947, but he was not going to sacrifice one generation on behalf of another. The economy should not be sacrificed to New Jerusalem; on the other hand, nor should the government abandon the plans it had been elected to introduce. Socialism, as Dalton argued, 'did best when it marched in step with the rules of arithmetic'.[4]

In total, Labour's economic policies were neither a startling success nor a miserable failure. Neither Labour's, nor Attlee's, reputation should hinge on economic management. But their stewardship did at least provide the possibility for success – or failure – in other realms.

Nationalisation

Labour had justified its proposals to nationalise key industries by pointing to the need for efficiency. Each industry was to have applied to it 'the test of national service': if it fell down on the job, the nation would have to see that things were put right.[5] Justified in this way, the policy seemed a matter of plain, uncontroversial common sense. Indeed for a time Labour's programme of public ownership did receive general acceptance. The Bank of England was the first measure of socialisation. The Old Lady of Threadneedle Street and the Old Man of the Treasury, Dalton reassured the nation, had been living in sin for some time: and now the marriage of nationalisation merely formalised arrangements. The joint stock banks were left untouched, and so there was nothing here to excite the Conservatives to unparliamentary language, let alone the unconstitutional obstruction which Labour had feared in the 1930s. Nor were most of the later measures of nationalisation – including coal, transport, gas and electricity – substantially more controversial. Compensation for existing owners, at a grand total of £2,700 million, erred on the side of generosity, and furthermore the public corporations set up to run the new undertakings were staffed mainly by people of capitalist outlook and convictions. Right-wing trade unionists were found seats on their boards, but there was no flirting with notions of workers' control or even participation in management decisions.

About 20 per cent of British industry was nationalised, but it was generally the public service industries and chronic lossmakers which were taken over by the state. The right-wing could therefore applaud, and the left could bemoan, that in a sense Labour's initiatives were supporting a 'mixed economy' which was still basically capitalist. Only the proposal to nationalise iron and steel was really controversial. The Conservatives were determined to oppose this measure as strongly as they could. After all, if the relatively profitable steel industry were nationalised, where would the process end? Would any industry be safe? Fearing the worst, therefore, private firms totally divorced from the 'commanding heights' of the economy – like Tate and Lyle – supported the Conservative campaign.

Furthermore, the Labour camp was divided over steel, which had been included in *Let Us Face The Future* only after pressure from the 1944 annual conference. Morrison, the mastermind behind both the manifesto and the nationalisation programme, was against it, and even the unions concerned were split on the issue.

The initial wave of enthusiasm for nationalisation had begun to recede both in the party and among workers by the time steel reached the cabinet agenda. Perhaps it was that the form which public ownership took was too conservative: certainly most workers did not feel that the industries belonged to them, and industrial relations did not suddenly improve. Attlee recognised that no *esprit de corps* was being developed in the pits, where the coal board was so distant from working men. In addition, Labour's economic thinkers were doubting the need for nationalisation. From 1947 physical controls as a means of directing the economy were being abandoned in favour of demand management, via the budget. Was there still a need, therefore, for government actually to own sectors of the economy? The government also wanted to establish good relations with private industry in order to encourage maximum export production. For this reason there was unprecedented consultation with the Federation of British Industries. Freeing businessmen from the fear of further state take-overs was another means of cementing good relations with the private sector.

On the other hand, left-wingers like Aneurin Bevan regarded steel nationalisation as the touchstone of Labour's socialist commitment. They had always believed in nationalisation on principle: private ownership generally meant the exploitation of workers in the interests of the wealthy few, whereas public ownership could ensure equitable prices, wages and conditions of service. Furthermore, they judged that public enterprise would be far more efficient than capitalism and would lead to desirable changes in the distribution of power in society. Labour's left believed that the case for nationalising steel, at the centre of the 'commanding heights', was unanswerable. In cabinet, not only Bevan but Dalton and Bevin were also strongly in favour. In August 1947 142 MPs petitioned Attlee that there should be no weakening in the determination to nationalise iron and steel.

Typically, Attlee's personal view on this issue was hard to

fathom. In a sense, his view did not matter: what did matter was securing consensus. His prime concern was that debate should lead to decision, not further, unresolved debate. He gave permission to John Wilmot, the Minister of Supply, to investigate schemes for government control of the industry which fell short of outright ownership, but when his proposals were debated in cabinet it was clear that there was substantial division. Attlee then swung in favour of full nationalisation but only for the 1948–49 session. This seemed like a sensible compromise, and it did receive cabinet assent. But it also complicated matters greatly. It seemed likely that the Steel Bill would be vetoed by the House of Lords for the maximum two-year period, which would mean that it could not be passed within the lifetime of the 1945 parliament. Hence Attlee also decided to introduce a new Parliament Bill, designed to limit their Lordships' power of veto to a single year. As it turned out, however, the steel bill was brought forward within a year of the 1950 election, and so the new powers over the Lords did not have to be invoked. The Iron and Steel Act was passed in 1949, but it was agreed with the Lords that it would not become operative unless Labour won the next election.

The Iron and Steel Corporation came officially into being on 1 January 1951. There was little time to get it up and running before Attlee's second government went out of office. Labour's delays, consequent upon the party's divided counsels, made it easy for the Conservatives subsequently to privatise the industry. Road haulage was the only other nationalised sector of the economy which Churchill's government returned to the private sector. The remainder of Attlee's programme remained intact until the Thatcher-Major period. There had in fact been a substantial consensus forged over nationalisation, as Attlee had hoped there would be. To some extent, this had existed during the war, as government reports showed the urgent need for a thorough reorganisation in several sectors of the economy, including the coal and gas industries. But a Conservative government after 1945 would certainly not have taken such a substantial number of industries and services under their wing. The Conservatives were won over to a somewhat reluctant acquiescence in state control, and partly because the newly nationalised industries were seen to be running tolerably well.

On several occasions, in the 1920s and 1930s, Attlee had

been keenly in favour of nationalisation, together with some measure of workers' control. As Prime Minister, however, his main concern was that the issue of nationalisation should not divide his party more than was necessary. Hence he wished to see a compromise between left and right. In 1950 he told Morrison that the removal altogether of nationalisation from Labour's manifesto would not do, but neither could he agree that it should have a prominent place. Hence in the manifesto for 1950, *Let Us Win Through Together*, the emphasis was put upon making each existing nationalised industry 'a model of efficiency and social responsibility'.[6] Yet beet sugar, sugar refining and cement were specified as targets for public owner-ship, while the chemicals industry was to be closely monitored. Such a token 'shopping list' showed quite clearly that Attlee had been able to arrange no more than an uneasy truce on this divisive issue. Similarly in 1951, Labour's manifesto announced that it would nationalise further industries 'if nec-essary'. All members of the party could accept this ambiguous form of words – which could mean entirely different things to different people – but in reality it did little more than paper clumsily over the cracks.

Industrial relations

Labour's economic hopes were based, primarily, upon getting people to work harder than before – once full employment existed – and to consume less. Hence much depended upon industrial relations, and these were generally good. Indeed the unions were, on the whole, important allies of Attlee's Labour administration, accepting several key government proposals. They agreed, for instance, that the wartime prohibition of strikes should continue into peacetime: all disputes had to be referred to the Minister of Labour, who would arrange for arbitration. This fiat did not in fact stop strikes: from May 1945 to September 1949, 10.25 million working days were lost. But this total was very small compared with the corresponding period after the First World War, which saw 170 million days lost. Nevertheless, the agreement did stop official strikes alto-gether. Furthermore, union leaders supported government measures against unofficial actions, even when the govern-ment used troops to carry on essential services, as it did on no fewer than eleven occasions, and even when it twice declared a state of emergency. Attlee was no more loath than MacDonald had been to invoke emergency legislation, though he had learned from the first Labour Prime Minister's failures the importance of having trade union leaders on his side.

The first state of emergency was declared in June 1948, when 20,000 dockers came out in London, holding up 140 ships. The declaration of the emergency, however, looked likely to exacerbate the situation, as industrial action soon spread to Merseyside. But then Attlee broadcast to the nation, appealing for the men to go back – and they did so within forty-eight hours. It was a remarkably effective performance, with a script provided by Bevin, leading the journalist J.L. Hodson to describe Attlee as having 'the gift of calm, of reason, of lucidity. He is the quintessence of a decent, fair man.'[7] The second state of emergency was also occasioned by a dock strike, this one in July 1949: the government sent in troops to unload ships in the London docks during an unofficial strike in support of Canadian dockers, which many thought was being organised by communists to sabotage Marshall Aid. The men voted to return to work two weeks later.

Most important of all, union leaders accepted the government's calls for pay restraint. In 1948 the TUC agreed to call for a temporary halt to rises in personal incomes, and the following year an even more severe wage freeze was accepted. This was the most successful 'pay policy' of the postwar period, and it constitutes a remarkable achievement for Labour. It almost seemed, for a time, as though the trade union leaders had become state agents, encouraging higher production and the ending of restrictive practices in the national interest. How can this be explained?

One factor was undoubtedly personnel. There were close connections between the party and the trade union world. One prominent member of the government, Bevin, had been the founder of the Transport and General Workers' Union, and in addition there were six union-sponsored MPs in the 1945 cabinet. Furthermore, seven TUC officials joined the boards of nationalised industries. In 1948 the unions were represented on over sixty government committees (compared with twelve in 1939). Attlee himself did his utmost to encourage close and cordial relations with the union world, becoming the first prime minister to address the TUC's annual conference. Also, there were three key union leaders – Arthur Deakin, Will Lawther and Tom Williamson – who were very loyal to Labour and pronouncedly anti-communist.

Yet from another point of view, the trade unionists were doing very nicely out of Labour. The government certainly delivered the goods when it revoked the hated Trade Disputes Act of 1927. Most important of all, government action against unofficial strikes was very much to the benefit of the official trade union leaders, whose grip on their membership had weakened during the war. In total, it was a cosy, symbiotic relationship.

Nevertheless, several factors served to undermine the government–union front. One of these was inflation, caused by devaluation and the Korean war. In 1950, at the TUC conference, a resolution against wage restraint was carried. The second factor is that the government seemed to many to overstep the mark in its action against unofficial strikers. Anti-strike legislation had had a deterrent effect: but it had not actually been invoked. However, in October 1950 summonses were issued against ten striking gas workers who, on pleading guilty, were sentenced to a month's imprisonment. Widespread opposition followed, and on appeal the sentences were reduced to fines. Nor was the government, once bitten, twice shy. In February 1951 seven striking dockers were prosecuted, an unpopular move which not only failed to produce convictions but exacerbated industrial conflict and led to a widespread call for the removal of the anti-strike legislation. In early 1951 the TUC itself called for an end to the ban on strikes, and in August the government complied. Close collaboration between government and the unions had undoubtedly benefited the government's economic policies, but it had been too good to last.

. . .

THE WELFARE STATE

By 1950 Labour was identified primarily as the party of the welfare state. This reputation rested on several substantial achievements. In terms of legislation, Labour had passed the National Insurance Act , the National Health Service Act and the National Assistance Act, as well as such second-tier acts as the Industrial Injuries Bill. The government also implemented family allowances, built over a million new houses and raised the school leaving age to fifteen. In addition, there were a host of reforms which tend to be ignored in text-book summaries, such as the extension of legal aid and the creation of twelve National Parks.

But did Attlee and Labour deserve much credit for introducing the welfare state – or was the postwar government merely following the plans of the wartime consensus? There is no doubt that, during the war, a degree of consensus had emerged between Labour and Conservative. Had it not done so, the Churchill coalition could not possibly have survived. We have seen that Attlee was one of the foremost creators of such consensus as existed, as he helped to restrain the reformers in his own party while, at the same time, chivvying the coalition in the direction of planning and implementing reform. But it is clear that, as well as consensus, there was also tension within the wartime government. Kevin Jefferys has described the situation well with his argument that wartime consensus was of the 'lowest common denominator' type: common Conservative–Labour plans represented the most which many Tories would accept and the least which many socialists would countenance.[8] This view is complemented by Brooke's insistence that Labour looked upon wartime reports 'not as blueprints for easy appropriation, but as platforms on which to build more radical measures'.[9] Furthermore, many landmarks in the wartime consensus had been anticipated by Labour. The famous 1944 Employment White Paper, for instance, in which the politicians pledged themselves to maintain a high and stable level of employment, had been preceded by Labour's *Full Employment and Financial Policy.*

After its election victory in 1945, Labour was certainly influenced by the ideas of Keynes, Beveridge and the other wartime planners. In introducing the National Insurance Bill, for instance, James Griffiths paid tribute to Beveridge and his Report of 1942. This fact should not be lost sight of. But neither should the degree of consensus – a relative not an absolute term – be exaggerated. At its 1942 annual conference, eight months before the Beveridge Report was published, Labour had committed itself to a comprehensive insurance scheme and to the abolition of the hated household means test; and, in addition, Attlee's government did not slavishly follow the Beveridge proposals. While Beveridge had called for pensions to be phased in over a period of time, in which those to become eligible would be paying contributions, Labour decided to implement the pension proposals in full

and immediately. Hence in some ways Labour was more generous than Beveridge. On the other hand, the government
decided to pay lower rates of benefit, in real terms, than
Beveridge had proposed. Here was a recognition of the country's parlous economic and financial conditions, in short a
recognition of reality.

Labour's social reforms were not self-financing, despite the
insurance element in them. Family allowances, pensions and
health reforms were to be paid for largely out of taxation.
Hence a good case could be made for at least postponing
reforms until a more prosperous period dawned, and it is certainly quite possible that a Conservative government might
well have done so. It is to Labour's credit, therefore, that ministers were determined to institute reforms, even if, in
consequence, benefits had to be kept low and, periodically, the
social services budget had to be pruned. Attlee realised, pragmatically and practically, that ideal circumstances might allow
ideal reforms, but that to wait for such times would be to wait
forever. In the real world, partial solutions would have to be
accepted. Half a loaf was infinitely better than no bread.

One area where expenditure mounted dramatically was
medical provision. Bevan did not create the National Health
Service from scratch. Much preliminary work had been done
and, more important, the wartime Emergency Hospital
Service, which saw all hospitals lay aside beds for war casual-
ties, fuelled public criticism of the old, inadequate system of
health care and, consequently, produced a general readiness
to accept thorough reform. Yet there were no blueprints for
Bevan to follow. Beveridge had merely posited the existence of
a national service as one of the assumptions in his Report. Nor
were the coalition's health plans to Labour's liking. Bevan
thought the issue out afresh, and there were battles to be
fought, with cabinet colleagues and the British Medical
Association, before acceptance was won.

When Bevan informed the cabinet of his proposal that the
state should take over all the hospitals, including those under
local authority control, Morrison fought hard to exempt
municipal hospitals. In his view, it would be 'disastrous if we
allowed local government to languish by whittling away its most
constructive and interesting functions'.[10] Morrison also played
skilfully on the Chancellor's fears that central control of all the
hospitals, with a consequent switch of funding from the

ratepayer to the taxpayer, might pose financial problems. Morrison was a formidable and tenacious opponent in cabinet; but Attlee gave Bevan consistent support and helped to swing the balance in his favour. The Prime Minister even accepted aspects of Bevan's schemes of which he disapproved. During the war Attlee had expressed his disapproval of plans to retain pay beds within NHS hospitals and of the proposal that doctors should be paid largely by capitation fees. But now he accepted, with Bevan, that such compromises were necessary. He was also aware that the imperfections of the system, from a socialist point of view, had the happy consequence of securing its acceptance by the Conservatives. Admittedly there were still administrative difficulties as well as spiralling costs, but the inauguration of the NHS on 5 April 1948 – with the participation of the general practitioners and the approval of the public – reassured Attlee that his daring appointment of Bevan to the Ministry of Health had been triumphantly vindicated. Britain became the first Western society to offer to all its people comprehensive health care free at the point of delivery.

Critics said that Attlee should have split housing from health (a criticism he tacitly accepted when, in 1951, housing responsibilities were transferred to the Ministry of Local Government). Bevan, said critics, could only keep 'half a nye' on housing. Certainly Labour was slow to start building houses and failed to provide anything like the quantities that were needed. Nevertheless, by 1951 several hundred thousand dwellings had been repaired and 160,000 'pre-fabs' had been erected. Most important of all, over a million new houses had been built – and of good size and quality. Admittedly this was not as many as were needed, but then this was a period of serious shortages in building materials and of competition for scarce resources. Perhaps more might have been achieved; but Attlee could take satisfaction from the Welshman's achievements in this sphere also.

Yet Nye's more visionary hopes did not come to pass. He hoped that council houses would be of so much better quality than privately built residences – erected quickly, and shoddily, for maximum profit – that everyone would want one. Similarly, private medicine would surely wither away, shamed out of existence by superior state provision. There would be no need to outlaw private housing or private medicine: the demand for them would simply cease as public enterprise showed its worth.

No doubt such visionary aims were impracticable from the start; but they certainly had little chance of success in an era of financial shortages. Bevan resigned in 1951 rather than accept charges for NHS spectacles and false teeth. Attlee, on the other hand, saw the need for strategic cuts in social spending, including housing subsidies and NHS funding, recognising philosophically the need to strike a balance between competing demands. Ideally, cuts would not have been necessary, and ideally the government could have undertaken a programme to construct new hospitals and modernise old ones. But it was not an ideal world: intractable realities undermined the pristine designs of the planners. Attlee had been in politics long enough to expect this. 'The aim of socialism is not to make the world perfect but to make it better':[11] the words were George Orwell's, but the sentiments were Attlee's.

Allocating resources after 1945 was a fiendishly difficult task. But it was one Attlee was peculiarly well equipped to tackle. His qualifications were impartiality, in that as the referee he was free of commitment to particular causes or ministers; a willingness to compromise; and a determination to reach a decision acceptable to the greatest number in the cabinet. He was not immobilised by the need occasionally to seek the lesser evil. On the other hand, he did genuinely wish to see beneficial change and would not lightly accept the status quo. If his foot had sometimes to be on the brake, it was also often on the accelerator.

In the field of education, for instance, Attlee realised the impossibility of achieving all that Labour supporters wished. Many new classrooms had to be 'pre-fabs', and many new teachers had to be hastily trained, in one year rather than the customary two. The demand for private education was not likely to dry up in such a climate, and nor did it. In addition, a reconsideration of basic educational philosophy had to be postponed, so that it was not until they were in opposition that the party came round to supporting the ideal of comprehensive schools. Nevertheless, the Labour government did make a positive difference to education in Britain. In January 1947, despite adverse financial conditions which might have led many a government to backtrack, the cabinet agreed to raise the school-leaving age to fifteen from April. Ellen Wilkinson fought hard in cabinet for acceptance of the reform, which involved an immediate increase of £100 million in the education budget. Three cabinet heavyweights – Dalton, Cripps and Morrison – were ranged against her, but Attlee gave his support to a woman who, in the past, had been one of his foremost critics, and the issue was finally won.

Assessment

Labour did not create the welfare state from scratch. They worked from the legacy of the past, unifying past welfare provisions into a new comprehensive system and making provisions universal. In 1938 there had been no fewer than eighteen separate means tests for benefits administered by seven separate government departments. Now Labour took this system (if such it can be called), and modernised, extended and improved it, building on wartime plans in the process. No doubt they were, in a sense, tackling yesterday's problems rather than anticipating those of the future: this is an easy criticism to make. But had they not done so, those same problems might well have continued to exist.

Sam Watson, the party's chairman, recapitulated Labour's achievements at the party conference in October 1950:

> Our Government has kept faith with the founders of our Party in spite of the difficulties which they themselves could not have foreseen. We have had to deal with the dollar gap, the destruction of our assets by war, the loss of our overseas wealth, the decay of certain industries in the hands of their private owners . . . But we need not apologise. The total amount of wealth – real wealth in real commodities – shared among our people was greater in 1949 than in any previous year, and it was shared out more fairly. Industrial production was higher than ever before in our history – 37 per cent higher than in 1938. Agricultural production too, was higher than ever before – 38 per cent higher than before the war. So were our exports, which were 51 per cent higher than in 1938 . . . I make a claim here and now which no other country, with few exceptions, can make: Poverty has been abolished. Hunger is unknown. The sick are tended. The old folk are cherished, our children are growing up in a land of opportunity. If we are allowed to carry on with the good work, a time will soon be with us when it will never again be possible to write on a man's grave the pitiless epitaph: 'He never had a chance.' At the base of this structure of liberty is a simple thing – the steady job and the living wage.[12]

There is an undeniable degree of hyperbole here. Nevertheless Labour's social achievements – resting on economic improvement, certainly, but also enacted in spite of financial dilemmas – were substantial.

Furthermore, the success of Labour's efforts undoubtedly helped to deepen the consensus which, to a lesser degree, had existed during the war. Labour success certainly made it much easier for progressive Tories to come to the fore in the Conservative party. Winston Churchill did not agree with a single word of a summary prepared for him of R.A. Butler's Industrial Charter, but he accepted that the prevailing political climate necessitated the inclusion of such ideas in the party's manifesto in 1950 and 1951. The period 1945–79 may not have been the 'Age of Attlee', as Morgan argues.[13] Such a blanket generalisation ignores the importance of the war years in producing a degree of consensus between the progressive wings of the parties, and it also minimises the often sharp party political differences that characterised the postwar years. In addition, it personalises political issues far too much. But Attlee had certainly played a leading role in producing a society which was more humane, less poverty-stricken and more civilised than the one he had known before 1914 and between the wars.

. . .

OMISSIONS

The 1945–51 governments, and especially the first administration, undoubtedly brought about significant, and relatively long-lasting, changes in British society. Some have even speculated that there was an actual revolution in these years and that socialism was introduced. Most historians, however, recognising that there was no fundamental shift in wealth or power between the classes, prefer the more cautious interpretation that Attlee's governments were profoundly reformist. It is indeed important to realise the degree of continuity, as well as change, between Labour's years in office and the preceding period. Furthermore, we should also note the failings of the governments and the omissions in their programmes. Several of these reflect the character of Attlee himself.

One area of weakness was undoubtedly public relations. Francis Williams, Attlee's adviser in this field, found it impossible to get him interested. Indeed the self-effacing Prime Minister told Williams that he was 'allergic to the press'.[14] He even urged his ministers to keep interviews with the media to a minimum – not that many of them, identifying advertising and publicity with the evils of capitalism, needed to be told. Forgetting that, sometimes, a great deal of sincerity can be absolutely fatal, Attlee tended to assume, quite wrongly, that if people were presented with a sincere statement of facts, they would respond in the appropriate manner, regardless of how the information was presented. Furthermore, he thought it would be constitutionally very dubious to spend state funds on issues – like nationalisation – of party political controversy. The result was that the public was fed predominantly with a diet of anti-Labour propaganda.

An important area of omission was Northern Ireland, Britain's forgotten province before the eruption of violence in the late-1960s. Nothing was done to improve the conditions of the Catholic minority, and nothing to stop the gerrymandering which prevented Catholics from securing representation even in areas where they were in the majority. Similarly, nothing was done to combat racism in Britain itself or to signal disapproval at the institution of apartheid in South Africa. Constitutionally, the first majority Labour Prime Minister did make changes. He arranged that ministers would no longer have no wear anachronistic court dress on ceremonial occasions, and he also abolished plural voting, except in Ulster; but there was no thorough reform of the House of Lords. Admittedly the power of veto by the Upper House was cut back to only one year, but this was, in a sense, the accidental by-product of the proposal to nationalise steel. Christopher Addison, whom Attlee had made Labour leader in the Lords, recommended the creation of life peers and also the abolition of the right to vote of the hereditary peers, but nothing along these lines was achieved. Reformers had to be content, instead, with the innovation from 1946 which allowed their Lordships to claim travelling expenses! Nor was anything done to reform the Civil Service, which was settling back into traditional ways after the brief but exhilarating infusion of new blood during the war.

There was no equal pay for women, and nor was the death sentence abolished. Hanging, Attlee once said, was an issue in which he had never been interested. Nor was there any reform of the Labour party Constitution: Attlee recognised that the constitution was the result of 'historical growth rather than of logical planning' and that if a fresh start were made a better structure could be constructed, but he lamented that 'the difficulty of introducing any change now is very great'.[15] Neither was anything done about the public schools. During the war Attlee had intimated that, while they should not be killed, they should in fact be adapted pretty drastically: certainly they should have a large proportion of scholars from the elementary schools. But, paradoxically, the period of Labour majority rule turned out to be something of a golden age for private education.

There is, of course, a limit to what can be achieved in six years in office, and the record of Attlee's government compares well with that of any other administration this century. Nevertheless the omission of important reforms from Labour's manifestos in 1950 and 1951 does suggest a lack of willpower. Certainly it is not easy to envisage Attlee, the Old Boy of Haileybury, attacking the public schools or even recasting fundamentally the House of Lords, which he joined a few years later. By 1951 he was proud, justifiably so, that so many of the injustices he had witnessed in Stepney before the First World War had disappeared. His governments could take an important share of the credit for this, as he could himself. But his administration bore the impress of his conservative as well as of his radical traits. Many believed that, for the future, Labour required the impetus of a new generation's energy and thought.

. . .

REFERENCES

1. C.R. Attlee, *As It Happened* (London, 1954), p. 163.
2. Dalton memo, 21 January 1947, Attlee Papers, dep 49, Bodleian Library.
3. Correlli Barnett, *The Lost Victory: British Dreams, British Realities, 1945–50* (London, 1995), p. 379.
4. Ben Pimlott (ed.), *The Political Diary of Hugh Dalton 1918–40, 1945–60* (London, 1986), 30 July 1947, pp. 403–4.
5. *Let Us Face the Future*, 1945, p. 6.
6. *Let Us Win Through Together*, 1950, p. 4.
7. *Listener*, 3 January 1980, p. 2.
8. Kevin Jefferys, 'British Politics and Social Policy during the Second World War', *Historical Journal*, vol. 30, no. 1, 1987, pp. 123–44.
9. Stephen Brooke, *Labour's War* (Oxford, 1992), p. 110.
10. Peter Hennessy, *Never Again* (London, 1992), p. 139.

11. *The Collected Essays, Journalism and Letters of George Orwell* III (Harmondsworth, 1970), p. 282.
12. *Report of the 49th Annual Conference of the Labour Party*, 1950, pp. 77–8
13. Kenneth O. Morgan, *Labour in Power 1945–51* (Oxford, 1984), p. 494.
14. Francis Williams, *Nothing So Strange* (London, 1970), p. 215.
15. C.R. Attlee, *The Labour Party in Perspective* (London, 1937), pp. 100–1.

Chapter 8

ATTLEE'S GOVERNMENTS, 1945–51: FOREIGN AND IMPERIAL AFFAIRS

There has been no weakness and no betrayal, nor will there be, but there are limitations to our powers.[1]

. . .

FOREIGN AFFAIRS

Attlee, like the members of his government and the vast majority of the electorate, hoped to concentrate on domestic reform after 1945. The natural reaction after five years of 'total war' was to seek to return to semi-isolation, especially in view of the need to cut back defence spending. The men from the swollen British forces were needed in the factories. Such common sense was reinforced by Keynes's expertise: he insisted that, at the end of the war, Britain must not only secure American aid and expand exports but also reduce overseas expenditure drastically and immediately. But could Britain disentangle itself from foreign affairs and focus on domestic issues? Towards the end of the war Attlee had spotted the possible menace from the Soviet Union, but now he adopted a hopeful and positive attitude. As a result, his relationship with his Foreign Secretary, Ernest Bevin, was far more complex and ambivalent that many historians, basing themselves on Attlee's own memoirs and recollections, have realised. Almost the first words Bevin spoke, on arriving at Potsdam as Foreign Secretary, were 'I'm not going to have Britain barged about'.[2] Attlee, however, was far less truculent; and though at Potsdam

161

he allowed Bevin to take the lead, and according to one observer receded in the background 'by his very insignificance',[3] he definitely had a mind of his own.

The new Prime Minister was determined to take a positive and optimistic view of the international situation. Certainly there were some grounds for caution as to Stalin's motives, but Attlee insisted that Britain had to make a real imaginative effort to see things from the Soviet point of view. In particular, he argued that no actions should be taken by Britain which might appear aggressive to the Soviets. He was also optimistic about the impact of the new United Nations Organisation. For the past quarter of a century he had believed in the vital necessity of an efficient and effective supra-national body, able to prevent war by its regulation of international affairs. Now it seemed possible that such a body was being born, and he for one would not help to strangle it at birth. Attlee was always in favour of playing the game, but not the game of traditional power politics.

Attlee saw a real chance to scale down Britain's commitments. Hence this reaction to the suggestion that Britain should administer some of the colonies taken away from Italy:

> Why should it be assumed that only a few great Powers can be entrusted with backward peoples? Why should not one or other of the Scandinavian countries have a try? They are quite as fitted to bear rule as ourselves. Why not the United States?[4]

In his view the existing British Empire could not possibly defend itself, and there was thus no possible justification for adding extra burdens. Instead Britain would have to withdraw from overseas bases, with a corresponding reduction in forces.

At the start of 1946 Attlee began asking questions which the service chiefs found highly embarrassing. Did Britain, for instance, really need a large fleet in the Pacific? What practical benefits were accruing to Britain from her massive overseas spending? In March he called for the adoption of a new strategy, based on real national needs and in line with economic strength. There should, in his view, be a timely retreat from excessive overseas commitments, and in particular from the Middle East. Correlli Barnett has praised Attlee's cabinet memorandum in this month as 'one of the most penetrating and perceptive written by any British statesman in the twentieth century'.[5] It was not that the Prime Minister wished to see the end of Britain's Great Power status. He believed that Britain still had a world role to play, and that her influence would, almost automatically, be beneficent. Indeed many colleagues were surprised at the virulence with which this veteran of the First World War defended the army against their criticisms. 'What the hell do you mean?' he once snapped. 'You can keep your bloody sneers to yourself. Some of us are damned proud of the British Army.'[6] But he did see the need to face facts. Britain could not continue to act as if she were still the world's premier economic power: this was the middle of the twentieth century, not the middle of the nineteenth. In his view the British could no longer defend the 'lifelines' of the Empire; and it followed from this that the Middle East was of dubious value, as was Greece in the eastern Mediterranean. In short, Britain should base its policy on present, not past, realities.

Attlee gave short shrift to left-wing critics who wished Britain to adopt a neutral position between the Superpowers of the Soviet Union and the United States. A memorandum by 'Comrade Zilliacus' (who was to be expelled from the party in 1949) drew forth from Attlee one of his classic put-downs: 'Thank you for your memorandum, which seems to me to be based on an astonishing lack of understanding of the facts.'[7] Nevertheless for a time, in 1946–47, Attlee was himself one of Bevin's foremost critics, and he did manage to temper his Foreign Secretary's policy. Despite Bevin, British aid to Greece and Turkey was ended in 1947, precipitating the Truman Doctrine, with its offer of aid to these countries, as to others attempting to resist totalitarian subjugation. But Attlee's influence was in fact limited. The forces arrayed against him seemed too great. Dalton, concerned to cut back defence expenditure, found Attlee's reasoning refreshing, but not so the Chiefs of Staff. The First Sea Lord, Lord Cunningham, confided in his diary the view that Attlee was an ass, whose policy amounted to little more than unilateral disarmament: his attitude was 'past belief'.[8] He, together with Montgomery for the Army and Tedder for the Air Force, threatened to resign if Britain pulled out of its bases in the Middle East. Furthermore, Bevin made his position very clear: to his mind, Britain's presence in the Middle East was vital to its status as a Great Power, while British withdrawal would only create a vacuum drawing in the Soviets.

Presented with such opposition, the Prime Minister capitulated, bowing philosophically to superior forces.

It was predictable that Attlee would back down – as would virtually any other premier. Hence neither Britain's commitments nor its expenditure were scaled down to the levels which to Attlee – let alone to later historians – seemed realistic. Perhaps the Prime Minister should have pressed his radical alternative more strongly. He believed in the proverb 'If you've a good dog, you don't bark yourself'; but it is a pity that he did not himself bark more often and more ferociously, especially since Bevin did exaggerate the Soviet threat to Western Europe. Instead, Attlee returned to his accustomed role in the cabinet, not arguing his own case but acting as referee. Two good cases were made by his colleagues, one for extra defence expenditure to meet short-term commitments and to reconstruct the services in the face of longer-term threats, the other for the scaling down of expenditure because of economic problems and the needs of social spending. Attlee generally managed to achieve a judicious compromise between them.

Nevertheless Attlee would probably have come round anyway to Bevin's way of thinking. The Soviet use of the veto in the Security Council and the Americans' unwillingness to internationalise nuclear power both led him to abandon, temporarily, his hopes for the United Nations, increasing the need for nations to look to their own defences. In addition, increasing signs of Soviet aggression convinced Attlee that Bevin's basic strategy was correct. Indeed even Labour's left wing acknowledged that earlier criticisms of Bevin had been faulty. After the Czech coup in February 1948, Michael Foot wrote in *Tribune* that the Soviet Union was no more than a 'fraudulent parody' of Marxism, an interpretation which seemed to be confirmed by the Soviet blockade of West Berlin from June; and the following year he insisted that the real threat of war came not from the USA – formerly described as 'a Rogue Elephant with a Bomb' – but from the USSR.[9] Britain had definitely entered the American camp in the Cold War, much to Attlee's satisfaction, for the benefits seemed to outweigh the disadvantages. Certainly Attlee, like Bevin, had reason to be thankful for Marshall Aid, of which Britain received almost $3,000 million out of Europe's total allocation of $12,000 million; and he too was fully behind the formation of the North Atlantic Treaty Organisation, in 1949. Labour had to adopt a much more realistic foreign policy than in the 1930s, and there was to be no appeasement: instead, there was straightforward collective resistance to aggression in Western Europe. Attlee thus accepted the Cold War as a fact of life. His initial reluctance to do so not only did Britain no harm but is to his credit, testifying to an open-mindedness which few Cold War warriors displayed.

Yet alliance with a Superpower almost inevitably meant subordination, and there are many who have argued that Labour gave up Britain's essential independence, becoming merely 'Airstrip One', from Orwell's *Nineteen Eighty-Four*. There was an American base – and nuclear weapons – on British soil in July 1948. A few years later the Americans had eight airfields in Britain, and the Labour government had little effective control over the deployment of nuclear weapons from its own soil. Furthermore the outbreak of the Korean War in 1950 meant that Britain had to accept American pressure for an unrealistically expensive rearmament programme, including an extension of conscription from 18 months to 2 years, which resulted in health service cuts and Bevan's resignation. Yet, on the other hand, Britain still retained some initiative. Had Britain been merely the puppet, the Americans would have danced her to a different tune on several issues, including Palestine and European unity. In addition, Britain recognised Mao's Communist China in October 1949, twenty years before the Americans. It is also arguable that Bevin and Attlee, rather than the Americans, provided the real impetus for the formation of NATO. The British saw the need to shelter under the wing of the United States and yet, at the same time, to stand up to the Americans – no easy posture to contrive.

Attlee had several long rows with President Truman, not least over the Americans' refusal to honour the wartime agreement to share nuclear know-how. It was partly in order to preserve an important degree of national independence and initiative that Attlee, and an inner core of ministers, decided to construct Britain's own nuclear weapons. The full cabinet was not consulted, Attlee explaining later that some ministers were simply not fit to be trusted with such important and sensitive information. The initial cost of £100 million was carefully camouflaged in the financial estimates. Here was not only a secrecy of which Ramsay MacDonald might have been proud but a constitutionally dubious sleight of hand of which few would have expected the orthodox Attlee to be capable. No longer the impartial chairman of committee, he was a man capable of bold, controversial action. Despite economic problems, the Prime Minister – as a Victorian, sharing delusions of British grandeur with almost all the members of his generation – had no intention of seeing Britain sink to the ranks of the second-rate powers. Some believed his expensive pro-nuclear stance to be misguided. For instance, Sir Henry Tizard, the chief scientific adviser to the government, judged that it was a mistake for Britons to persist

> in regarding ourselves as a Great Power, capable of everything and only temporarily handicapped by economic difficulties . . . We are not a Great Power and never will be again. We are a great nation, but if we continue to behave like a Great Power we shall soon cease to be a great nation. Let us take warning from the fate of the Great Powers of the past and not burst ourselves with pride.[10]

Such criticisms seem all the more pertinent after the passage of time, and subsequent British decline. Yet in the late-1940s Britain was still the third most powerful nation on earth, and its citizens were still congratulating themselves on victory in the war: it would therefore take time for the British imperial psyche to readjust itself thoroughly to new world realities.

Certainly Attlee was treading a fine line between asserting Britain's voice in world affairs and diminishing that voice by overstretching the economy. He also had to steer a course between the Scylla of conciliating, and possibly falling dependent upon, his American paymasters, and the Charybdis of standing up to, and possibly alienating, them. In 1951, for instance, he accepted an inflated defence budget – at around 14 per cent of total national income a heavier burden per capita than that accepted by the Americans themselves – and agreed that British troops should be deployed in Korea, an area of no real strategic value from Britain's point of view; but he also flew to Washington to argue strongly against the use of atomic weapons and the spreading of the war into China. Described by Dean Acheson as 'a damn good lawyer', he even managed to get Truman to accept that Britain should have a veto on the deployment of the atomic bomb, before US officials hastily convinced the President of the need for caution.[11] Attlee's was the sort of balancing act which successive governments have tended to find ever more difficult.

His expertise in foreign affairs was perhaps shown to best effect in 1951. When on 2 May the Iranian Prime Minister, the eccentric, pyjama-clad Dr Mossadegh, nationalised the Anglo-Iranian Oil Company, amidst a plethora of anti-British propaganda, there were some in the cabinet who called for immediate retaliatory action. Morrison, Bevin's successor as Foreign Secretary, was one of these, and so was Shinwell, the Minister of Defence, while the First Sea Lord insisted that the public 'were tired of being pushed around by Persian pip-squeaks'.[12] The cabinet considered Operation Buccaneer, which involved occupying the island of Abadan, where Britain had built the world's largest oil refinery. But it was Attlee who, in Roger Louis's words, 'steadied nerves and guided his colleagues towards restraint'.[13] He showed a real understanding not only of the nature of Arab nationalism, which an expedition would have inflamed throughout the Middle East to the harm of British interests, but of American opinion, which would not have supported British aggression. Some at the time regarded Attlee's policy as dismally defeatist; we, on the other hand, with the benefits of hindsight, are likely to compare it very favourably with Eden's policy during the Suez crisis of 1956. Certainly the issue ended highly satisfactorily from Britain's point of view. In 1953 the CIA and MI6 engineered a coup against Mossadegh, and the Oil Company (re-named BP) soon re-entered Iran as part of an international consortium in which it had a 40 per cent stake.

Europe

The Americans would have preferred Britain to join wholeheartedly with the movement for closer association in Europe. That way, there would be a firmer barrier to the spread of communism, and US diplomatic relations would be much simplified. Acheson has called Britain's failure to adhere to the 1950 Schuman plan – designed to construct a European Coal and Steel Community (ECSC) as the 'first foundations of the European Federation which is indispensable to the maintenance of peace' – her 'great mistake of the postwar period'.[14] But though Britain took part wholeheartedly in NATO and in the Organisation for European Economic Co-operation, as the means of receiving Marshall Aid, Attlee's government was convinced of the need to steer well clear of further connections with Europe.

Attlee had, in the past, insisted that Europe must federate or perish. Even now, he retained the same view in theory, but he also stressed that the merging of sovereignties could come about only very slowly and that the time for Britain's participation in such a scheme was a long way off. Memories of the war were too alive for him – and for many others – to welcome wholehearted co-operation with France, let alone Germany. Once, when someone said that the French were critical of Britain for not doing more for European defence, Attlee responded with: 'What the hell right have they got to criticise us? Tell them to go and clear up their own bloody stable. They haven't got any decent generals. They haven't had a good general since Prince Eugene, and he served their enemies.'[15] More humourously, he once insisted 'Can't trust the Europeans – they don't play cricket'.[16] Britain was not emotionally ready, as continental Europeans were, for the fresh start which European union offered. In the perceptive words of Jean Monnet, 'Britain had not been conquered or invaded. She felt no need to exorcise history.'[17] It was natural for the British to be more concerned about sovereignty than the states on the continent which had been overrun by Hitler. As Bevin once commented, in his inimitable way, of the Council of Europe, 'If you open that Pandora's box, you never know what Trojan Horses will jump out'![18]

There were several other, more precise reasons why Attlee's government stood aside from the ECSC. Economically, the Schuman Plan and European integration seemed to make little sense for Britain. British trade with the Empire and Commonwealth was more important than European commerce; and few, around 1950, foresaw that trading patterns were to change in the future. The advice of an official committee was that there were no compelling economic arguments in favour of entry into the proposed Community. In addition, the government was not prepared to hand over its newly nationalised coal industry and its about-to-be nationalised steel industry to the Western European capitalists. Morrison, deputising in cabinet for Attlee, judged that the Durham miners would not stand for it. Furthermore, the French made few attempts to appeal to British *amour propre*. Although Dean Acheson and West Germany's Adenauer were informed of the scheme before its launch, Bevin was kept in the dark, despite an earlier promise that he would be forewarned before any initiatives were taken. The French ambassador in London criticised his own government for this. Then Britain was given only twenty-four hours to decide whether or not to attend an inaugural conference. Several members of the government interpreted France's ultimatum as an attempt to exclude Britain from the Schuman Plan and steal the leadership of Europe for herself. This was, in fact, a misinterpretation, but it was an understandable one. It is also notable that the Conservative opposition, which criticised Labour's lukewarm attitudes towards Europe, followed Labour's policies when in government. Criticisms of Attlee's government, such as Acheson's, therefore lack real substance.

. . .

IMPERIAL AFFAIRS

Labour's 1945 manifesto spoke of the need to concede responsible self-government in India and to achieve the 'planned progress of our Colonial Dependencies'.[19] Attlee cared little about the latter, and he never appreciated the fine work done by Creech Jones in promoting nation-building – both economic and political development – in Africa. By the time Labour went out of office the Gold Coast and Nigeria had taken giant steps along the road to decolonisation, which not even the reluctant decolonisers in Churchill's second government could reverse. But Attlee did care about India and had done since he joined the Simon Commission in 1928. He was determined to end the British Raj. Any other policy, he believed, would have been flying in the face of reality. The virulence of the Quit India campaign, described in 1942 by the Viceroy, Lord Linlithgow, as the most serious rebellion since the Indian Mutiny of 1857, had been concealed from the British public for reasons of military security; but Attlee knew that nationalist forces had been unleashed which no imperial power could hope to defeat, except perhaps at entirely disproportionate costs, in terms of manpower, money and international obloquy. If the Indians were unable to expel the British, they were certainly able to paralyse British rule. Soon the Viceroy, Lord Wavell, was bemoaning the fact that he and his staff had lost nearly all power to control events. He doubted whether the army would remain loyal if asked to quell a rebellion, and in February 1946 mutinies occurred in the navy and the air force.

Attlee chose at his Secretary of State the aged Pethick-Lawrence, who was in the House of Lords, and thereby took charge of Indian policy himself. He had two tasks. The first was to convince the Indians that, at long last, Britain was sincere in its wish to transfer power. This was difficult. The second was to devise some means of leaving. This proved virtually impossible, since power had to be transferred in an orderly fashion, and if possible to successors friendly to Britain. For eighteen months British policy seemed to flounder. Neither conferences of local politicians, an all-party delegation from the House of Commons, nor a three-man cabinet mission served to produce a solution. It seemed that nothing could engineer an agreement between the Indian National Congress, which wanted above all a united India, and the Muslim League, insisting on a separate Muslim State of Pakistan. Several people, including Gandhi, suggested that Attlee should himself come to India. Or should responsibility be handed over to the fledgeling United Nations? Instead Attlee decided on another course of action, which his supporters called bold and his detractors rash.

On 31 January 1947, amid severe economic problems at home, Attlee took the initiative. He sacked the Viceroy, Lord Wavell. This was a good decision. Essentially a soldier, Wavell was out of his depth with loquacious politicians: his single eye would glaze over as Gandhi prattled on, and a look of intense misery would settle on his face. As his diary reveals, he was sleeping badly, waking up early and obviously suffering from depression. In his place, Attlee chose the suave Lord Mountbatten, who had impressed him while Supreme Allied Commander of South East Asia at the end of the war. Here was a man, Attlee believed, who would have the finesse to secure agreement from the local politicians. Moreover he would add a touch of dignity, if not grandeur, to the last days of British rule. In addition, in February 1947, a few days before Britain made known its determination to withdraw aid from Greece and Turkey, Attlee announced that, come what may, British rule in India would end by June 1948. By this means, he revolutionised Indian policy. Earlier he had deprecated 'setting paper dates';[20] but now he saw the need to gamble. The announcement, Attlee hoped, would concentrate the minds of the Indians and force them to face realities.

The time-limit did indeed transform the situation, and soon the Congress leaders finally became reconciled to partition.

Mountbatten later insisted that he had demanded such a dead-line. But although his role was important and it was he who judged that the date should be brought forward to August 1947, Attlee had decided on the need for a withdrawal date before Mountbatten's appointment. Instead of doodling in cabinet, he had briskly taken the lead, overcoming opposition not only from Bevin, an old-fashioned imperialist, but also from Cripps, the cabinet's second expert on India. Shortly afterwards Attlee was equally impressive in the Commons, responding to Churchill's charges of scuttle. It was a familiar indictment, having been already made in cabinet by Bevin. Attlee was therefore able to put aside his notes. He seemed to speak from the heart and even, according to one observer, with a genuine eloquence:

> This man burns with a hidden fire and is sustained by a certain spiritual integrity which enables him to scale the heights when the occasion demands. Churchill was raked with delicate irony. It was close in-fighting, which is sometimes lost upon the general public, but which scores points with the judges and wins bouts in the Parliamentary ring.[21]

What mattered henceforth, however, was whether Mountbatten could justify Attlee's gamble.

Most British observers decided that the transfer of power, despite being hastily improvised, went well. The announce-ment of a deadline may have worsened communal tensions, but on 15 August 1947 both India and Pakistan (comprising present-day Pakistan and Bangladesh) became independent and agreed to join the Commonwealth. The president of the new Indian parliament called independence 'the consumma-tion of the ideals of the British race', an interpretation devoutly to be wished from Attlee's point of view. The Prime Minister was able to insist that Britain was not so much losing an Empire as gaining a multi-racial Commonwealth: what was happening, he told the House of Commons, was 'not the abdi-cation but the fulfilment of Britain's mission in India', and it was occurring 'without external pressure or weariness at the burden of ruling'.[22] He was of course creating a historical myth, and one which redounded to his own historical credit as well as to Britain's image in the world. His handling of Indian affairs in 1945–47 is generally thought to have been masterful.

Yet in fact the transfer of power was not planned or orderly but improvised, and Attlee himself had felt his way forward, though admittedly without fumbling. Nor was it a glorious end to empire: it was scarred by mass communal slaughters in which hundreds of thousands of lives were lost, as millions of refugees left their homes and struggled to cross the newly constructed, and highly contentious, political borders.

A slower pace, some say, might have produced far more deaths, perhaps two million; but others insist that a less frenetic and more orderly transition would have resulted in far fewer fatalities. There is really no way of knowing – which does not, of course, prevent the argument from raging on. Attlee himself, having made the key decisions, was philosophical. He wrote on 18 August 1947 that he doubted if things would go smoothly in India, as their leaders knew little of administration, 'but at least we have come out with honour instead [of], as at one time seemed likely, being pushed out ignominiously with the whole country in a state of confusion'. It was this honour which seems to have mattered most to him; but it was at least tactless on his part to judge in retrospect that, broadly speaking, 'the thing went off well'.[23] At all events, it must be admitted that the course of events could have worked out far more badly. Attlee had acted boldly. On no other single issue had his voice in the government been so authoritative, and he had assuredly left his mark on history. Another success came in April 1949 with the 'London Declaration', which changed the rules for Commonwealth membership. Henceforth the Crown was merely the 'symbol' and the Monarch the 'head' of the Commonwealth, a simple but ingenious form of words which meant that republics could henceforth be members of the multiracial club.

Yet if the government's Indian policy won them praise, no applause was won by their handling of Palestine. Nor could any realistically be expected. The British had made incompatible promises to Zionists and Arabs in the First World War, and as holders of the Palestinian Mandate from the League of Nations Britain had to take the consequences. It was a classic no-win situation, as Jews and Arabs – each with important allies, the former in the United States and the latter in the oil-rich Middle Eastern kingdoms – struggled for control of the territory. Once, when his wife asked him to unravel a tangled skein of wool, Attlee accepted with alacrity, musing that it was refreshing to find a problem which actually had a solution. He may well have had Palestine in mind as the archetypal problem without a solution.

Before 1945 Labour had been more pro-Zionist than the Conservatives. The party had criticised the 1939 White Paper, which set limits to the number of Jewish immigrants, and at its 1944 conference endorsed a pro-Zionist policy ('Let the Arabs be encouraged to move out as the Jews move in'). But this policy was the humanitarian response of a small number of men on the International Sub-Committee of the NEC, rather than the considered view of the party as a whole. After their election victory, Labour ministers back-tracked and accepted the 1939 limitations as the basis of their policy. President Truman called for the immediate admission of 100,000 Jews into Palestine, but Bevin became convinced that an Arab backlash against unrestricted Jewish immigration would harm British interests throughout the Middle East. Ideally he wanted to see two autonomous Arab and Jewish provinces, each controlling its own immigration. Yet neither side would accept, and so Britain had the unenviable and expensive task of barring entry to the holocaust survivors, most famously aboard the *Exodus*, and trying to keep law and order amid escalating violence, seen most spectacularly in the destruction of the King David Hotel in Jerusalem in July 1946. Altogether, 338 British lives were lost in Palestine after the war. In the words of one of the men on the spot – tactless words, it must be said, given Muslim and Jewish dietary laws: Britain was 'the ham in the sandwich'.[24]

In the end British exasperation caused the Labour cabinet to wash its hands of the problem. The future of Palestine was handed over to the United Nations, and Britain refused the thankless task of trying to implement its proposed partition of the country. The British High Commissioner left on 14 May 1948, as Israel was proclaimed. The Attlee government had abdicated. War would determine the political geography of the region.

Britain's role had been an ignominious one. Neither Attlee nor Bevin had been able to provide any constructive end to British involvement. Others, for instance Dalton, would have followed a more pro-Jewish policy, though the end results of this cannot be foreseen. But we can be reasonably certain that Attlee's view had to a large extent been guided by Bevin. For instance, Attlee accepted his Foreign Secretary's view of

American Zionism as 'a profitable racket . . . A Zionist is defined as a Jew who collects money from another Jew to send another Jew to Palestine. The collector, I gather, takes a good percentage of his collections.'[25] It was natural of Attlee to resent dictation from Truman about British policy in Palestine, and the two men exchanged acrimonious comments on the subject. The President had been less than guarded in some of his criticisms of the British. On the other hand, Attlee's own remarks were not always above reproach. When Ian Mikardo and Austen Albu were recommended for office, Attlee commented that 'they both belonged to the Chosen People, and he didn't think he wanted any more of them'.[26] Attlee's role in external policy is, on the whole, a creditable one, especially when considered in the context of the magnitude of the international problems facing him and of the other, multifarious claims on his time and on that of his ministers. But his reputation for wisdom, which always rested partly on his taciturnity, would be higher still had he said even less.

. . . .

REFERENCES

1. C.R. Attlee to Lord Salisbury, 18 December 1946, Attlee Papers, Bodleian Library.
2. *The Memoirs of General The Lord Ismay* (London, 1960), p. 403.
3. David Dilks (ed.), *The Diaries of Sir Alexander Cadogan 1938–1945* (London, 1971), p. 776.
4. R.D. Pearce, *The Turning Point in Africa* (London, 1982), p. 93.
5. Correlli Barnett, *The Lost Victory: British Dreams, British Realities, 1945–51* (London, 1995), p. 54.
6. George Mallaby, *From My Level* (London, 1965), pp. 56–7.
7. Kenneth Harris, *Attlee* (London, 1985), p. 295.
8. Raymond Smith and John Zametica, 'The Cold Warrior: Clement Attlee reconsidered, 1945–7', *International Affairs*, vol. 61, 1984–85, p. 245.
9. Jonathan Schneer, *Labour's Conscience: the Labour Left 1945–51* (London, 1988), pp. 39, 44.
10. Peter Hennessy, *Never Again* (London, 1992), p. 431.
11. Harris, *Attlee*, pp. 462–3.
12. K.O. Morgan, *Labour in Power* (Oxford, 1984), p. 469.
13. William Roger Louis, *The British Empire in the Middle East* (Oxford, 1984), p. 669.

14. Hennessy, *Never Again*, p. 364. On Attlee's government and the Schuman Plan, see John W. Young, *Britain and European Unity, 1945–1992* (London, 1993), pp. 28–43.
15. Mallaby, *My Level*, p. 57.
16. Harris, *Attlee*, p. 315.
17. Hennessy, *Never Again*, p. 364.
18. Ibid., p. 359.
19. *Let Us Face the Future*, p. 11.
20. Nicholas Owen, '"Responsibility without power": The Attlee governments and the end of the British rule in India', in Nick Tiratsoo (ed.), *The Attlee Years* (London, 1991), p. 158.
21. Alan Campbell-Johnson, *Mission with Mountbatten* (London, 1985 edn), p. 29.
22. Owen, 'Responsibility without power', p. 167.
23. Attlee to Tom Attlee, 18 August. 1947, Attlee Papers, Bodleian Library; Francis Williams (ed.), *A Prime Minister Remembers* (London, 1961), p. 212.
24. Robert Pearce, *Attlee's Labour Governments, 1945–51* (London, 1994), p. 69.
25. Attlee to Tom, 29 December 1946.
26. Ben Pimlott (ed.), *The Political Diary of Hugh Dalton 1918–40, 1945–60* (London, 1986), 20 February 1951, p. 508.

Chapter 9

ANTI-CLIMAX: OPPOSITION AND AFTER, 1951–67

In any party one is bound to have people who dislike each other. One has got to get on with them. And, frankly, the last year has been the unhappiest in my seventeen years of leadership . . . . The enthusiastic Socialist has a fire in himself which burns up the straw of selfishness and ambition.[1]

. . .

PARTY LEADER, 1951–55

Labour daggers were sheathed in October 1951. There was no call for Attlee to go. A party which had been so reluctant to accept him as a permanent leader now decided he could stay as long as he liked. Even Dalton, antagonistic since 1912, hoped that he would carry on for several more years. Why should anyone attempt to unseat a leader who was manifestly more popular than the party as a whole and therefore an electoral asset? It seems that only his wife wished Clem to give up. He was re-elected leader unopposed, and his acceptance of the Order of Merit was received well, despite the party's traditional contempt for honours. In the first debate of the new parliament Richard Crossman described him as 'snappy and witty'. He was also impressed with a skill Attlee had perfected over the years, that of 'staying in the Centre of the Party, wherever it is at the moment'.[2] The mood in the party was in fact buoyant, despite the Conservative victory. Dalton even went so far as to call the election results splendid. Labour needed a rest, while the narrowness of the Conservative victory made it seem unlikely that the new government would last long.

Yet, on the whole, Attlee, now aged almost seventy, proved a poor leader of the opposition. He was too reasonable, and too little the partisan. In addition, he was as poor as ever at courting publicity. In particular he, like Winston Churchill, never came to terms with television. The party leaders had both refused to give a party political broadcast on television in 1948 and 1950, and now they both upheld the Fourteen Day Rule (operative until 1956), which specified that no topic likely to be debated in the Commons within the next fortnight could be discussed on television. But Attlee went further than Churchill in his dislike of the proposal for a commercial channel. Fearing that politicians would be turned into entertainers, he pledged Labour in 1954 to abolish Independent Television. In addition, Attlee was too aloof in his party. Detachment was an advantage to a prime minister, allowing him to get on with affairs of state, but not to an opposition leader, with the job of rallying the troops and spearheading the creation of policy.

Soon Attlee was ill at ease in the affluent dispensation, with an unfamiliar working class clutching their new household goods, bought on credit. While appreciating the importance of material well-being, he had always rejected a materialist outlook on life. Furthermore his health was not good. In 1953 he had an appendix operation, and in early 1955 he fainted into Churchill's arms. 'Poor Attlee,' lamented Winston, who was nine years his senior, 'he is getting old; he is 72.'[3] In August 1955 he suffered a slight stroke.

So why did Attlee stay on so long, in fact until December 1955? There are several explanations. First, there was a general demand for him not to go. A general election could be called at any time – Attlee himself thought that the Tories would not last beyond 1953 – and therefore it seemed unwise for the PLP to change horses in mid-stream. Attlee had always described himself as the servant of the party, and it is possible to argue that the needs and wishes of the party kept him in the saddle. Such an explanation, however, falls far short of providing a full explanation. His image as the humble, unambitious figurehead, willing to go or stay as others chose, had always been largely a myth. Furthermore, Attlee's age now told against him, and the initial overwhelming consensus in his favour began to evaporate. It was not long before speculation about a successor began – and not only speculation but rumours, plots and counter-plots. Might Bevan have a chance of leading the party, or would his followers be better off backing a compromise candidate, say Jim Griffiths, as an alternative to Morrison, who would be likely to be succeeded in time by fellow right-winger Gaitskell? Attlee was in fact more of a caretaker leader than ever before.

The next explanation is that Attlee could foresee no suitable successor and therefore had to hold the ring until one emerged. It was just possible that Bevan, whom Attlee had at one time favoured as a future party leader, might cease being a rebel and settle down to respectability. But this would obviously require time, after his resignation in 1951. Meanwhile any immediate resignation by Attlee was likely to lead to the election of his long-time rival Herbert Morrison. When it was put to Attlee that his period as leader had been prolonged in order to exclude Morrison, only five years his junior, he reacted sharply and vehemently. He even went so far as to assert that one of his reasons for staying was to give Morrison's reputation a chance to recover after his recent failures at the Foreign Office. 'Herbert's chance would have been even smaller in 1951 than it turned out to be in 1955.'[4] He was protesting too much, and it is likely that dislike of Morrison did indeed form part of his motivation.

Another possibility is that the splits in the Labour party required Attlee to stay on as a conciliator. There was indeed a major fissure between the left-wing fundamentalists and the right-wing revisionists, and Attlee – never as modest as he seemed – may have felt he was needed to heal, or at least contain, it. But if so, it can be argued that he did a poor job. Arguably the Labour party needed firm leadership, but Attlee was loath to provide it. He preserved his own position, but he did little to remedy the splits in the party – either by soothing or lancing the boil.

Labour MPs spent far more time after 1951 fighting themselves than attacking the Conservative government. The first serious problem erupted in March 1952, when 57 Labour MPs defied the whip and voted against the government's Defence White Paper. Attlee thought they should be censured and called for them to promise in writing to abide in future by majority PLP decisions. Yet he failed to support a resolution to this effect with any passion or conviction, and it was defeated by a large majority. Standing Orders were reimposed, but the paradoxical result was that the 'Bevanites' became a more tightly knit group. The leader's attitude, complained Gordon Walker and other critics on the right, was 'almost that of a detached observer', and Morrison judged that 'he doodled where he ought to have led'.[5] Certainly Attlee impressed no one at the annual conference in Morecambe, in September–October 1952, where the Bevanites won six out of the seven NEC seats reserved for the constituencies. Morrison and Dalton both lost their seats, and divisions between the two wings of the party undoubtedly widened. Attlee was unhappy at what was happening, suspecting 'a considerable infiltration of near Communists into the Constituency delegations';[6] but it was Hugh Gaitskell, in a fighting speech at Stalybridge (which the left branded as McCarthyite), who attacked the Bevanites, winning in the process the plaudits of the trade union leaders. Attlee, as usual, preferred the middle ground. Nevertheless, he did subsequently call for the PLP to ban all unofficial groups (branding the 'party within the party' as 'intolerable') and for party members to refrain from attacking each other. This passed by a large majority, after which the Bevanites were disbanded as a group, though they still spoke and acted in unison. Yet it was only a truce not a real reconciliation.

The right of the party continued to think that Attlee was pusillanimous. Attlee wants 'the middle of the road all the while', complained Morrison in 1953, adding – in a swift change of cliché – that 'sometimes you have to come down off the fence and fight. He won't do that.'[7] Nor was the left any more enamoured of his leadership. When, at the 1954 conference, Attlee urged that emotionalism was a poor guide to foreign affairs, Bevan insisted that he was guilty of such emotionalism, adding, ironically, that the right kind of leader was a 'desiccated calculating machine who must not allow himself in any way to be swayed by emotion'.[8]

Once again foreign policy was the divisive issue within Labour ranks. In March 1954, acting on impulse, Bevan dissociated himself in the House of Commons from a statement Attlee had just made, and the next day he resigned from the shadow cabinet, disappointing his friends and confirming his enemies' charges of instability. Wilson took his place on Labour's front bench. Nye now spoke in private of his wish to 'destroy the bogus reputation of Clement Attlee'.[9] Further problems arose the following year. In January 1955, in defiance of the leadership, Bevan tabled an unofficial motion, with over a hundred signatures, deploring the government's refusal to hold direct talks with the USSR. He also disapproved of Attlee's approval of the Tories' decision to manufacture the hydrogen bomb. Attlee could not avoid taking action, but he did so in highly ambiguous ways. He introduced a PLP resolution rebuking Bevan, which was passed by 132 votes to 72; but at a meeting of the shadow cabinet on 7 March, when the vote was heavily in favour of withdrawing the whip from Bevan, Attlee made no real intervention, just a few mumbled comments against drastic action. A week later, when the PLP voted, though much more narrowly, to endorse this decision, Attlee spoke out more strongly, insisting that this was a vote of confidence in his leadership. Yet he had done so only when pressed, and to colleagues like Gaitskell, the leader's attitude was still too equivocal. Attlee later complained that he had been made the spearhead of a policy in which he did not really believe. In the end, Bevan avoided expulsion, but only narrowly. When the key decision was taken, at the NEC, Morrison and Gaitskell were strongly for expulsion, but now Attlee spoke firmly against, and a face-saving formula – passed by a single vote – allowed him to stay. Had Churchill not just resigned and an election not been in the offing, perhaps even Attlee's cautious moderation – some called it wisdom, others weakness – might not have prevailed.

Attlee was balancing, nimbly but precariously, between the two wings of the party. Nevertheless, he had managed to keep the party together. To his supporters – including biographers Harris and Burridge – this was a vindication of his decision to stay on as leader. Was Attlee the only one to keep his head while all around – to the left and the right – were losing theirs and blaming it on him? Such an heroic interpretation is possible. Certainly left and right did come together eventually. At the Brighton conference in 1957, Bevan, then shadow foreign secretary, repudiated unilateral nuclear disarmament (prompting the comment that he had been transformed into Bevin). This new-found party unity struck one journalist as belonging somewhere 'between the merely incredible and the plainly impossible',[10] but it had happened. Did Attlee foresee it? Was that why he stayed on, sacrificing his own comfort for the party in a final act of disinterested statesmanship?

Attlee did indeed hope that the party's troubles would blow over. (Most things do, in the long run, though, as Keynes once said, in the long run we are all dead.) But, on the other hand, he had no proper strategy to heal the divisions. He simply hoped that the party would pull itself together. In short, there was a complacency about him in this period. At times he did seem, as the *New Statesman* profile put it, untroubled by his own inadequacies.[11] Admittedly, he had done much to avoid expulsions. But he deserves little credit for his work in 1951–55, and for several reasons. First, his efforts really served little purpose. In the 1955 election, Labour's divisions over nationalisation and defence were barely camouflaged. Nor did its unity from 1957 achieve very much. After all, the Conservatives won a third successive election in 1959, and Labour was only re-elected after both Gaitskell and Bevan had died. It is difficult to envisage that, had Attlee retired in the early-1950s, the party could have fared any worse. Second, it seems unlikely that Attlee stayed on primarily to secure party unity. No doubt his motives were mixed, but it seems certain that an important factor in his remaining as leader was, quite simply, his wish to do so. It is true that he had never seemed an ambitious man, and indeed for years he had paraded his humility and his willingness to step down, but this was merely a shy man's convenient political persona. In reality he enjoyed power. Leading the party was his life: it had become a familiar and reassuring habit.

There was a certain conceit in Attlee's staying on as long as he did. The words he applied to Beveridge – 'Always a mistake to think yourself larger than you are'[12] – also apply to him. Like many another politician, late in his or her career, he had fallen into the trap of regarding himself as indispensable. Harold Wilson drew several lessons from Attlee, and it is well known that he tried to follow his style in chairing the cabinet. But may he not also have learned a negative lesson – the importance of not lingering on for too long?

. . .

1955: GENERAL ELECTION AND RESIGNATION

Attlee several times expressed the wish to become prime minister again. But the Labour party really had little chance of being elected on 26 May 1955. Attlee gave his usual sort of performance, travelling 1,200 miles with his wife at the wheel and addressing forty meetings. In his speeches he stressed moral issues – the brotherhood of man and the importance of working towards a classless society and utilising the wealth of Britain for the benefit of the many not the few. He and Churchill crossed swords, but parrying not lunging. Churchill called Attlee piebald, and the Labour leader responded that this came rather oddly from Churchill, always something of a chameleon. It all seemed remarkably unreal. The most unusual aspect of the campaign was the prominence of television. Attlee could not avoid giving one of Labour's broadcasts, though David Butler judged it Labour's least inspired: he neither said anything new nor anything old in a new way.[13] It was a placid campaign, in which the Conservatives did little to exploit the dissension in Labour ranks. They did not need to, and there was a steep fall in the Labour vote. The Tories won a comfortable victory of 59, with a national swing in their favour of 1.8 per cent.

The Times advised Labour against precipitate changes in leadership, for without Attlee the party might not have even the semblance of unity. Certainly the Bevanites wished him to stay on: an immediate party election would probably see Morrison's elevation but, if Attlee remained, Morrison would soon appear too old, and there might still be a chance for Nye. In fact, Attlee stayed another six months. For about a year, he admitted privately, he had been feeling 'a relic of the past'.[14] Then, on 7 December 1955, he announced his retirement, and in typically terse fashion: 'Offered an earldom. Shall I accept? Right. Then that's agreed.'[15] It was said that several MPs, including the formidable Edith Summerskill, wept at the announcement, while Attlee sucked hard on his pipe. He gave up the leadership of the party and his seat in the House of Commons with definite reluctance, describing it as 'rather a wrench after 33 years . . . but this break is, of course, inevitable, unless one wants to carry on into senility'.[16]

By this time Morrison's chances of the leadership had indeed faded, but Nye's behaviour ruled him out as well. Gaitskell was elected on the first ballot. It seemed to many that now was the time for the sort of unambiguous leadership which Attlee had been unwilling or unable to provide.

. . .

RETIREMENT, 1955–67

Now in the House of Lords, Attlee could still put up a good performance. His speech at the beginning of the Suez Crisis, for instance, was described as a 'small masterpiece of foresight and deadly exposure'.[17] In old age he was still active, his main political theme being the vital necessity of world government – a long-term interest of his, though one he had done little to foster while in office. Also, he was still reading. He turned once more to his favourite authors, like Jane Austen; and *Wisden* was a great consolation, as was the annual *Haileybury Record*. He was also writing, and now his reviews were much in demand. A brief piece for *Time-Life* magazine received the 'ridiculous' sum of £710, which he calculated worked out at £200 an hour. He was still to be seen on ceremonial occasions, like Churchill's state funeral, but not often. He also took some part in the 1964 election, despite the sudden death of his wife only a few months earlier. He spoke for Douglas Jay in Battersea, producing thunderous cheers with his insistence that though he was an old man, who did not expect to live much longer, he hoped to live until the end of the general election: and 'if I hear that a Labour Government has been elected, I shall die happy'.[18] Soon, however, he was critical of Wilson's administration, with its adoption of 'Tory policy in everything'.[19]

By 1965 he was writing that he expected to be dead soon and that, when they heard the news, people would say they thought he had died ages ago. He did not mind. He took comfort from the thought that for over eighty years he had lived in the greatest country in the world and that he had known friendships and kindness: he would die with 'lots of poetry in my heart and perhaps on my lips'.[20] Clement Attlee had often seemed one of the least dramatic and most humdrum of men. But he had a rich inner life, and until the end his imagination was an indestructible dominion. Furthermore, he could rest assured that he had undoubtedly made his mark: Britain would have been a poorer place without his imprint. He died on 8 October 1967.

· · ·

REFERENCES

1. Janet Morgan (ed.), *The Backbench Diaries of Richard Crossman* (London, 1981), 23 October 1952, p. 163.
2. Ibid., pp. 31, 68.
3. Lord Moran, *Winston Churchill: The Struggle for Survival* (London, 1968 edn), p. 622.

4. Francis Williams (ed.), *A Prime Minister Remembers* (London, 1961), p. 255. Francis Williams, *Nothing So Strange* (London, 1970), p. 307, accepts that Attlee delayed retiring in order to give Morrison a chance of succeeding to the leadership.

5. Robert Pearce (ed.), *Patrick Gordon Walker: Political Diaries 1932–1971* (London, 1991), p. 32; Lord Morrison of Lambeth, *Herbert Morrison* (London, 1960), p. 295.

6. Attlee to Tom Attlee, 5 October 1952, Attlee Papers, Bodleian Library.

7. Bernard Donoughue and G.W. Jones, *Herbert Morrison: Portrait of a Politician* (London, 1973), p. 522.

8. Kenneth Harris, *Attlee* (London, 1984), p. 522.

9. Morgan (ed.), *Backbench Diaries*, 21 April 1954, p. 315.

10. Leslie Hunter, *The Road to Brighton Pier* (London, 1959), p. 9.

11. *New Statesman*, 24 April 1954.

12. Williams (ed.), *Prime Minister Remembers*, p. 57.

13. Michael Cockerell, *Live from Number 10* (London, 1988), p. 33.

14. Attlee to Winterton, 31 December 1955, Winterton Papers, Bodleian Library.

15. Roy Hattersley, *Between Ourselves* (London, 1994), p. 329.

16. Attlee to Tom Attlee, 6 December 1955.

17. Frank Pakenham, *Five Lives* (London, 1964), p. 74.

18. Douglas Jay, *Change and Fortune* (London, 1980), p. 296.

19. Attlee to Patricia Beck, 6 February 1967, Attlee Papers, Bodleian Library.

20. Ibid., 25 October 1965.

CONCLUSION: ATTLEE IN PERSPECTIVE

You don't need to be a master-batsman forever scoring centuries or a demon bowler skittling out the other side to be a great captain in the field when the pressure is at its height.[1]

Clement Attlee is one of the most important figures in twentieth-century British political history. No one should make the mistake of so many of his contemporaries and dismiss him as a nonentity. Admittedly he sometimes seemed unimportant, merely the silent, insignificant servant carrying out the decisions of bigger personalities; but this image, stemming from his ingrained shyness, was in fact a highly effective – because deceptive – political persona. It enabled him to scale the greasy political pole almost unobserved. Nor, on the other hand, was he the ultra-efficient, impersonal, somewhat one-sided figure – selfless but also stunted – of another historical legend. Neither stereotype will fit even his years as Prime Minister, from 1945 to 1951, let alone his career as a whole. The reality is much more complex and interesting – and difficult to unravel, given the man's enigmatic personality. George Thomas was not the only one to compare Attlee to the Buddha, impassive and unfathomable. To the historian he is often the witness who repeats endlessly – and infuriatingly – 'No comment'.

Attlee prompts questions rather than answers. Was he on the left of the Labour party, or in the centre or on the right? He often said that the best place from which to lead was left of centre: but did he mean of the party or the political spectrum? Was he a decisive executive, with ideas of his own and steel in his will, or merely a good chairman of committee and deft follower of majority decisions, able to harness the creative talents of others? Furthermore, was he essentially radical or conservative? Surely he was all of the above, by turns. In his long political life he played many roles – from 'a damned socialistic tub-thumping rascal',[2] as he seemed to an army colleague, to the personification of Labour's respectability and moderation. But Attlee was no one-dimensional figure, and he exhibited contrasting qualities not only at different times but in the same periods of his career. Generally he was the leader who followed, but occasionally he could be the dominant executive scarcely bothering to consult other ministers. He could act decisively and he could also dither; and in addition he was the master of judicious compromise. Hence he is no easy figure to pigeon-hole.

So many political labels can be applied to Attlee because he was so often ambivalent. Many thought him a hollow man, lacking substance, but in fact he was pulled by strong emotions and convictions – not surprisingly, given both his respectable, middle-class upbringing and his partial rebellion and escape into social work and socialism. He was a reformer and an establishment figure. At times he espoused quasi-revolutionary views, and yet he also 'played the game' as consistently as Austen Chamberlain (though certainly Attlee did not always lose). Out of office, his heart tended to be on the left, and he favoured major structural change; but in office, whether in local or national government, his head convinced him of the need always to work from the existing system and to foster moderate, practical change. He was certainly not the resigning type – and nor could he understand anyone wanting to resign on a matter of conscience, which he dismissed as usually one's own conceit.[3] In general, his head won out over his heart, so that in his view the 'cardinal political sin' was to run away from responsibility.[4] But his heart played its part in the decisions of his head. As Prime Minister, he always saw the need to secure the general acceptance of reforms: it was therefore necessary to work through some form of consensus in the nation, just as it was in the Labour Party. But Attlee as Prime Minister still contained within him the young romantic whose poetry testified to his deep abhorrence of poverty and exploitation. He aimed to use power for positive ends, especially to improve the lot of those worse off than himself.

Attlee would never have agreed with Morrison that socialism is simply what Labour governments do. No doubt the cares of high office sometimes dimmed Attlee's idealism, but he was never that cynical. To his mind, power had to be purposive. He was never much of a theorist – and indeed his pragmatism was in many ways peculiarly English – but he was a moralist. His appeal was always to a morality which transcended selfishness. In 1922 he wrote that 'what is needed in political life is first of all principle, secondly principle; and thirdly principle'.[5] He was a man who believed in plain living and high thinking. Again and again, throughout his career, he appealed not to human cupidity or selfishness, nor to the profit motive, but to higher instincts and 'the motive of service'.[6]

It was Attlee's dual concern with both practical consensus and radical reform which goes a long way to explain the peculiar achievements of his 1945–50 government. To idealists on the left it was profoundly disappointing, especially in its abandonment of socialist theory; to hard-headed realists on the right, it attempted too much too soon, overstraining the industrial base in the process. Yet to others it was doggedly realistic in its idealism – in its determination to press on with reform, despite adverse conditions and the need to trim before the storm. Attlee was, at one and the same time, one of the most idealistic and realistic of modern political leaders. Had he been merely the one or the other, he would be a far less substantial, and unusual, political figure.

Attlee's important place in Labour history is secure. He helped the party recover from the débâcle of 1931 and to retain its basic unity during the traumatic late-1930s; and he then presided over its most creative and successful period in office, from 1940 to 1951. Also notable is his ability to survive. There were many rivals to Attlee's crown, but none who could ever topple him. The key to his success was that he was never out of step with party policy or majority opinion. Gaitskell noted that Attlee had always 'played the game of leadership by not leaning too heavily on one wing or another'.[7] Like Stanley Baldwin, he was a much shrewder politician than most people believed, and, like Baldwin again, he perfected the art of seeming to be politically innocent, even inept. Attlee seemed the archetypal honest, guileless and modest man – an image he fostered with little sign of true humility. Neither Attlee nor Baldwin was an accidental prime minister. The Labour leader undoubtedly enjoyed power, not ostentatiously but with genuine satisfaction, and he took care to be in a position to enjoy it for as long as possible. But, unlike Baldwin, Attlee got things done.

He was undoubtedly the most successful prime minister in Labour history, managing to harness the forces of left and right into an, albeit brief, period of constructive government. He showed that idealism and practicality could go together: indeed he felt that either one without the other was futile. Similarly he knew that discussion without decision was barren, and one of his most notable qualities was the ability to shut people up. This was a quality he shared with Churchill, though Churchill silenced others by talking incessantly himself. No wonder the civil servants tended to prefer Attlee. The Labour leader also contrasted with the Conservative in that he was aloof and without favourites. Hence he was the perfect referee, mediating between his seemingly more talented and able colleagues.

Attlee had other strengths too. Despite his shyness, which led so many to underestimate him, he had remarkable determination and self-confidence. Indeed Francis Williams believed that there was 'a strong streak of ruthlessness' in him.[8] He was also hard-working and dedicated. He got on with the job. He did not strut or fret: instead, he spent his hour on the stage most constructively. In 1950 Hugh Gaitskell judged that he had 'more political sense' than almost anybody else. He also mused that 'the qualities needed for success in peacetime are by no means the ones usually associated with greatness'.[9] Attlee showed that a prime minister does not need to have charisma or extravagant flamboyance – providing, of course, that he has the Attleean personal qualities and an able team of ministers under him.

Yet Attlee's reputation for wisdom – like his reputation for inadequacy – stemmed partly from his taciturnity, and in truth he was not the perfect politician or prime minister. He had definite intellectual limitations. In addition, having the defects of his virtues, he rarely understood his colleagues, and he certainly made mistakes in his career. He was slow to call for rearmament in the 1930s. During the war he insisted that divisions between the parties in Britain were as 'little ditches' compared to the 'great gulf' that separated the British from Hitler and Mussolini.[10] But he had not said this during the late-1930s: perhaps hostility to Chamberlain blinded him to what was so obvious under Churchill. His efforts to avoid the general election in June 1945 constitute another error. Had his voice been authoritative, the crowning glory of his career, his administration in 1945–50, would not have come about. As Prime Minister, of course, he did have his way – and his successes. But he handled Nye Bevan badly, and he was certainly wrong in his timing of the general election of 1950. Similar bad judgement harmed the Labour cause in 1951. Had he listened to advice and chosen a date to suit the party rather than the king, Labour would probably not have embarked on its fratricidal period in opposition. Finally, it must be admitted that he stayed on as party leader for too long, harming his own reputation and failing to boost Labour's cause.

On a personal level, Attlee had a shyness and a taciturnity which is unique in modern British politics. A small number of people are like this in all walks of life, yet none but Clem Attlee has ever become prime minister. His shyness camouflaged his ability. In some circumstances, such diffidence would inevitably have minimised his political impact. In the circumstances of the post-1931 'betrayal', however, it was an advantage. No one seemed less like Ramsay MacDonald than Attlee. His character also effectively camouflaged his ambition and his skills, making him a deceptively adept political colleague.

Perhaps Attlee's shyness delayed an appreciation of his merits, but it also, in the end, made him into a political 'personality'. His habitual terseness made him capable of witty one-liners, and many people in political life cherished their favourite Attlee story. Once, for instance, after Churchill had got excited over a government policy, Attlee commented: 'Trouble with Winston: nails his trousers to the mast. Can't climb down.'[11] On another occasion, when news of Labour's decision to manufacture the atomic bomb leaked out, a Welsh MP treated the PLP to a ten-minute speech of great passion, in which he detailed the gruesome consequences of nuclear war, with the untold horrors that would be reaped by generations yet unborn, after which Clem removed his pipe and agreed 'Yes, we must watch it. Next business.'[12] Often such stories bring out his well-developed sense of right and wrong. When a Labour MP betrayed a royal confidence in an American magazine, Attlee insisted that this was not the behaviour of a gentleman. When the MP insisted that he did not know what

Attlee meant, the retort came – 'Exactly'.[13] More often, however, his very colourlessness gave him character. Elizabeth Longford decided to offer the Prime Minister the last bottle of her grandfather's vintage port, which was over fifty years old. She mused, as she carefully decanted the precious liquid, that it might have been served to her great-uncle, Joe Chamberlain himself. Yet whether the historical associations were appreciated by Clem she could not judge, for his only comment was 'Seems all right'.[14] Attlee was often described as ordinary, but in fact he was not ordinary at all; or, to put it another way, he was so amazingly ordinary as to be positively extraordinary. Malcolm Muggeridge saw this very clearly. He described Attlee's memoirs, *As It Happened*, as a 'quite fabulous work, completely flat, but so flat, so fabulously flat, as to be quite fascinating . . . It would be interesting to consider how he'd describe the day of Judgment.'[15] The ugly duckling had been a cygnet all along. There is no doubt that Clement Attlee has a unique niche in British political history.

. . .

REFERENCES

1. Attlee quoted by James Margach, *The Anatomy of Power* (London, 1979), p. 4.
2. Roy Jenkins, *Mr Attlee* (London, 1948), p. 73.
3. *Clem Attlee: Granada Historical Records Interview* (London, 1967), p. 47.
4. Trevor Burridge, *Clement Attlee: A Political Biography* (London, 1985), p. 267.
5. C.R. Attlee, 'Liberal and Labour Co-operation', *Socialist Review*, March 1922, p. 134.
6. C.R. Attlee, *The Labour Party in Perspective* (London, 1937), p. 132.
7. Philip M. Williams (ed.), *The Diary of Hugh Gaitskell 1945–1956* (London, 1983), 2 April 1955, p. 401.
8. Francis Williams, *Nothing So Strange* (London, 1970), p. 219.
9. Williams (ed.), *Diary of Gaitskell*, 26 May 1950, p. 189.
10. Kenneth Harris, *Attlee* (London, 1984 edn), p. 181.
11. Geoffrey Dellar (ed.), *Attlee As I Knew Him* (London, 1983), p. 44.
12. Ibid., p. 36.
13. Ibid., p. 47.
14. Elizabeth Longford, *Pebbled Shore* (London, 1986), p. 259.
15. Malcolm Muggeridge, *Like It Was* (London, 1981), p. 469.

FURTHER READING

(Place of publication is London unless otherwise stated.)

SOURCES

Attlee was remarkably careless about his historical reputation, and as a result he disposed of considerable quantities of his papers. The largest extant collection is housed in Oxford's Bodleian Library, with a smaller number, including his draft autobiography, at Churchill College, Cambridge. A number of personal papers have been retained by his family.

Attlee's own writings include *War Comes to Britain*, ed. John Dugdale, 1940, a selection of his speeches on foreign policy from October 1932 to February 1940. Another set is *Purpose and Policy: Selected Speeches*, ed. Roy Jenkins, n.d. but 1947, from Attlee's speeches made between June 1945 and November 1946. The papers in the Bodleian contain numerous type-scripts for Attlee's speeches, especially as Prime Minister, but Hansard remains the prime source. The Labour party's annual conference reports are also extremely useful. His own books include *The Social Worker*, 1920; *The Will and the Way to Socialism*, 1935; and *The Labour Party in Perspective*, 1937. All of these contain autobiographical passages. His memoirs, *As It Happened*, 1954, constitute a classic example of Attlee's low-key, unemotional and guarded approach. Francis Williams, *A Prime Minister Remembers*, 1961, is largely a transcript of interviews with Attlee in retirement, as is the much shorter *Clem Attlee: The Granada Historical Records Interview*, 1967. They are both of value: and the contradictions between them underline the need to treat all such works as, to some degree, rationalisations.

The diaries of Attlee's colleagues are a major source, though all need to be treated with care. The most important are *The Political Diary of Hugh Dalton 1918–40, 1945–60*, ed. Ben Pimlott, 1986; *The Second World War Diary of Hugh Dalton 1940–45*, ed. Ben Pimlott, 1987; and *The Diary of Hugh Gaitskell 1945–1956*, ed. Philip M. Williams, 1983. Also of value are *Labour and the Coalition: From the Diary of James Chuter Ede, 1941–1945*, ed. K. Jefferys, 1987; *'Chips': The Diaries of Sir Henry Channon*, ed. Robert Rhodes James, 1993 edn; *The Empire at Bay: The Leo Amery Diaries 1929–1945*, eds John Barnes and David Nicholson, 1988; and *Patrick Gordon Walker: Political Diaries, 1932–1971*, ed. R. Pearce, 1991. There are some useful titbits of information in Tony Benn, *Years of Hope: Diaries, Letters and Papers 1940–1962*, 1994; and more, for Attlee from 1951, in *The Backbench Diaries of Richard Crossman*, ed. Janet Morgan, 1981.

Memoirs are another important source. Those which reveal something of Attlee, as well as their authors' often biased opinions, include Roy Jenkins, *A Life at the Centre*, 1991; Douglas Jay, *Change and Fortune: a Political Record*, 1980; Lord Morrison, *Herbert Morrison: An Autobiography*, 1960; Lord Wigg, *George Wigg*, 1972; Ian Mikardo, *Back-Bencher*, 1988; Francis Williams, *Nothing So Strange*, 1970; and James Griffiths, *Pages from Memory*, 1969. Memories and opinions of Attlee, from over thirty of his contemporaries, have been collected in Geoffrey Dellar (ed.), *Attlee As I Knew Him*, 1983: these can be occasionally revealing, as well as sometimes banal. A filial tribute has been paid by Lady Felicity Harewood, *Clem, Father and Politician*, the third memorial lecture of the Attlee Foundation, 20 February 1985. The memoirs of those on the political fringes are legion: two of the most useful for their recollections and judgements of Attlee are George Mallaby, *From My Level*, 1965, and James Margach, *Anatomy of Power*, 1979.

. . .

BIOGRAPHIES

Attlee has fewer biographical studies than any prime minister of his stature. The first was Cyril Clemens, *The Man from Limehouse*, International Mark Twain Society, Missouri, 1946; the second – Roy Jenkins, *Mr. Attlee: An Interim Biography*, 1948

– was a more professional piece of work. J.T. Murphy, *Labour's Big Three*, 1948, which focuses on Bevin and Morrison as well as Attlee, is a challenging left-wing analysis, though not always reliable. Far more substantial are Kenneth Harris, *Attlee*, 1982 (but the 1984 paperback edition, with references, is more valuable), and Trevor Burridge, *Clement Attlee: A Political Biography*, 1985. Jeremy H. Brookshire, *Clement Attlee* (Manchester), 1996, appeared when this present work was all but completed. Also important is William Golant, 'The Political Development of C.R. Attlee to 1935', B.Litt. thesis, Oxford University, 1967: this is most easily consulted in several articles, including 'The Emergence of C.R. Attlee as Leader of the Parliamentary Labour Party', *Historical Journal*, 1970, pp. 318–72 and 'C.R. Attlee in the First and Second Labour Governments', *Parliamentary Affairs*, 1972–73, pp. 318–35.

Among the plethora of biographies of Attlee's colleagues, the most notable include Raymond Postgate, *The Life of George Lansbury*, 1951; Alan Bullock, *The Life and Times of Ernest Bevin*, 3 vols, 1960–83, the third of which is indispensable for Attlee as Prime Minister; Bernard Donoughue and G.W. Jones, *Herbert Morrison: Portrait of a Politician*, 1973; Ben Pimlott, *Hugh Dalton*, 1985; Ben Pimlott, *Harold Wilson*, 1993; Michael Foot, *Aneurin Bevan*, 2 vols, 1962 and 1973; John Campbell, *Nye Bevan and the Mirage of British Socialism*, 1987; Philip Williams, *Hugh Gaitskell*, 1979. There are brief, but stimulating, biographical sketches in Kenneth Morgan, *Labour People* (Oxford), 1987; David Marquand, *The Progressive Dilemma*, 1991; and Peter Clarke, *A Question of Leadership* (Harmondsworth), 1990.

.   .   .

ASPECTS

For the 1930s, see Ben Pimlott, *Labour and the Left in the 1930s*, 1977, an indispensable and thought-provoking work; Dean E. McHenry, *The Labour Party in Transition*, 1939, which has been unduly neglected; and Elizabeth Durbin, *New Jerusalems*, 1985, which is particularly strong on economic aspects. On foreign policy, the standard work is John F. Naylor, *Labour's International Policy: The Labour Party in the 1930s*, 1969, which is remarkably sympathetic to Labour. See also M.R. Gordon, *Conflict and Consensus in Labour's Foreign Policy, 1914–1965* (Stanford, California), 1969.

Good background on the war years is provided by A. Calder, *The People's War*, 1969; P. Addison, *The Road to 1945*, 1975; S. Brooke, *Labour's War* (Oxford), 1992; K. Jefferys, *The Churchill Coalition and Wartime Politics, 1940–1945* (Manchester), 1991; and K. Jefferys (ed.), *War and Reform: British politics during the Second World War* (Manchester), 1994. See also Harold L. Smith (ed.), *War and Social Change* (Manchester), 1986.

There are many stimulating books on Attlee's 1945–51 governments. The two best starting points are Kenneth O. Morgan, *Labour in Power, 1945–1951* (Oxford), 1984, and Peter Hennessy, *Never Again 1945–51*, 1992. Also useful, though certainly not as readable, are the essays in Nick Tiratsoo (ed.), *The Attlee Years*, 1991. There is an excellent bibliography in Kevin Jefferys, *The Attlee Governments 1945–1951*, 1992. Other studies include Henry Pelling, *The Labour Governments 1945–51*, 1984, and Robert Pearce, *Attlee's Labour Government 1945–51*, 1994. For a more critical, left-wing viewpoint of the governments and of Attlee, see J. Hinton, *Labour and Socialism* (Brighton), 1983, and John Saville, *The Labour Movement in Britain*, 1988.

On the economy, Alec Cairncross, *Years of Recovery*, 1985, is a standard work; Correlli Barnett, *The Lost Victory: British Dreams, British Realities, 1945–50*, 1995, is immensely stimulating and challenging. Also valuable are Jim Fyrth (ed.), *Labour's High Noon: the Government and the Economy 1945–51*, 1993; H. Mercer, N. Rollings and J. Tomlinson (eds), *Labour Governments and Private Industry* (Edinburgh), 1992; William Ashworth, *The State in Business*, 1991; and Justin D. Smith, *The Attlee and Churchill Administrations and Industrial Unrest, 1945–55*, 1990.

Other aspects are covered in Jonathan Schneer, *Labour's Conscience: The Labour Left 1945–51*, 1988; Ritchie Ovendale (ed.), *The Foreign Policy of the British Labour Governments, 1945–51* (Leicester), 1984; Raymond Smith and John Zametica, 'The Cold Warrior: Clement Attlee reconsidered, 1945–7', *International Affairs*, vol. 61, 1984–85, pp. 237–52, a stimulating revaluation of Attlee's role in the immediate postwar period; R.J. Moore, *Escape from Empire* (Oxford), 1983; Wm. Roger Louis, *The British Empire in the Middle East 1945–51* (Oxford), 1984; and Charles Webster, *The Health Services since the War*, vol. 1, 1988.

For the 1950s, Leslie Hunter, *The Road to Brighton Pier*, 1959, is an engaging account by a pro-Morrison journalist. More scholarly are Mark Jenkins, *Bevanism: Labour's High Tide* (Nottingham), 1979, and Stephen Haseler, *The Gaitskellites*, 1969. Kevin Jefferys, *The Labour Party Since 1945*, 1993, also contains a valuable summary.

CHRONOLOGY

1883	3 January	Born in Putney
1896		Pupil at Haileybury
1901		Student at University College, Oxford
1904		Graduated with a 2nd in History
1905		Passed Bar Exams
1907		Manager of Haileybury Club in Stepney
1908		Joined Independent Labour Party, soon becoming branch secretary in Stepney
1912		Tutor in Social Services Department at LSE
1914		Joined 6th Battalion of South Lancs Regiment
1915		Fought in Gallipoli
1916		Fought and wounded in Mesopotamia
1917		Promoted Major; fought in France with 5th Battalion, South Lancs
1918	August	Wounded in action
1919		Defeated for London County Council seat; organised Labour victory in borough elections; appointed first Labour Mayor of Stepney

1920		Elected an Alderman
1922	January	Married Violet Millar
	October	Elected MP for Limehouse division of Stepney; PPS to Ramsay MacDonald
1923	December	Under-Secretary at the War Office in the first Labour Government
1926		Reluctant supporter of the General Strike
1927	November	Appointed to the Simon Commission
1930	May	Chancellor of the Duchy of Lancaster in second Labour Government
1931	February	Postmaster-General
	October	Won Limehouse by 551 votes; elected deputy leader of the Labour Party
1932		Accepted need to introduce 'definite socialist legislation'
1933		Accepted need for an emergency powers act
1934		Deputised for Lansbury; became more moderate, distancing himself from Cripps and the Socialist League; elected to NEC for first time
1935	October	Lansbury resigned, after Brighton conference
	November	Acting leader during 1935 election
		Defeated Morrison and Greenwood for party leadership
1936		Wrote *Labour Party in Perspective*
1937	May	*Labour's Immediate Programme*
	July	PLP agreed not to vote against arms estimates
	December	Visited Spain

1939	January	Cripps expelled over Popular Front issue
	June	Prostate operation
1940	11 May	Lord Privy Seal, with seat in War Cabinet
1942	19 February	Dominions Secretary and Deputy Prime Minister
1943	July	Chairman of Committee on Postwar Europe
	September	Lord President of the Council
1945	May	Coalition ended; made Companion of Honour
	26 July	Labour victory announced in general election; Prime Minister
1946	March	Bank of England nationalised
	May	Trade Disputes Act repealed
	July	King David Hotel in Jerusalem blown up
1947	January	Manufacture of atomic bomb authorised
	February	Mountbatten appointed Viceroy; deadline for withdrawal from India announced
	1 April	School-leaving age raised to 15
	15 July	Sterling was made convertible into dollars
	15 August	India and Pakistan became independent
	21 August	Sterling convertibility suspended
	September	Cripps moved to unseat Attlee: he was made Minister of Economic Affairs
	November	Dalton resigned: Cripps as Chancellor
1948	27 February	Communist coup in Czechoslovakia

1948	14 May	End of mandate in Palestine
	26 May	Berlin Airlift began
	June	State of Emergency declared during dock strike
	5 July	NHS inaugurated
1949	4 April	NATO set up
	27 April	London Declaration on the Commonwealth
	July	Second State of Emergency, during another dock strike
	18 September	Devaluation of sterling from $4.03 to $2.80
	26 October	Britain recognised Communist China
1950	23 February	Narrow Labour victory in general election
	25 June	Cabinet rejected the Schuman Plan
	2 September	TUC discontinued wage freeze
	19 October	Gaitskell became Chancellor
1951	March	Morrison became Foreign Secretary
	April	Death of Bevin; Attlee in hospital; Bevan resigned over NHS charges
	25 October	Labour defeat in general election
		Award of Order of Merit
1952	March	Bevan defied Labour whip
		Reintroduction of Standing Orders
	September	Battle at Morecambe conference
1954	April	Bevan challenged Attlee over foreign policy
1955	March	Whip removed from Bevan, but no expulsion

1955	26 May	Secure Conservative victory in general election
	7 December	Resigned as Labour leader (aged 72); accepted an earldom; succeeded by Gaitskell
1967	8 October	Died (aged 84)

INDEX

Main entries are in alphabetical order, sub-entries are in broadly chronological sequence.